Using AutoCAD

An Introduction to Computer-Assisted Design for the Theatre

L. J. DeCuir

HEINEMANN
PORTSMOUTH, NH

Heinemann
A division of Reed Elsevier Inc.
361 Hanover Street
Portsmouth, NH 03801–3912
www.heinemanndrama.com

Offices and agents throughout the world

© 2000 by L. J. DeCuir

The author and publisher wish to thank those who have generously given permission to reprint borrowed material:

Screen shots reprinted by permission of Autodesk, Inc.
AutoCAD is a registered trademark of Autodesk, Inc.

In the accompanying CD-ROM:

Photograph "Taiwan Dark Green, Taiwan" courtesy of Casatelli Marble & Tile Imports.

Image from *Surfaces: Visual Research for Artists, Architects, and Designers* by Judy A. Juracek. Copyright © 1996 by Judy A. Juracek. Reprinted by permission of W. W. Norton & Company, Inc.

Library of Congress Cataloging-in-Publication Data
DeCuir, L. J.
    Using Autocad: an introduction to computer-assisted design for the theatre / L. J. DeCuir.
        p. cm.
    Includes bibliographical references and index.
    ISBN 0-325-00122-7
    1. Theater—Stage-setting and scenery—Computer programs.
PN2091.S8D37 2000
792'.025'0285—dc21   99-33506

Editor: Lisa A. Barnett
Production: Elizabeth Valway
Cover design: Monty Lewis
Technology coordinator: Dan Breslin
Manufacturing: Louise Richardson

Printed in the United States of America on acid-free paper
04 03 02 01 00   RRD   1 2 3 4 5

CONTENTS

iv   **Contents**

ACKNOWLEDGMENTS

A book such as this one never gets written without a lot of help, and that is certainly the case here. Writing about all that help, however, is always a difficult task for the author. One cannot list every single person who has been of assistance, and inevitably, someone does get left out. So, I'll start this off with a big thank-you to all of those who have not been mentioned directly. Everyone's help has been appreciated, whether you are mentioned here or not.

The number one acknowledgment for helping this work actually make it into print has got to go to my wife, Mari. She's the one who struggled through the proofing of the early copies, kept track of the expenses necessary to keep the IRS happy, put up with my mumbling to myself at the dinner table about "commands" and "formatting," and has generally had to pick up the slack while I spent hour after hour pounding keys at the computer. Thank you, my dear!

After Mari there is a whole list of folks whose input and support have also been essential: Lisa Barnett at Heinemann, who has offered intelligent and down-to-earth advice; the Innovative Technologies Center at the University of Tennessee, which provided the grant that gave me the first hardware and software necessary to work with these programs; the Student Technology Fee at the University of Tennessee, which provided the grants that have created a functioning computer laboratory for our students and the opportunities to test out the ideas in this book in practice; the Department of Theatre at the University of Tennessee, which supported me both with time to write and the facilities necessary to see if many of the ideas in this book really work in practice; the students in my classes, who served as guinea pigs to ensure that the instructions are actually comprehensible when one is sitting in front of the computer trying to figure out how to make a program work; Marianne Custer, who let me use some of her designs in the exercises in this book; and Judy Juracek, who let me use some of the files from her own *Surfaces* book. Thanks to all of you as well.

The emotional support that is necessary for an author to keep going day after day has come from Mari as well, but also from Raphael, Rocky, Belle, and Nellie. These are our four English Bulldogs, who have all put in time snoring on the doggy bed next to the computer, giving me an affectionate nuzzle, and providing a friendly head to pat while I was puzzling over a problem.

My thanks to all of you,

L. J.

INTRODUCTION

With the explosion of computer use in all of our lives over the past few years it was inevitable that the rapid expansion of applications to the theatrical design process would quickly follow. By now most of us in the area of theatrical design have seen examples of computer-aided designs either in practice, at conventions, or on the World Wide Web, and many designers and technicians who have not yet begun to use computer programs in their work have at least started to wonder about the process and exactly what is required to begin.

Lighting designers were among the first to utilize the computer as an aid, primarily with such "drafting" tools as AutoCAD, Mini-CAD, etc. They recognized that computer-assisted drafting greatly sped up the process of modifying, refining, and changing drawings that is so much a part of the theatrical process. These computer-assisted "drafting" programs also had the capability of three-dimensional "drawing" that would let one, after creating a ground plan, quickly turn it into a perspective view of the scenery from any viewpoint desired. While these perspective views could be highly detailed, they usually lacked the capability of being turned into artistic visions without returning back to the drawing board or painter's easel.

There were already on the market a number of programs for the artist that would let one create artistic visions on the computer, but it was still extremely difficult if not impossible to work back and forth between the draftings necessary to communicate the vision to the lighting and scenery crews and the "renderings" that communicated the vision to the other designers and the director of a production. With the advent of a number of new programs, it is now possible to do exactly that.

This book and its companion are intended to serve as aids in understanding several computer programs that the designers on a theatrical production can use both in the creation of a rendering of their artistic vision and in the communication of that vision to the technicians responsible for transforming it into wood, plastic, metal, fabric, and lighting instruments. I have specifically chosen four programs that I have found to be highly useful to the scenic designers, lighting designer, costume designer, and technical director in this process. In addition to offering instruction in the basic understanding and use of these programs, I have further attempted here to deal with the integration of these four programs into the entire design process. Using these four programs, the set designer can begin with a simple ground plan, a rough "thumbnail" sketch, or a 3-D model on the computer and turn it into a rendering that is as detailed or open to interpretation as desired. The set designer can also, as a part of the same process on the computer, create the draftings necessary for the construction of the scenery or turn that part of the process over to the technical director. The costume designer can begin working from a "figure model" that is in whatever suitably dramatic pose or body type desired for a character or even begin working from a photo of the actor who will be playing the character in the actual production. The lighting designer can work from the renderings of the scenic designer and then experiment with lighting applications on top of that or start drafting the lighting plot from a highly accurate ground plan or 3-D model created by the scenic designer or technical director. At any part of the design process the three designers can also exchange information. The costume "sketches" can be imported into the scenic rendering for presentation to the director, for example, or the lighting designer's ideas can be expressed in the same 3-D model in which the scenic designer is working. By working together in these four programs all of the designers on a production can greatly enhance both their communication with one another and their visual communication with the rest of the production staff.

None of these four programs was originally designed for use in a theatrical application. As such they do have some shortcomings when adapted to our needs. Unfortunately, the theatrical market for computer programs has not yet expanded to the point where someone has attempted to create a single integrated program that fulfills all of the requirements and desires listed in the previous paragraph. Maybe sometime that will actually happen, but until that time we shall have to continue to adapt the best available programs to our own uses. The four programs covered in this book and its companion volume currently form one of the best groups of programs that will satisfy as many of these needs and desires as possible and offer the closest integration of all three design areas. All four are available for PC-based computers, which is the most widely distributed format today. Three of them are also available for Mac-based computers, the second most widely distributed format.

The four programs that I have chosen for this work are AutoCAD, 3D Studio MAX, Poser, and Painter. AutoCAD is the premier program currently on the market for both two-dimensional and three-dimensional drafting. This volume is intended primarily as an introduction to the use of AutoCAD for the theatrical designer and technician. There are many other works currently available that explore each program in a great deal more depth and breadth if you are interested in further applications of this program. See the Bibliography for a listing of the works that I have found to be especially useful. One of AutoCAD's greatest virtues for us in theatrical design, however, is its ability to export both individual objects and entire three-dimensional views into other programs such as 3D Studio MAX or Painter. These objects and/or views can then serve as the basis for a highly detailed three-dimensional computer model in 3D Studio MAX or a rough sketch for a rendering in Painter. Once a model has been created in 3D Studio MAX or a rendering has been created in Painter, a variety of lighting techniques can be applied in these programs to create visions of individual scenes. It is a relatively easy matter to work between these three programs. The fourth program, Poser, is extremely easy to learn and can be used to make human figures for the renderings created in Painter or the 3-D models and drawings of 3D Studio MAX and AutoCAD. In Painter these figures can be used as the underlying figures in a costume rendering that can then be imported into a set rendering created in Painter. Using these four programs together as a part of the overall design process can enable the designers on a production to quickly and easily exchange ideas and information both among themselves and with the other members of the production staff.

The purpose of this book and its companion volume is to introduce these four programs in their theatrical applications. My hope is that this will form the basis of your own exploration of the possibilities inherent in these and other programs to your own design process. None of the sections on the individual programs is intended to be the definitive work on all possible aspects of the program's uses, but rather to offer you a beginning for understanding how the program works and how to integrate the four programs with one another in the theatrical design process. Above all, I have also attempted to use simple English in all of the instructions in this book. Anyone in theatre not already highly skilled in the areas of computers who has attempted to learn almost any computer program is only too familiar with the difficulties of doing so from the usual instruction manual supplied. Highly important steps in the use of the program seem invariably to be entirely left out or "assumed" to be already at your command. I have done my best to avoid those pitfalls in this work so that it can truly be accessible to even those with the most rudimentary of computer skills. Throughout the book I have tried to focus on the commands in each program that will be most useful to theatrical artists and to give detailed instructions on how to import and export files from one program to another. These import and export instructions along with your own imagination are the key to integrating the four programs with one another and the theatrical production process.

One final word of caution is necessary. One must remember that a computer is nothing more than a tool to assist you in your own artistic process. If you can't already draw, you won't be magically transformed into an artist by using a computer. If you don't understand the construction of scenery, drafting it on a computer will not suddenly turn a physically weak or poorly supported platform or step unit into one that will hold elephants. The computer will not turn a poor designer into a good one. Whatever your own levels of skills with a paintbrush or drafting board already are, they will remain the same. Once mastered, however, the computer programs covered in this book and its companion will allow you to utilize those skills, talents, and knowledge in ways that previously may not have been possible and often to do so at a great savings of both time and difficulty.

THE PROGRAM, HARDWARE, AND DRIVE BASICS

The Program

AutoCAD

AutoCAD, produced by AutoDesk, is one of the first sophisticated drawing programs that found widespread use in theatrical applications. As has been usual with computer applications in the theatre, the lighting designers were the first to make use of this program. The lighting designer probably now thinks of the program primarily as a drafting tool that allows one to quickly create and rapidly modify lighting plots, and the use of AutoCAD in this way will indeed be covered in this book. Included on the accompanying CD-ROM, for example, is a complete instrument library that one can simply copy onto one's hard drive and then use, as is, in creating lighting plots.

Following quickly on the heels of the lighting designers came the technical directors in finding uses for AutoCAD. They also realized that this program, once learned, offered them the opportunity to rapidly create and modify technical drawings for use in the scene shop, prop shop, etc. These uses of AutoCAD will also be covered in this book with particular attention to some of the commands that the technical director will find especially useful.

It is only more recently that many scenic designers have come to realize that AutoCAD is a tool that they can utilize also in more creative ways than simply creating ground plans. The three-dimensional aspects of AutoCAD allow the scenic designer to create not just a ground plan, but an entire "virtual" 3-D model of a set and all of its components. These models can then be exported from AutoCAD into Painter to create a rendering. The components can be exported into 3D Studio MAX and have textures added to create a 3-D model that can then have lighting applied so that the setting can be realistically viewed under a variety of different lighting conditions.

For the costume designer, the applications of AutoCAD are probably a bit more limited. He or she might find it useful, however, as the basis for yet another program that will allow him or her to quickly draft and resize patterns.

AutoCAD is available in a variety of versions for different platforms. The oldest version is for MS-DOS and operates primarily from keyboard commands. Release 12 is the first version that was available for Windows and will operate in Windows 3.1, Windows95, WindowsNT, and Windows98. Release 13 is available for both Windows and Macs. The latest version, Release 14, is only available for Windows95, NT, and 98. There are also inexpensive versions of AutoCAD called AutoCAD Lite or LT that are very similar in operation to the full versions, and because of their cost they are finding widespread use in theatrical applications, but are only available for Windows. AutoCAD LT2 is extremely similar to R12. LT95 is similar to R13 and LT98 is similar to R14. If you have any of the versions of AutoCAD Lite or LT, refer to the AutoCAD sections dealing with the full version to which it is similar. You will find that most of the commands covered in this book work exactly the same in the Lite or LT versions. There are a few commands that you will not be able to use in Lite or LT, and these will be noted in the text.

AutoCAD is an expensive program. If you are affiliated with a college or university, check with your computer center about its arrangements for securing site licenses from AutoDesk and you will find that you should be able to buy copies at a considerable discount. If you are not connected with a college or university then you might seriously look into one of the older releases or AutoCAD Lite versions for your use. These will cover the needs of the vast majority of theatrical situations. There actually are very few "new" commands in R13 and R14. The biggest difference between these and R12 is a lot more graphics and a bit more "user-friendly" layout. All of the exercises in this book and all of the integration of work between AutoCAD and 3D Studio MAX, Painter, and Poser can be done with any of the AutoCAD releases or versions.

3D STUDIO MAX

3D Studio MAX is one of the most capable programs available today for the creation of simulated three-dimensional modeling on the computer. You can create your 3-D features directly in 3D Studio MAX or more accurately create them in AutoCAD and then import them into 3D Studio MAX. This second method allows you to save considerable time in the process because the features created in AutoCAD can also be turned directly into working drawings for the shop. The scenic designer can easily manipulate the components of the set in the program and move them around to try out different configurations. The basic components are easily "covered" with a wide variety of textures available in the program or imported from outside so that one can quickly change the color and texture of walls, furniture, etc. to try out different looks. Once a virtual model of the setting is created, the lighting designer can apply lighting "instruments" to it that can be controlled for spread, intensity, color, and edge. You can also create gobos or patterns for use in the program. This is a program that really allows the set designer, the lighting designer, and the technical director to work together in the creation of the scenery and lighting requirements for a production.

Like AutoCAD, 3D Studio MAX is from AutoDesk. Unlike AutoCAD, which has a fairly steep learning curve, 3D Studio MAX is more "user-friendly" and is accompanied by a number of extremely helpful tutorials. At this time it is available only for Windows95, Windows98, and WindowsNT.

3D Studio MAX is an expensive program that is usually available for academic use through site licenses secured through your college or university at a considerably reduced cost. This program will represent a serious investment for the freelance theatrical artist or for theatrical companies without academic affiliations.

3D Studio MAX has so far gone through two releases with a number of smaller changes within those releases. This work covers both R1 and R2. For the sake of an introductory manual, the differences between the two programs are minor. The biggest difference is that R2 can read R1 files, but R1 cannot read R2 files. R2 can also accept files directly from AutoCAD R14.

PAINTER

Painter is one of the easiest to learn of the "rendering" programs available today for the traditionally trained theatrical artist. In conception and terminology it closely approximates all of the familiar techniques used in creating pencil, ink, watercolor, acrylic, oil, etc. work by hand with some greatly appreciated extras like the ability to use watercolor that doesn't dry until you tell it to. All of the rendering skills that you have spent years developing are available to you when you work in Painter. The scenic designer can easily import realistic-looking perspective views from AutoCAD or 3D Studio MAX and then create all the mood, atmosphere, and feeling that he or she would in a traditional rendering. The costume designer can import a figure from Poser, import a pencil sketch, or start with a photograph of an actor and create a costume rendering that will be as photo-realistic or stylized as he or she desires. There are a limited number of lighting effects available as well, but with nothing like the more sophisticated control available in 3D Studio MAX. Painter can also be used to create textures, gobos, etc. that can be exported for use in 3D Studio MAX and Poser.

Painter is available from MetaCreations, formerly Fractal Design, for all Windows and Mac platforms. The latest full version is Painter 5 and it comes packaged in a clever gallon paint bucket. As of this writing, there was also a 5.5 "Web Edition" upgrade available. While there are cheaper rendering programs out there, there are few that are as well conceived, offer as much variety of technique, and are as easy to use as Painter. Painter is at its most effective when it is used in combination with a graphic tablet such as a Wacom ArtPad, since this tool will allow you to control your stroke in a manner similar to a brush or pencil.

POSER

Poser is a program with applications in all three of the others. An extremely simple program to master, Poser allows you to create a wide variety of human figures that can then be imported into Painter, 3D Studio MAX, or AutoCAD for use with renderings or drawings. The basic figure is available in a large number of different sizes and body types—everything from giant figures to adults to children from svelte to obese. The program also literally lets you control the dimensions of specific parts of the figure to match a particular body type or actor. The figures can be covered with a simple wireframe, exposed muscle, or skin as desired and can be moved into any simulated three-dimensional pose that you wish. You can also control the lighting of the figure from up to three directions in both intensity and color. It also has basic animation capabilities for the figures and the ability to import props and backgrounds.

Poser is made by MetaCreations, formerly Fractal Design, and is available for all Windows and Mac platforms. The latest version is Poser 4, which is an expanded version of Poser 3. While this book primarily covers Poser 3 the procedures and operations of Poser 4 are identical. The major difference in the two programs are in the size of the figure library and other libraries that are available within the program. You will have no difficulties working with Poser 4 using the instructions in this book. Both Poser 4 and Poser 3, however, represent a radical change in layout, graphics, and operation from Poser 2. If you should have Poser 2, there are several files on the CD-ROM that accompanies this book that contain instructions for working with this older version of the program. You can print out one of these files or work with it directly from the CD-ROM if you like. The files are all located in the Poser folder on the CD-ROM and are in formats for a variety of word processor programs in both PC and Mac formats. There are files named Poser2.wpd for WordPerfect in both PC and Mac, files named Poser2.doc for Word in both PC and Mac, a file labeled Poser2.txt for any generic word processor on a PC, and a file labeled Poser2.rtf for any generic word processor on a Mac.

Hardware Requirements

Processor: For this group of programs I would recommend a computer with a minimum processor speed of 200 MHz. More important than processor speed, however, is the RAM of the computer.

RAM: Random access memory will keep these programs from turning into slow-motion exercises on you. Ignore what the manufacturers of the programs say here. An absolute minimum 64 MB of RAM is really necessary to run these programs properly, especially with modern operating systems, and the more you can get, the better.

Hard Drive: The size of hard drive necessary can vary considerably from one user to another, but many of the files created in these programs can get rather large. I would recommend a minimum of at least 4 to 6 GB of hard drive, and if you can afford an 8 GB drive, that would be preferred. It is always better to get a much larger hard drive than you think you will need so that you can easily add more programs and files at a later date without having to delete ones that are already there.

Video Card: The video card in the computer will determine the quality of color that your monitor will be able to display. For a larger size monitor such as is recommended for graphics work, a 2 MB video card will display 64,000 colors, which is OK for general use, but if you really want photo-realistic color resolution you will need a 4 MB video card to be able to handle 16.7 million colors.

Tape Backup Systems or Zip Drives: Many of the files that you will be creating may be so large that they cannot fit on a "floppy" disk, which has 1.0 to 1.4 MB capacity. A tape backup system, a Zip drive, or a large-capacity disk system—100 MB or greater—will allow you to transfer these files to storage other than your hard drive as well as move them from your computer to another. Seriously consider one of these as an option.

Modem or Ethernet Capability: Depending upon your location and linkage with other computers, either a modem or an Ethernet card will allow you to transfer files between your computer and others as well as over the Internet. The resources available to the designer on the Internet are already numerous and are increasing daily. Check with your network server for information on what kind of Ethernet or network card is recommended for your system. If you are using a modem to connect to the Internet, then a modem of 33.6 K bps or above is strongly suggested. Again, check with your server for details on a modem.

CD-ROM: CD-ROM drives are now standard on almost all computers. Be sure that your computer does come with a CD-ROM drive as well as a 3.5-inch "floppy" drive. There is a considerable amount of design material available to you today on CD-ROMs.

Audio Card, Wavetable MIDI, Speakers, etc.: If the computer is going to be used by your sound person, talk to him or her about what you should be getting here. If it's just going to be used for graphics, don't even worry about it. Take the basics that come with the system and put your extra money into one of the other items above.

Accessories

Monitor: When using a computer for theatrical graphics, buying the largest monitor that you can afford is a real plus. The 14- or 15-inch monitor that comes with most computers becomes a problem when dealing with large draftings or details on drawings, forcing you to constantly zoom or adjust your viewpoint. A 17-inch monitor is the basic size I would recommend for this kind of work. Unfortunately, the price of monitors goes up rapidly after they get larger than 17 inches in diagonal screen size. Larger sizes are nice, but they can get quite costly. By the time that this book actually goes into print, however, much of that may have changed, considering how quickly the prices of computers and their accessories are dropping. So, buy the largest monitor that you think you can afford.

When considering a monitor, look at dot pitch, resolution, and refresh rate in addition to screen size. The smaller the dot pitch the better, with .28 mm being the largest you would want. Small differences in dot pitch, however, are really not that noticeable. The higher the resolution, the more detail that will be displayed, with $1,024 \times 768$ being minimal and $1,280 \times 1,024$ preferred. Don't be tempted, however, by a cheaper monitor with a high resolution and a slow refresh rate. The refresh rate will keep the screen from flickering at you and driving you crazy. The faster the refresh rate the better, with 75 Hz being the slowest you would want and a 85 Hz rate preferable.

Printer/Plotter: A good-quality color printer is a must for doing any kind of rendering work with your computer. If you are interested in printing on different kinds of papers, then one with a paper path that flows almost straight through the printer is necessary rather than one with a paper path that reverses itself. If possible, try to compare different printers for color and sharpness before buying. In an ink-jet printer, look for a minimum resolution of 600 dpi. Laser printers can give you a considerably higher resolution but are much more expensive. Do not even consider a dot-matrix printer.

If you are going to be using the computer for drafting work, then a plotter is a recommended accessory. While these are considerably more expensive than printers, it can be a godsend to have your own plotter in the theatre rather than having to wait for a commercial operator to do your plots for you. For most theatrical applications a plotter that can handle paper at least 36 inches wide is necessary.

Scanner: A good-quality flatbed scanner, 300×600 dpi resolution or better, is a must for working with these programs. This will allow you to convert almost anything that you desire from a photograph or a flat image directly into a file that can be used by the programs. Scanner prices have now also dropped to the point where almost anyone who can afford a computer can easily afford a scanner as well. Be sure that you get a flatbed scanner rather than the kind that has a flow-through path. Another option to consider is a slide scanner. These will allow you to scan a 35 mm slide and turn it into a computer image. However, they are usually more costly than a flatbed scanner.

Graphic Tablet: A graphic tablet or "artpad" is a must for use with Painter. When drawing with a mouse, you will only be able to achieve one density of "line." A graphic tablet allows you to use the pen that accompanies it much as you would use a paintbrush, pen, or pencil. You will be able to taper, flare, and control the density of your strokes in the same way. The most useful size for theatrical work is probably a 6 × 8-inch or 9 × 11-inch size. They are available in smaller sizes at quite reasonable prices or larger sizes at considerably more cost.

Digital Camera: While rather expensive, a digital camera can be an extremely useful tool to combine with your computer. It will allow you to "photograph" an actor, an object, or an image directly as a digital image that can be used by the computer. If you have found a texture that you want to apply to the set, for example, you can shoot it with the digital camera and then apply it directly to the rendering of the set in the computer. A costume designer could also take a digital image of an actor and then create a costume rendering in Painter over the image of the actor.

Drive Basics

In order to integrate and work between the above programs it is necessary that you understand the drive system of your computer. If you do not already understand the layout and use of your hard drive, floppy drive, CD-ROM drive, and Zip or other drives, now is the time to learn. I strongly recommend that you find someone familiar enough with your computer to explain the use of these systems to you in detail. I will try to cover the basics behind them here, but the exact layout of any particular system will vary from computer to computer and you need to be familiar with your own.

The drive system of the computer organizes programs, files, etc. so that the computer and you can access them. These are the storage systems of the computer and how they are laid out. Today, most computers have at least three drive systems: a hard drive, or "permanent" storage; a 3.5-inch "floppy" drive, for storage on small disks with 1.0 to 1.4 MB capacity; and a CD-ROM drive, usually used to hold programs and large amounts of data. There are also a number of other drive systems that are now being offered for use such as Zip or auxiliary drives that offer you the option of external data storage in capacities of 100 MB or larger. Somewhere on your computer there is a program that will let you examine these drives to see how they are organized and what they contain. In Windows 3.1 this program is called File Manager. In Windows95 and Windows98 one program is called Explorer or Windows Explorer and a second is called My Computer. On Macs this is your Hard Drive and Floppy or A: drive icons. Before you continue with this book, become familiar with the program used on your computer and how to use it to navigate around your drive system. Many of the instructions in this book assume that you already know how to get around on your drive system. If you don't, you will quickly end up losing files and getting quite lost yourself.

On most computers today the "floppy" drive is referred to as the A: drive. If you want to read a file from a 3.5-inch disk or save one to it, you have to select the A: drive. The drive that lets you read what is on a CD-ROM is referred to by different letters on different computers. Depending upon your computer this may be the D:, E:, or F: drive. Find out how to access the CD-ROM drive on your particular computer. For most computers the hard drive is the C: drive. It may also be referred to by a name or a number. The hard drive is divided up into sections called folders or directories. When you install a program, it is usually placed into a folder or directory that is created by the installation part of the program. It is important to know what folder or directory these programs have been placed in so that you can access them later. When you install a program, it will usually ask you if you want it to create a folder or directory with a particular name similar to the name of the program or the program's manufacturer. Remember the name of this folder or directory. You can also create folders or directories yourself to help you organize your files and make them easier to find. When I'm working on a show, for example, I may create a folder using the name of the show and place all of the files that I create in that folder so that it will be easier for me to find them later. I highly recommend this procedure so that you will not have to search all over your hard drive to find a particular file. You can also create subfolders and subdirectories under folders and directories. Learn how to create folders, subfolders, etc. so that you can organize your files. It will save you vast amounts of time in the long run.

The other important part of learning to use the drive system on your computer is learning to use your "floppy" A: drive to back up and/or save any files that you create. Hard drives crash, and when they do any material that is on them will usually be lost. Hours, months, or even years of work can be completely destroyed this way. I cannot say this too strongly: *BACK UP EVERYTHING THAT YOU PUT ON YOUR HARD DRIVE!* If you save a file onto the hard drive, save it onto a disk as well. Some people even recommend that you do a double backup and save it onto two separate disks. The 3.5-inch disks can go bad, too. If that happens, anything on that disk is lost. I would recommend saving important files onto two different disks. When I was writing this book I had it saved onto two different hard drives on two different computers and also onto a separate set of 3.5-inch disks and onto a Zip disk. When it comes to backup, the old "suspenders and belt" philosophy is a good idea.

The problem with 3.5-inch disks is that they will hold only about 1.0 to 1.4 MB of storage. When you start creating graphics files, you'll find this is not a lot of space. As a result a number of different kinds of tape and large disk systems have been introduced with storage capacities of 100 MB to 4 to 8 GB.

If you have one of these systems, often called tape drives or Zip drives, you can use it to back up large files or large groups of files so that you don't have to deal with ten to twenty 3.5-inch disks for a particular group of files.

Files that you create using these programs can also be saved only to 3.5-inch disks, tapes, or large disks in order to save room on your hard drive. If you have a small hard drive, you may find that it has very little room left on it after you install all the programs. You will then have to save your files to one of these storage systems because there is not enough room left on the hard drive. It is quicker and easier to get at files from the hard drive than it is from one of these external storage systems, but eventually if everything is saved to the hard drive you will run out of storage space. When I'm working on a show I usually save the files to the hard drive, back them up on an external drive, and then when that show is over I delete the work from the hard drive and just keep it on the external disks or tapes. If it is an important project, I will normally have two copies of the external disks or tape(s) on which the project has been saved. Following this practice can prevent you from having to replicate hours or weeks of work from scratch if a disaster happens. When you're working with computers there is always the possibility that something can go wrong . . . go wrong . . . go wrong! *Always* back up your work.

AutoCAD

Introduction

AutoCAD is the most widely used drafting program throughout the world. Practically every engineering or architectural firm has multiple copies of this program and utilizes it for the vast majority of its drawings. It is also the most widely used drafting program in professional and academic theatre. Unfortunately for the theatre practitioner, it is one of the most complex drawing programs that exists and has one of the "steepest" learning curves. Many people in theatre are intimidated by AutoCAD. Contributing to this is an obscure set of instruction manuals that accompany the program. They seem to be written by someone who goes out of his way to make learning the program as difficult as possible. This certainly does not have to be the case.

AutoCAD offers many advantages to the theatrical designer beginning with the fact that there are more copies of it being used in theatre than any other drafting program. Its ability to work in three dimensions and capacity for exporting drawings to 3D Studio MAX or Painter for sophisticated renderings sets it at a level far above many other drafting programs. AutoCAD is much more than just a drafting program. An AutoCAD drawing can be presented in a three-dimensional format that offers a highly detailed perspective view of a setting or can serve as the "sketch" that underlies a highly presentational rendering. It does not have to be nearly as intimidating as the instruction manual makes it appear. AutoCAD does not have to be learned in its entirety for use by the theatrical practicioner. You will find that in a lot less time than you expected you will be able to use every aspect of AutoCAD that is important for theatrical applications. Then you can proceed on to many of the more complicated aspects at your own leisure if you desire.

AutoCAD, like all programs, is constantly being updated. There are a number of versions of the program currently in use. Unlike many programs, however, the older versions may not get updated by users as rapidly as the new versions appear. The main reason for this is cost. AutoCAD is an extremely expensive program. As a result, there are a lot of theatres and theatre departments that are still using R12 even though R13 and R14 have been out for quite some time. AutoDesk has also made available several versions called AutoCAD LT2, LT95, and LT98 at an extremely reasonable price to students. LT2 is almost identical to R12 with some minor differences, LT95 is extremely similar to R13, and LT98 is extremely similar to R14. If you are working with one of the LT versions of AutoCAD, follow the instructions for the corresponding versions 12, 13, or 14. In this volume I have tried to cover all of the currently available versions of AutoCAD—R12, R13, and R14—because there are so many copies of the older versions still in use. Because theatres and theatre departments are relatively poor compared to architectural and engineering firms, most of them simply can't afford to run right out and acquire multiple copies of the latest version of AutoCAD. It therefore will be necessary for you to pay close attention to the differences between the versions and use the particular instructions that apply to your edition. The Command Box that you will find described below is designed to assist you in sorting out the differences in how to activate a command in the various editions.

This book includes the instructions for configuring AutoCAD and how to work with the commands that are most useful for theatrical applications. These instructions have been written in English rather than the "computerese" of most instruction manuals and follow the "prompts" that appear on the AutoCAD screen at each step in the command process. If you take each command one step or prompt at a time as you work through it you will find that you will quickly understand how to go about drawing in AutoCAD.

At the end of each section there is also an exercise for you to practice the commands learned in the section in many cases with a sample on the accompanying CD-ROM of how the finished exercise should appear. The exercises are all based on the sample prototype drawing that is also given on the CD-ROM that accompanies this book. This will allow you to begin actually drawing in AutoCAD as rapidly as possible and begin to feel comfortable with the program. The exercises, like AutoCAD, are cumulative. In most cases you will need to have mastered the commands in one section and exercise before you can attempt the commands in the next. There are also sections intended specifically for the lighting designer with an accompanying set of lighting symbols based on the latest USITT Lighting Design Graphic Recommended Practice as well as sections that focus on the uses of AutoCAD for the technical director and on exporting three-dimensional figures into 3D Studio MAX or Painter for realistic rendering by both the scene designer and the lighting designer. Throughout the book I have attempted to focus on those tools and techniques that are specifically most useful in theatrical applications and to make the instructions for their use easily understood by theatre designers and technicians.

**THE COMMAND
BOX**

AutoCAD Command	Function	
Name of Command	**Purpose of Command**	

Keyboard Command	Pull Down Menu Path	Icon
Type this on the keyboard	**Click on this path on the pull down menu**	**Click on this Icon** **R13 or 14Toolbar Name**

A word of explanation about the Command Box that accompanies the text on each AutoCAD command in this book: I have included a Command Box in a graphic box near the text that explains each command. This box contains the basic information about how to activate each command in an easy-to-read format. The top of the box contains the name of the command and a simple statement of what the command does. The bottom of the box contains information on the three different methods by which most commands can be activated in AutoCAD: by keyboard, through a pull down menu, or with an icon.

- Keyboard: The first way most commands can be activated is by using the keyboard. The keyboard command is identical in almost all versions of AutoCAD. To activate the command by using the keyboard method you must first type in the letters shown in the Command Box in capital letters and then hit Enter. Note that you do not have to use capitals when you type these letters. I have just put the commands in capital letters in the Command Box so you can easily see which letters you need to type for the commands.

- Pull Down Menu: The second way most commands can be activated is by using the pull down menu. The pull down menu path may vary from one version of the program to another. I have noted any differences between the versions in the pull down menu path in the Command Box. To use the pull down menu path, click on the word before the first slash (/) that appears on the pull down menu bar at the top of the screen. This will open a pull down menu. The word after the first / will be on that pull down menu. Click on it to start the command. If there is more than one / you will have to keep clicking on each subsequent word until you reach the last one.

- Icon: The third way most commands can be activated is by using icons or "buttons" that appear on the toolbars. If you click on the icon shown in the Command Box, it will activate the command. When the icon used varies from one version of the program to another, the differences are noted in the Command Box. In R13 and R14 there are also a number of different toolbars that can be opened or closed at any given time. Given in text in the Command Box underneath the icon is the name of the particular toolbar on which an icon for a command can be found in R13 and R14.

Most AutoCAD commands can be initiated by any of the above methods. There are a few that are only accessible through the keyboard or pull down menu. You will quickly learn which of these methods is faster for the way that you use the program.

An Important General Note About Using AutoCAD

The program uses both the left and the right mouse buttons. If I do not specify a mouse button to be used, assume that you should use the left one as you normally would. If the right mouse button is to be used it will be noted.

Another property of AutoCAD the theatrical designer must get accustomed to is the manner in which scale is treated. When you are drawing in AutoCAD you draw full size. That is to say, when you want a line 10 feet long on stage you instruct the program to draw a 10-foot line without worrying about what scale the drawing will be printed in later. After the drawing is completed and you begin the print/plot process you must instruct the program in the scale desired, for example, 1/4 inch = 1 foot, 1/2 inch = 1 foot, etc. It actually is a little more complex than that simple example. There are some other elements of the drawing that have to be instructed for scale such as linetype—proportion of dashed and dotted lines—and dimensions—proportional size of dimensions and dimension lines—but these instructions are simple to add in the drawing process. Each of these areas will be covered in detail later in the book.

This is not to say that AutoCAD is a simple program to learn. It is a complex program and will take time and practice to master. When you first began to learn to draft or draw by hand you had to spend many hours at the drawing board learning hand-eye coordination. Similarly, as you begin to learn AutoCAD you will find that you will have to take the time to make the "right click," "left click" sequence of operation second nature rather than having to pause at each step to remember what comes next. Just like hand drafting or drawing, AutoCAD requires physical learning to master. There is no way to conquer this kind of learning without practice. The more that you use the program the better you will become at its use and the more rapidly you will find yourself able to execute each of the steps that are part of the process of drawing in AutoCAD. If you are skilled at drafting or drawing you will find that it will take some time before you will even be able to work in AutoCAD as quickly as you can work by hand. With practice, however, you eventually will find that working in AutoCAD is faster than working by hand and that changes are infinitely faster and easier to make.

CONFIGURING THE PROGRAM AND SETTING PREFERENCES

To install AutoCAD follow the instructions that come with the program carefully. The Install Shield that accompanies the installation will ask you some questions such as whether to use its name for the folder on the hard drive it will be installed in, etc. You should answer yes to all of the questions that it asks unless there is something about your system that is particularly different, in which case you should consult with someone familiar with your system. It will be important later to remember the name of the folder in which the program has been installed. You will need to know this for some aspects of AutoCAD.

Configuring AutoCAD

After you have installed AutoCAD and you try to open it for the first time you will get a message that tells you the program has not been configured and this must be done before you can use it. It is possible to customize the program to your own tastes through the configuration process, and as you get more familiar with it you may want to go back and change the configuration to make it more suited to your particular needs. For now though, I will talk you through a simple configuration that will get you up and running. Some of the specifics of the configuration process will vary depending upon the version that you are using, but the process will be similar to the steps below. Read through the following set of instructions completely before beginning. There is information that you must have to configure AutoCAD that you may not know immediately. Find this out before you start the configuration process. Differences between the versions of AutoCAD are noted in the description of the configuration process.

CONFIGURING AUTOCAD IN R12 OR R13

1. Typically, after the message appears on the screen telling you that AutoCAD must be configured, an AutoCAD text box will open automatically to ask you some of the following questions. **Note:** If you want to change the initial configuration later, click on File in the upper left-hand corner of the screen. In the pull down menu box that opens under File, click on Configuration. The AutoCAD text box will open, displaying the Configuration menu.

2. The first question usually asks you to make a choice among available video displays. If you are not sure about the display driver on your computer, then for R12 select the Driver by AutoDesk by typing in the

number next to it and hitting Enter. For R13 you would select the Windows Display Driver by AutoDesk, Inc.

3. The second question usually asks if you have measured the height and width of a "square" on your graphics screen and whether you would like to use these measurements to correct the aspect ratio. Unless you are familiar with your aspect ratio, just go with the default selection <N> and hit Enter.

4. The next question regards digitizers. If you are not using a digitizer along with the program—and most of us aren't—select 1. Current System Pointing Device and hit Enter. If you are using a digitizer, check the manual and material that accompanies it to select the proper device from the list.

5. The next question usually regards Available plotters. If you have both a printer and a plotter for use with the program you will need to select two different numbers from this list. Let's cover the printer first. If you have a printer that you want to use with AutoCAD, select System Printer ADI # - by Autodesk Inc. and hit Enter. Depending upon the printer associated with your system, a System Printer Configuration box may open. Answer the questions asked in the box. When in doubt go with the default selections—you can always change them later. Then you will get another list of options starting with Plot Optimization Level = 0 and you will be asked if you want to change anything. Unless you are already familiar with some of these options and know that you want to change them, go with the default selection <N> for no and hit Enter.

6. Next you will be asked to enter a description for this plotter, even though it is a printer. Just type in an abbreviation for your printer such as HP1150C. This just gives a name to the printer in the AutoCAD Print/Plot control box. Hit Enter.

7. Next you will be asked to enter a login name. If you want to control access to the program you can enter a name that must be used when logging in. If you don't want to have to log in with a name, select the default <****> by hitting Enter.

8. The next prompt will be a question about the maximum numbers of users for this package with a default of <1>. Just hit Enter unless you are running on a network.

9. Next you will be asked if you wish to run the executable from a read only directory? Select the default <N> by hitting Enter.

10. Then you will be asked if you would like to enter a password that will be required in order to use the program. Unless you want to control access with a password, select the default none < > by hitting Enter.

11. The next question is Do you wish to enable file locking? Here, even though the default is <Y> for yes, I would recommend that you enter an N on the keyboard and then hit Enter. You can always go back and change this later and until you completely understand how file locking works this can get you into trouble because your computer won't allow you to make changes to files.

12. For R13 you will then be asked to select an Available Spelling Dialect:; choose American English by hitting its number on the keyboard and then hitting Enter. This question will not appear as part of the configuration for R12.

13. The current configuration will then be displayed, and you will be prompted to press Return (Enter) to continue. Do so.

14. This will return you to the Configuration menu.

15. If you have a plotter associated with your system in addition to the printer, now is the time to configure the plotter as well. If you don't have a plotter then simply hit Enter to select <0> Exit to drawing editor. Skip to step 23 in this section.

16. If you would like to configure a plotter, type the number next to Configure plotter and hit Enter.

17. This gets you to the Plotter Configuration menu. Type the number next to Add a plotter configuration and hit Enter.

18. You should now be back at the Available plotters list that you saw earlier when you were configuring your printer. Select the number associated with your plotter manufacturer by typing that number in and hitting Enter. Each of the selections on this list will take you to another list with a more detailed description of Supported Models. Select the model number of your plotter and hit Enter. If you cannot find the manufacturer's name and/or model number of your plotter, go to your plotter's instruction manual. You may be told that it simulates a certain plotter. Select this manufacturer's name and model number instead. If the plotter instructions do not have this kind of information, read the entire instruction manual carefully for information on how to install the plotter and follow these instructions. If you have done this and still can't get the plotter working, it is time to call the store where you bought the plotter or the plotter's manufacturer.

19. Next you will be prompted for how long you want AutoCAD to wait for the plotter port to time out. The default is <30> for thirty seconds. Select this by hitting Enter.

20. Then you will be prompted for the serial port name for the plotter. The default here is <COM1>, which is the usual port being used. You can

select it just by hitting Enter. If you know that your plotter is installed on a different serial port, type the name of the serial port here and then hit Enter. If in doubt, check with whoever installed your plotter, where it was purchased, or the plotter's manufacturer.

21. The list of information beginning with Plot optimization level will again appear on the screen. Again select <N> as the answer to the question Do you want to change anything? by hitting Enter.

22. You will be prompted to Enter a description for this plotter:. Type in an abbreviation for the manufacturer's name and model number such as HP7585 and hit Enter. Remember that this is just the name that the plotter will be identified by in the Print/Plot box in AutoCAD. This does not have to be precise, but you do need to remember what name you used.

23. You should now be returned to the Plotter Configuration menu. Type in the number for Exit to configuration menu and hit Enter.

24. You will be returned to the Configuration menu. Type in the number for Exit to drawing editor and hit Enter.

25. You will be asked if you want to keep the configuration changes. Select the default <Y> by hitting Enter. If you enter <N> for no instead, all of the choices that you have made will be discarded and you will have to start the configuration process over again.

Note: The same process outlined in steps 16–25 above can also be used to configure AutoCAD for a plotter that you do not actually have, but instead is owned by a commercial plotting operation in your location. Many local blueline/blueprint stores now also run AutoCAD plots for architects, engineers, etc. and will be only too happy to run yours as well. You will have to check with them about what plotter they are using and will have to configure AutoCAD for that plotter.

SETTING AUTOCAD PREFERENCES IN R12 OR R13

In addition to configuring AutoCAD, this would also be a good time to set your preferences. Remember that these can be changed later if you find that you don't like them. The preferences control the look of the drawing environment.
    To set your preferences:

1. For R12, click on File in the upper left-hand corner of the screen. In the pull down menu box that opens under File, click on Preferences. For R13, click on Options on the top of the screen. In the pull down menu box that opens under Options click on Preferences. The Preferences box will open, looking something like the ones in the figures labled The Preferences Box: R12 and The Preferences Box: R13.

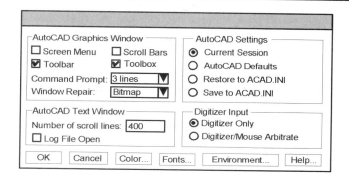

In the AutoCAD Graphics Window section I do not recommend making any changes initially. At a later time you may want to try adding a check mark by Screen Menu. This will give you yet another way to access AutoCAD commands. For R12, leave Toolbar and Toolbox checked and the Command Prompt set at 3 lines. Later you will learn about how these parts of the drawing environment are used. Similarly for R12 leave the settings in the AutoCAD Settings, AutoCAD Text Window, and Digitizer Input sections alone. For R13, under Keystrokes, check AutoCAD Classic.

2. For R12, one area that you might want to change right away is the Color section. You may have noticed that the opening screen is a dark grey. In its default settings you will be drawing in white lines on a dark grey screen. Many people that I know in theatre don't care for this setting. If you would like to draw in black lines on a light grey or a white screen, the Color section of this box is where you can change the colors. Click on

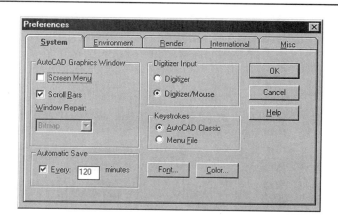

Color. The AutoCAD Window Colors box will open. In the upper right-hand part of this box you will see a window labeled Window Element with an arrow by it. Select the window element that you would like to change by clicking on the arrow and then clicking on the element. The Graphics Window Background is the background color for the main drawing screen. The Crosshair Color is the color of the cursor or crosshairs that you will use for drawing. These are the two main color elements that you might want to change. To change them, while the Color box is open select the element that you want to change so that it appears in the Window Element box. Then click on the color that you want to associate with it in the Basic Colors palette. A preview of the end product will appear in the samples to the left of the screen.

When you have all the color choices the way that you want them click on OK at the bottom of the box and you will return to the Preferences box. If you don't want to make any changes to the default colors, click on Cancel to return to the Preferences box. If you play around in the Color box long enough you can get quite complicated with your color choices. You can even get extremely weird if you prefer. R13 opens with a screen that is black lines on a white background.

3. The Fonts button in the Preferences box is another place that you can get cute if you would like. This is where you can select the font that you want to be used on the parts of the screen surrounding the AutoCAD drawing screen. You can select any font that is loaded into your computer. The default font is a MS Sans Serif. Please note that this has nothing to do with the font that is used on the AutoCAD drawing screen. Changing the font for the text in an actual drawing is a part of the AutoCAD command system and will be covered later in this book. If you make any changes in the Fonts box and want to apply them to the program, click on OK at the bottom of the box to return to the Preferences box. If you don't want to make any changes from the defaults then click on Cancel to return to the Preferences box.

4. The Environment button is something that you really don't want to mess around with at this point. If you completely understand the material in the AutoCAD manual concerning these elements then you may not need this book to understand how AutoCAD works.

5. For R12, if you have made changes in the Preferences box that you would like to apply to AutoCAD for just this drawing session then be sure that there is a dot in the circle next to Current Session under AutoCAD Settings. If you would like to apply the changes that you have made for a longer period of time then click on the circle next to Save to ACAD.INI under AutoCAD Settings. Then exit the Preferences box by clicking on OK.

If you chicken out at the last minute and don't want to save any of the changes that you have made, click on Cancel. For R13, all settings apply to all drawing sessions until you change them again in the Preferences box.

CONFIGURING AUTOCAD R14 AND SETTING PREFERENCES

When you first start version 14 the text box described above for R12 and R13 does not appear. Instead you get a Start Up dialogue box. If the Start from Scratch button is not depressed, click on it. Under Select Default Setting:, English should be highlighted. Under Description, it should read: Uses the default English (feet and inches) settings. Click on OK.

The next step is to click on the word Tools on the pull down menu bar running across the top of the screen. Click on the word Preferences on the pull down menu that opens. This will open the Preferences box shown in the figure labled The Preferences Box: R14.

1. Click on the Display tab.
   A. Under the Drawing Window Parameters: section place a check by Display scroll bars in drawing window. The other two boxes should not be checked.
   B. Under the Text Window Parameters: section there should be a 3 in the box next to Number of lines to show. . . . There should be a 400 in the box next to Number of lines of text. . . .

THE PREFERENCES BOX: R14

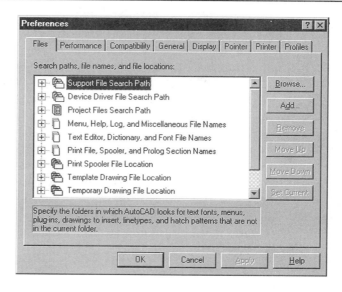

C. Click on the Colors button under the AutoCAD window format section. In the AutoCAD Window Colors box that opens, change the Graphics Windows Background to white. When you do that, the Crosshair Color should change to black. Click on the arrow next to the box under Window Element to check that. Scroll down and then select Crosshair Color. The color box in the middle lower center of the AutoCAD Window Colors box should turn to black.

D. Click on OK in the AutoCAD Window Colors box. The box will close and you will return to the Preferences box.

2. Click on the Pointer tab.

A. Unless you have a digitizer or one of the pointing devices listed, the Current System Pointing Device should already be highlighted in the scrollable window. Do not change anything. If you are going to be using a mouse, do not change anything. If you have a digitizer or one of the pointing devices listed in the scrollable window, you will need to find it and select it.

3. Click on the Printer tab.

A. If your computer is connected to a standard printer you should see Default System Printer highlighted in the large window. If you are only going to be printing to this printer leave everything alone.

B. If you are going to be working with a plotter or need to configure for creating .plt files that can be plotted on a commercial plotter you will need more information on your plotter's driver and/or the commercial plotter's driver that you will be using. Find out the manufacturer, name, and model number of the plotter with which you will be working and as much information about its driver as you can. Click on the New button. The Add a Printer box opens. If you do not have enough information to make a selection among the choices available in this box, go back to your plotter information and locate the information that you need to make a selection. For a Hewlett Packard plotter, for example, you will need to know whether it requires an ADI 4.2 or ADI 4.3 driver. Once you have enough information to select a driver for your plotter click on that driver to highlight it. Then click in the box next to Add a description:. Type in a description for your plotter. This can be a shortcut that is just used to identify it; it does not have to be extremely precise. If you have added a printer, click on the OK in the Add a Printer box. Anytime that you want to add a printer/plotter to the system you will need to return to this box to update it.

4. Click on OK on the bottom of the Preferences box.

THE AUTOCAD SCREEN AND ITS LAYOUT— MODIFYING THE OPENING SPACE

Differences Between Versions

The biggest immediately noticeable difference between the AutoCAD releases is in the screen layout and how you access the commands. The result is that the three versions of AutoCAD covered in this book have a very different look and sometimes access the commands in different ways. Therefore, I have divided this section, which deals with the AutoCAD screen and layout, into three separate parts for each of the three versions—R12, R13, and R14. Refer to the part for your particular version.

Modifying the Opening Space in R12

The figure titled The Opening Screen: R12 shows the main AutoCAD screen in a typical layout for Release 12. Many of these features may not mean much to you at this point, but familiarize yourself with them so you will be able to identify them later. If you are having trouble identifying a feature that is referred to in the text, come back to this section. Working from top to bottom on the screen, here are the main features:

The Title Bar

Working from left to right:

AutoCAD Icon: Double click here to exit the program.

The Date

THE OPENING SCREEN: R12

Title of Open File

Minimize Bar: Click here to reduce program to smallest size.

Maximize Box: Click here to make the AutoCAD window fill the whole computer screen or appear in a smaller size.

Close Button: Single click here to exit the program. Has an X on it.

The Pull Down Menu Bar

This bar contains the main headings for all of the pull down menus. Clicking on one of these names opens the pull down menu underneath. This is one way of accessing AutoCAD commands. The pull down menus are: File, Edit, View, Assist, Draw, Construct, Modify, Settings, Render, Model, and Help.

The Toolbar

The number of buttons on the toolbar will vary depending upon the size monitor that you are using and the screen resolution that you have selected for that monitor. Working from left to right, these are the main features:

Layer Color Button: The color of this button tells you the color of the currently active drawing layer.

Layer Control Button: The button labeled Layer activates the Layer Control box, which lets you create and change the properties of layers.

Layer Selection Box: The box with the arrow on its right side lets you change the active drawing layer. Click on the arrow to select from the available layers.

Ortho Button: The button labeled O turns the ortho feature of AutoCAD on and off.

Snap Button: The button labeled S turns the snap feature of AutoCAD on and off.

Paper Space Button: The button labeled P lets you enter and exit paper space.

A Small Group of Command Buttons: This next group of buttons between the Snap button and the coordinate display are toolbar buttons that can be changed to activate different AutoCAD commands. The exact number of buttons located here will vary with the size of your monitor and the resolution selected.

The Coordinate Display: This window shows you the exact position of the crosshairs or cursor in X and Y coordinates. See the detailed explanation of how the coordinate display works later in this section.

A Large Group of Command Buttons: The last and larger group of buttons can also be changed to activate different AutoCAD commands.

The Drawing Space

The main part of the screen is occupied by the **drawing space**. This is where you will do the actual drawing in AutoCAD. Move the mouse and you will see the crosshairs or cursor move around in this space. In the lower left-hand corner of the drawing space is the **UCS** icon. This looks like two arrows with an X and a Y in them. This is a constant reminder of the orientation of the drawing space in X and Y directions. Also located in this space is the toolbox.

The Toolbox

The box located in the drawing space with columns and rows of icons on it is the **toolbox**. The command buttons on the toolbox can be changed to activate different AutoCAD commands. Click on the bar at the top of the toolbox and hold the left mouse button down to move the toolbox to a new location in the drawing space. Release the left mouse button, and the toolbox will stay in its new location.

The Command Line

The window at the bottom of the AutoCAD screen contains the three **Command lines**. These lines show you keyboard commands that you have just typed in and commands that have been activated by the pull down menu or icons on the toolbar or toolbox and prompts you for the next part of a command. Until you learn the commands very well it pays to watch these Command lines closely.

MODIFYING THE TOOLBAR AND TOOLBOX

Both the toolbar and the toolbox in AutoCAD hold icons that can be used to activate the drawing commands in the program. When you first open the program you will find common commands assigned to the buttons on the toolbar and toolbox. Usually you will also find several blank buttons on the toolbar. Most of these commands will prove extremely useful, but the program also allows you to change the commands assigned to these buttons. The process for doing this is covered below.

1. Move cursor to the button you want to change and click once with right mouse button.

2. This opens the **Toolbox** or **Toolbar Customization** box, depending upon whether the button that you clicked on is on the toolbox or the toolbar. Here you can associate a command with an icon on the toolbox or toolbar. The buttons on the toolbar allow you to create a command that is not associated with a standard icon or to create a multiple-part command. The buttons on the toolbox will only accept commands that are associated with standard icons.

**THE TOOLBAR
CUSTOMIZATION
BOX: R12**

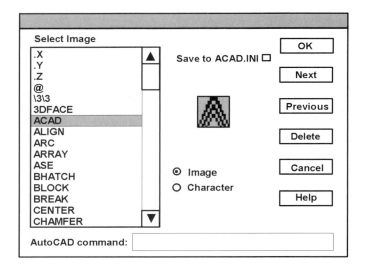

3. Modify a button on the toolbar:
   A. Click once on the button that you want to change with the right mouse button. This opens the Toolbar Customization box.
   B. Select the command and its associated icon by scrolling up and down in the Image Name box.
   C. When you have found the command that you want, click on the command in the Image Name box; the icon associated with it will appear to the right.
   D. The Toolbar Customization box offers these other options that are not available in the Toolbox Customization box:
      1. You can write your own command in the AutoCAD command: box and this can be a multiple-part command with a space between the parts.
      2. You can select a letter or character to represent the command rather than just an icon.
   E. Again, place an X in the Save to ACAD.INI box to save this change permanently. Do not put an X in the box if you want the change to only take place for this session.
   F. Click once on OK. This places the command icon on the button that you have selected.
4. Modify a button on the toolbox:
   A. Click once on the button that you want to change with the right mouse button. This opens the Toolbox Customization box.

    B. Select the command and its associated icon by scrolling up and down the Image Name box.

    C. When you have found the command that you want, click on the command in the Image Name box; the icon associated with it will appear to the right.

    D. If you do not want to make the change a part of the permanent setup, be sure that there is not an X in the Save to ACAD.INI box. If you do want to make the change a part of the permanent setup, be sure that there is an X in the Save to ACAD.INI box.

    E. Click once on OK. This places the command icon on the button that you have selected.

5. Modify the size of the toolbox:

    A. To add a button to the toolbox:

        1. Click once on the last button on the toolbox with the right mouse button. This will open the Toolbox Customization box.

        2. Click on the Insert button. You will go back to the main screen with a duplicate of the button that you had clicked on created. To modify this button to the new button that you would like, follow the procedures in step 3 above.

    B. To change the width of the toolbox:

        1. Click once on any button on the toolbox with the right mouse button. This will open the Toolbox Customization box.

        2. In the lower right-hand part of the Toolbox Customization box you will see a box labeled Toolbox Width. If you change the number under Toolbox Width and then click on OK it will modify the width of the toolbox to the number of buttons that you have specified.

6. Move the position of the toolbox: By using the toolbox command, you can also move the position of the toolbox to the left side of the screen, the right side of the screen, keep it free-floating as it originally opens, or make it disappear entirely. Each time that you issue the toolbox command, the toolbox will move to a new position on the screen. Issue the command again and it will move again. Keep moving it until you get it to where you would like it to appear.

THE COORDINATE DISPLAY

The coordinate display window on the toolbar helps you keep track of where you are in the drawing space in terms of X and Y coordinates, with X being the horizontal component and Y being the vertical component. It can be set in three modes by either clicking with the left mouse button on the display itself

AutoCAD Command	Function
Toolbox (R12 only)	**Moves position of toolbox on screen**

Keyboard Command	Pull Down Menu Path	Icon (R12)
TOOLBOX	**None**	

or pressing **F6** or **Ctrl-D** *after* you have started a drawing command such as
line. The three modes are:

1. **On, with polar coordinate display during commands,** which allows polar
   coordinate input. This mode has a "split personality" in most commands.
   When the crosshairs pull a rubber band line, such as in a line command,
   the second mode automatically switches into a polar distance/angle
   display relative to the last point. This mode is useful if you want to pick
   the initial point for a command with absolute X,Y coordinates and then
   pick subsequent points with relative polar coordinates.
2. **On, with absolute coordinate display,** which constantly updates the X,Y
   display as you move the cursor.
3. **Off,** which is sometimes called static coordinates. These coordinates are
   updated each time a point is specified. The default mode is **on, with polar
   display.** Clicking on the coordinate display or pressing **F6** switches to the
   absolute position, then to the off position. If this sounds confusing, it is!
   Switch the display mode until you get the coordinate display that you
   want.

Remember: Click on the display and press **F6** or **Ctrl-D** *after* you have started
a drawing command such as line.

THE SCREEN MENU

In addition to the pull down menu above the toolbar, most AutoCAD commands can be accessed from a **Screen** menu that will appear on the right-hand
side of the screen when it is toggled on. The Screen menu is activated by clicking on **File** and then on **Preferences**. This opens the **Preferences** dialogue box.
In the Preferences dialogue box, click on **Screen Menu** and then on **OK**. The
AutoCAD Alert box will open. Click on **Continue**.

   If you are using any of the choices that you make in the Preferences dialogue box on a continual basis then you can save them to the ACAD.INI file by

**THE OPENING
SCREEN: R13**

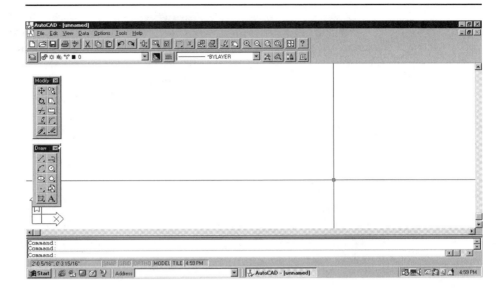

clicking on the Save to ACAD.INI File in the Preferences dialogue box. These preferences will then be automatically activated every time that you open AutoCAD. If you want that option activated only for the current session, do not click on the Save to ACAD.INI File in the box.

To use the Screen menu you move the cursor to highlight the menu selection and then click on it with the left mouse button. This will open the Branch menu under that menu selection, which can then be activated in a similar manner. These Branch menu items are the same as the items under the pull down menu above the toolbar. You return to the main Screen menu by clicking on AutoCAD at the top of the Screen Menu box.

Whether you want to use the pull down menu or the Screen menu depends upon personal preference and how large you want the drawing space to be. Both the pull down menu and the Screen menu activate the same commands. The Screen menu was a feature of pre-Windows versions of AutoCAD that was retained in the Windows version, which added the pull down menu.

Modifying the Opening Space in R13

The above figure labeled The Opening Screen: R13 shows the main AutoCAD screen in a typical layout for Release 13. This is actually what the screen looks like the first time that you open a new copy of the program. Many of these features may not mean much to you right now. However, with AutoCAD opened on your computer, work through the following so that you start to become familiar with these features. If you are having trouble identifying a feature that is referred to in the text, come back to this section. If you are working with a program that has been used by others it may have been customized to their preferences. This means that things may not be exactly where they are illustrated in the figure. Read the orientation below carefully to find out about most of these customization features. Working from top to bottom on the screen, these are the main features:

The Title Bar

This is the blue bar at the top of the screen. Working from left to right:

AutoCAD Icon: Double click here to exit the program.

The Name of the Program: AutoCAD.

The File Name of the Open File: This will be Untitled if no file is open.

Minimize Button: Click here to reduce the program to an icon.

Restore/Maximize Button: Click here to switch display sizes for AutoCAD screen.

Close Button: Click here to close program.

The Pull Down Menu Bar

This is just below the blue bar at the top of the screen.

This bar contains the main headings for the pull down menus. Clicking on one of these names opens the pull down menu underneath. This is one way to access AutoCAD commands. The pull down menus available are: File, Edit, View, Data, Options, Tools, and Help.

Note: The toolbars in AutoCAD R13 can be modified and moved about the screen as desired. The Standard toolbar and the Object Properties toolbar described below are usually left open by most people when they are working in AutoCAD. If they should not be open, refer to the section on floating toolbars (see page 32). When you initially open a new copy of AutoCAD R13 the Standard toolbar and the Object Properties toolbar will be in the locations described below. If you suspect that they are not open, click on Tools/Toolbars/Standard Toolbar and/or Tools/Toolbars/Object Properties on the pull down menu.

The Standard Toolbar

The Standard toolbar usually appears just below the pull down menu bar. Each of the icons on this toolbar can be quickly identified by moving the cursor over the icon. The name of the icon will appear when the cursor is left over the top of the icon for a short period of time. Right click on the icon and the Toolbars box will open. This box will let you customize the toolbar, change it for another one, and delete toolbars. I do not recommend any of these operations until you become much more familiar with the program. Right click on the icon a second time and the Button Properties box opens. This box will tell you the name of the button and give you a simple description of its function. This box can also be used to customize buttons. If you have opened either of these boxes, close them by clicking on the X in the upper right-hand corner.

There are some other properties of the icon buttons with which you should be familiar. You will notice that some of the buttons have a small arrowhead in their lower right-hand corner. This indicates that there are pop-up buttons underneath that button. Click on the button and hold the mouse switch down. The pop-up buttons will appear. Still holding down the mouse, move the cursor over the line of buttons that have just appeared. Pause over each one and the name of that button will appear. If you release the mouse over any of the pop-up buttons it will activate that command and that button will move up to the top of the pop-up, replacing the button that was there before.

This would also be a good point to quickly familiarize you with another important AutoCAD command: Cancel. If you activate a command and would like to get out of it without executing the command, hit Esc on the keyboard. This is the cancel command. Since you have probably just activated commands by checking out the pop-up buttons, it is extremely useful to know how to get out of them. Another quickie command that can be useful until you become more familiar with AutoCAD is one located on the Standard toolbar: the Undo command. The icon that looks like a curved arrow pointing left is the icon for the undo command. Undo, as its name implies, reverses or undoes the effect of the last command. So if you accidentally activate a command that you don't want, you can use the undo command to reverse it. Both the cancel and the undo commands will be covered in more detail later in this book.

The right-hand end of the Standard toolbar is the Help button. It is easily identified by a question mark (?). This button can also answer questions that you might have about the program.

The Object Properties Toolbar

Just below the Standard toolbar is the Object Properties toolbar. The buttons and windows on this bar are used to control the layers in AutoCAD and the properties associated with those layers such as color, linetype, etc.

The AutoCAD Drawing Space

The major portion of the AutoCAD screen is occupied by the drawing space. This is where you will be creating drawings. As you move the cursor around this space, it appears as crosshairs. The crosshairs will be an important part of the drawing function of AutoCAD. In the lower left-hand corner of the drawing space is the UCS icon. This looks like two arrows with an X and a Y in them. This is a constant reminder of the orientation of the drawing space in X and Y directions. Also in the drawing space are the floating toolbars.

Floating Toolbars

If you have just opened a new version of AutoCAD R13 you will see two boxes filled with icons in the left-hand side of the drawing space. One will have a blue bar at the top labeled Draw and the other will have a blue bar labeled Modify. These are two of the floating toolbars available in AutoCAD R13. If you are working with a version of AutoCAD R13 that has already been used, these boxes may not be in that location or they may not exist on the screen at all. The floating toolbars are another method of accessing commands in AutoCAD. The reason that they may not be where I have described them is that they can also be moved around the screen, aligned in different manners, and even made to completely disappear. This is one of the customization features of AutoCAD that you will be using on a regular basis. There are many other floating tool-bars besides the two that typically appear when you first open the program. You can quickly have just the toolbars that you need open on the screen, close toolbars that you are not using at present, and then reopen them when you want to use them.

These toolbars may be free-floating as I have described above. If that is the case, you can click and drag on the blue bar at the top of the toolbar to move it about the screen to any location that you desire. If you click and drag on the blue bar and move the toolbar to the top or the side of the drawing space the blue bar and title will disappear and the toolbar will appear as a single row or column along the top or side of the drawing space. If these toolbars should appear along the top or side of the drawing space you can turn them back into floating boxes again by clicking and dragging on the small border just outside the icons. This operation of turning toolboars into floating ones or stationary ones can also be done to the Standard toolbar and the Object Properties tool-bar. I do not really recommend it for these two toolbars, however, as they are constantly in use when working in AutoCAD. Floating toolbars can also be reshaped into vertical or horizontal configurations. Move the cursor to the edge of the toolbar that you would like to contract or expand. A double-ended arrow will appear. Click and drag to resize that side of the toolbar.

When toolbars are in their free-floating state, in addition to the blue bar along the top and a title they will also have an X in the upper right-hand corner. If you click on this X it will close the toolbox entirely. To reopen a tool-box, go up to the pull down menu and click on Tools/Toolbars/ and then on the name of the desired toolbox. The options under this menu are: Draw, Modify, Dimensioning, Solids, Surfaces, External Reference, Attribute, Render, External Database, Miscellaneous, Select Object, Object Snap, Point Filters, UCS, View, Object Properties, Standard Toolbar, and Close All. If you have trouble remembering which toolbars are open and which are closed or are trying to identify a particular toolbar it can be useful to Close All and then open the toolbars one at a time. Each of the toolbars will be covered one at a time in later lessons.

Command Line

Just below the drawing space is the Command line window. It can be customized in the Misc. section of the Preferences box (Options/Preferences) to be as many lines as you would like, but most people working in AutoCAD use the three-line default that is the standard setting with the program. The Command line window is divided into two parts. The top part shows the last two lines of commands that have been issued to the program. The bottom part is where any commands that you are currently issuing will appear. As you type on the keyboard, for example, each letter that you type will appear on this bottom line. To the right of the top two lines are scroll arrows. These will let you scroll up and down through previous commands so that you can view in text form any commands that you have issued in the past.

Coordinate Display

Just below the Command line window in the lower left-hand corner of the screen is the coordinate display window. You will notice that there are two numbers in this window separated by a comma. As you move the cursor about the drawing space these numbers will change. The first of these numbers indicates where on the screen you are located relative to the X coordinate. The second number indicates the value of the Y coordinate. X and Y values are given from the origin point of the drawing, which is usually in the lower left-hand corner of the drawing space. You can turn the coordinate display on and off by double clicking in the coordinate display window.

Toggle Buttons

To the right of the coordinate display window along the bottom of the screen are a series of buttons that let you toggle features of AutoCAD on and off. Displayed in either grey or black letters you will see the words: Snap, Grid, Ortho, Model (or Paper), and Tile. If the word is displayed in grey, it means that function of AutoCAD is toggled off. If the word is displayed in black then that function of AutoCAD is toggled on. Double click on a button to toggle it on or off.

Modifying the Opening Space in R14

The figure labeled The Opening Screen: R14 shows the main AutoCAD screen in a typical layout for Release 14. This is actually what the screen looks like the first time that you open a new copy of the program. Many of these features

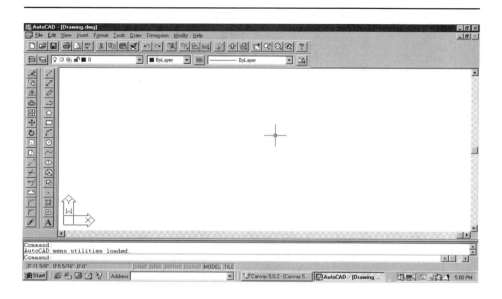

may not mean much to you right now. However, with AutoCAD opened on your computer, work through the following so that you start to become familiar with these features. If you are having trouble identifying a feature that is referred to in the text, come back to this section. If you are working with a program that has been used by others it may have been customized to their preferences. This means that things may not be exactly where they are shown in the figure. Read the orientation below carefully to find out about most of these customization features. Working from top to bottom on the screen, these are the main features:

The Title Bar

This is the blue bar at the top of the screen. Working from left to right:

AutoCAD Icon: Double click here to exit the program.

The Name of the Program: AutoCAD

The File Name of the Open File: This will be Untitled if no file is open.

Minimize Button: Click here to reduce the program to an icon.

Restore/Maximize Button: Click here to switch display sizes for AutoCAD screen.

Close Button: Click here to close program.

The Pull Down Menu Bar

This is just below the blue bar at the top of the screen.

This bar contains the main headings for the pull down menus. Clicking on one of these names opens the pull down menu underneath. This is one way to access AutoCAD commands. The pull down menus available are: File, Edit, View, Insert, Format, Tools, Draw, Dimension, Modify, and Help.

Note: The toolbars on AutoCAD can be modified and moved about the screen as desired. The Standard toolbar and the Object Properties toolbar described below are usually left open by most people when they are working in AutoCAD. If they should not be open, refer to the section on floating toolbars (see page 36). When you initially open a new copy of AutoCAD R14 the Standard toolbar and the Object Properties toolbar will be in the locations described below. If you suspect that they are not there click on View/Toolbars to open the Toolbars dialogue box. Check to see that there is an X in the box to the left of Object Properties and Standard Toolbar. If there is not, place one there by clicking in the box.

The Standard Toolbar

The Standard toolbar appears just below the pull down menu bar. Each of the icons on this toolbar can be quickly identified by moving the cursor over the icon. The name of the icon will appear when the cursor is left over the top of the icon for a short period of time. Right click on the icon and the Toolbars box will open. This box will let you customize the toolbar, change it for another one, and delete toolbars. I do not recommend any of these operations until you become much more familiar with the program. Right click on the icon a second time and the Button Properties box opens. This box will tell you the name of the button and give you a simple description of its function. This box can also be used to customize buttons. If you have opened either of these boxes, close them by clicking on the X in the upper right-hand corner.

There are some other properties of the icon buttons with which you should be familiar. You will notice that some of the buttons have a small arrowhead in their lower right-hand corner. This indicates that there are pop-up buttons underneath that button. Click on the button and hold the mouse switch down. The pop-up buttons will appear. Still holding down the mouse, move the cursor over the line of buttons that have just appeared. Pause over each one and the name of that button will appear. If you release the mouse over any of the pop-up buttons it will activate that command and that button will move up to the top of the pop-up, replacing the button that was there before.

This would also be a good point to quickly familiarize you with another important AutoCAD command: Cancel. If you activate a command and would like to get out of it without executing the command, hit Esc on the keyboard. This is the cancel command. Since you have probably just activated commands by checking out the pop-up buttons, it is extremely useful to know how to get out of them. Another quickie command that can be useful until you become more familiar with AutoCAD is one located on the Standard toolbar: the undo command. The icon that looks like a curved arrow pointing left is the icon for the undo command. Undo, as its name implies, reverses or undoes the effect of the last command. So if you accidentally activate a command that you don't want, you can use the undo command to reverse it. Both the cancel and the undo commands will be covered in more detail later in this book.

The right-hand end of the Standard toolbar is the Help button. It is easily identified by a question mark (?). This button can also answer questions that you might have about the program.

The Object Properties Toolbar

Just below the Standard toolbar is the Object Properties toolbar. The buttons and windows on this bar are used to control the layers in AutoCAD and the properties associated with those layers such as color, linetype, etc.

The AutoCAD Drawing Space

The major portion of the AutoCAD screen is occupied by the drawing space. This is where you will be creating drawings. As you move the cursor around this space, it appears as crosshairs. The crosshairs will be an important part of the drawing function of AutoCAD. In the lower left-hand corner of the drawing space is the UCS icon. This looks like two arrows with an X and a Y in them. This is a constant reminder of the orientation of the drawing space in X and Y directions. Also in the drawing space are the floating toolbars.

Floating Toolbars

If you have just opened a new version of AutoCAD R14 you will see two columns filled with icons along the left-hand side of the drawing space. These are two of the floating toolbars available in AutoCAD R14. If you are working with a version of AutoCAD R14 that has already been used, these boxes may not be in that location or they may not exist on the screen at all. The floating toolbars are another method of accessing commands in AutoCAD. The reason that they may not be where I have described them is that they can also be moved around the screen, aligned in different manners, and even made to completely disappear. This is one of the customization features of AutoCAD that you will be using on a regular basis. There are many other toolbars besides the two that typically appear when you first open the program. You can quickly have just the toolbars that you need open on the screen, close toolbars that you are not using at present, and then reopen them when you want to use them.

When you initially open a new copy of AutoCAD R14, the toolbars Draw and Modify are located along the left-hand side of the screen. These toolbars can also be turned into free-floating toolboxes. Click and drag on the border around the icons and the toolbar will become a row of icons that can be moved about the screen. When a toolbar is free-floating you can click and drag on the blue bar at the top of the toolbar to move it about the screen to any location that you desire. If you click and drag on the blue bar and move the toolbar to the top or the side of the drawing space, the blue bar and title will disappear and the toolbar will appear as a single row or column along the top or side of the drawing space. If these toolbars should appear along the top or side of the drawing space you can turn them back into floating boxes again by clicking and dragging on the small border just outside of the icons. This operation of turning toolbars into floating ones or stationary ones can also be done to the Standard toolbar and the Object Properties toolbar. I do not really recommend it for these two toolbars, however, as they are constantly in use when working in AutoCAD. Floating toolbars can also be reshaped into vertical or horizontal configurations. Move the cursor to the edge of the toolbar that you would like to contract or expand. A double-ended arrow will appear. Click and drag to resize that side of the toolbar.

When toolbars are in their free-floating state, in addition to the blue bar along the top and a title they will also have an X in the upper right-hand corner. If you click on this X it will close the toolbar entirely. To reopen the toolbar, go up to the pull down menu and click on View/Toolbars. This will open the Toolbars dialogue box. The Toolbars dialogue box can also be opened by right clicking on the border around the icons of any toolbar. Open the Toolbars dialogue box. In the window labeled Toolbars: there is a list of available toolbars. Those with an X in the box next to their name are being displayed on the screen. To close any toolbar, click on the box next to the name of the toolbar that contains the X. If you want to open any toolbar, click on the box next to the name of the toolbar so that an X appears. When you have finished opening and closing toolbars you can close the Toolbar dialogue box by clicking on Close or on the X in the upper right-hand corner of the box. The Toolbar dialogue box also allows you to create, delete, and customise your own toolbars.

Command Line

Just below the drawing space is the Command line window. It can be customized in the Display section of the Preferences box (Tools/Preferences) to be as many lines as you would like, but most people working in AutoCAD use the three-line default that is the standard setting with the program. The Command line window is divided into two parts. The top part shows the last two lines of commands that have been issued to the program. The bottom part is where any commands that you are currently issuing will appear. As you type on the keyboard, for example, each letter that you type will appear on this bottom line. To the right of the top two lines are scroll arrows. These will let you scroll up and down through previous commands so that you can view in text form any commands that you have issued in the past.

Coordinate Display

Just below the Command line window in the lower left-hand corner of the screen is the coordinate display window. You will notice that there are two numbers in this window separated by a comma. As you move the cursor about the drawing space these numbers will change. The first of these numbers indicates where on the screen you are located relative to the X coordinate. The second number indicates the value of the Y coordinate. X and Y values are given from the origin point of the drawing, which is usually in the lower left-hand corner of the drawing space. You can turn the coordinate display on and off by double clicking in the coordinate display window.

Toggle Buttons

To the right of the coordinate display window along the bottom of the screen are a series of buttons that let you toggle features of AutoCAD on and off. Displayed in either grey or black letters you will see the words: Snap, Grid, Ortho, Model (or Paper), and Tile. If the word is displayed in grey, it means that function of AutoCAD is toggled off. If the word is displayed in black, that function of AutoCAD is toggled on. Double click on a button to toggle it on or off.

OPENING, CLOSING, AND SAVING AN AUTOCAD FILE

OPENING A FILE (open)

You use the open command to open a file in AutoCAD. Like most AutoCAD commands it can be done with the keyboard, the pull down menus, or by clicking on an icon. Since this is the first command that I'm covering, this time I will talk you through each method. After this you should refer to the Command Box near the related text in this book for the command and then pick the method that you prefer.

THE OPEN COMMAND

AutoCAD Command	Function
Open	Opens a new file (closes old one).

Keyboard Command	Pull Down Menu Path	Icon
OPEN	File/Open	

- Keyboard: To use the keyboard method, type the word **open** and then hit **Enter**. As you are doing this, watch the three command lines that are in the lower left-hand corner of your screen. What you are typing will appear here as you type it. The part of the Command Box labeled Keyboard Command shows what you have to type using the keyboard method. Note that you can type the letters that appear here either in capitals or in both capitals and lowercase. Also note that you do not have to use capital letters when you type in the command. I am just using capital letters in the Command Box to indicate the simplest example that can be typed on the keyboard. When you hit **Enter** a prompt from AutoCAD will appear here on the line below the line that you just typed in. This prompt will ask you for the next part of the command. In the case of **open** and some other commands, a dialogue box such as the **Open Drawing** box (R12) or **Select File** box (R13 and R14) will appear on the screen. When a dialogue box appears, you must work in the dialogue box instead of using any other method.
- Pull Down Menu: To use the pull down menu method, click on the word **File** on the pull down menu bar at the top of the screen. Then on the pull down menu that appears below the word **File**, click on **Open**.
- Icon: To use the icon method, locate the icon shown in the Command Box and click on that icon on your screen.

The **Open Drawing** box or **Select File** box will appear on the screen. After the Open Drawing or Select File box appears, you need to locate the file that you want to open. The box typically opens in the **c:** drive. If you click on the arrow in the box labeled **Drives:**, the other drives that are available on your computer will appear. Remember that the **a:** drive is your "floppy" or 3.5-inch drive. There is a file located on the CD-ROM that accompanies this book that you will be using in the exercises for AutoCAD. Place the CD-ROM that came with the book in the CD-ROM drive of your computer. Locate the CD-ROM drive for your computer in the **Drives:** box and click on the icon or letter for that drive. The folders on the CD-ROM drive will appear in the box labeled **Directories:** above the Drives: box. Locate the folder labeled **AutoCAD** in this box and double click on it to open it. Find the file labeled **Proto.dwg** in the box labeled **File Name:** on the left-hand side of the Open Drawing box, then click on it once to highlight it. Next, click on **OK** to open the file.

Note: If you have AutoCAD R12, you may not be able to open a CD-ROM file unless you reconfigure the location of temporary files, see the following section on R12 and Read Only Files if you cannot open the file on the CD-ROM.

Another way to open the file is to double click on the file name once you have located it. The Open Drawing box will disappear and the file that

AutoCAD Command	Function	**Saves current drawing to**
Save As		**new location and/or name.**

Keyboard Command	Pull Down Menu Path	Icon
SAVEAS	**File/Save As**	**None**

you have selected will open on the drawing screen. You use the same technique to open a file from the c: (hard) drive or the a: (floppy) drive.

Note: AutoCAD R12 users should see the About the CD-ROM section on page 259.

Saving a File: The Save As (saveas) Command

Now that you have a file opened in AutoCAD, let's save it to another drive. The command to use is the **save as (saveas)** command.

Activate the **save as** command with the file **Proto.dwg** opened on the drawing screen. The **Save As** box will open. Place a 3.5-inch disk in your **a:** drive. Click on the arrow in the box under **Drives:**. Click on **a:** to select the floppy drive. If you want to change the name of the file you can also do that now. Click to the right of the name in the **File Name:** box, and then use the **Backspace** key to erase what is there. Enter the new name followed by **.dwg** to indicate that it is an AutoCAD file if you would like to rename the file or, in this case, just save it with the same name to the floppy disk. When everything in the box is as you want it, click on **OK**. You can also use the Save As box to save to a folder or directory in your hard drive by selecting **c:** in the **Drives:** box, then clicking in the **Directories:** box until you select the folder you want to place the file in. Go ahead and save the file **Proto.dwg** to a floppy disk in your **a:** drive. This disk can then be used in many of the exercises located later in this book.

Saving a File: The Save (**save**) Command

The **save (save)** command only works for a file that has already been named and that you want to save back to the same location from which it was opened. Neither the **save** nor the **save as** command will work with the CD-ROM drive. Remember that ROM stands for read only memory, meaning you can't change anything on or save anything to a CD-ROM.

**THE SAVE
COMMAND**

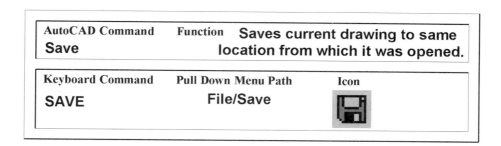

AutoCAD Command	Function	Saves current drawing to same location from which it was opened.
Save		

Keyboard Command	Pull Down Menu Path	Icon
SAVE	**File/Save**	

SAVING A FILE AS AN EARLIER VERSION OF AUTOCAD

As with most programs, when a new version of AutoCAD comes out it can read files from the older versions, but files from the new version cannot be read in the older versions. Files created in R14 cannot be read in R12 or R13. Files created in R13 cannot be read in R12.

AutoCAD does offer a feature that will let you save a file as a lower version so that it can be read in that version. Under the File pull down menu in R13 is the command Save R12 DWG. If you click here the Save As Release 12 Drawing box will open. This box will allow you to save a file that you created in R13 as a drawing that can be used in R12.

In R14 the procedure is a little different. In R14 you must first activate the save as command as indicated in the section on the save as command (see page 40). Then when the Save As box opens, click on the arrow next to the Save as Type: window. Then click on the file type that you would like to create in the selections available. You will notice that R12 and LT2 are the same file type and R13 and LT95 are the same file type. If you have LT98, it is the same file type as R14. Select the file type for the version that you desire and then continue with the other parts of the save as Command Box as indicated in the section on that command. All of the files located on the CD-ROM that accompanies this book have been created in AutoCAD R12 so that they can be read in any version. After you work with a file in your version and save it once, however, unless you have specifically saved it to an earlier version format it will be saved in the format for your version.

THE EXIT (exit) COMMAND

To exit AutoCAD and close the program, use the exit command. This may be done while a file is still open, but if you have not saved the changes that you have made to the file, AutoCAD will automatically ask you if you want to save those

**THE EXIT
COMMAND**

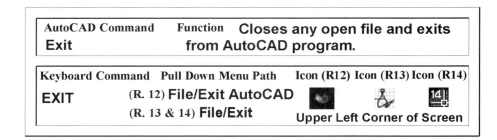

AutoCAD Command	Function	**Closes any open file and exits from AutoCAD program.**
Exit		

Keyboard Command	Pull Down Menu Path	Icon (R12) Icon (R13) Icon (R14)
EXIT	(R. 12) **File/Exit AutoCAD** (R. 13 & 14) **File/Exit**	**Upper Left Corner of Screen**

changes before it allows you to exit. You can also exit AutoCAD by double click-ing on the AutoCAD icon at the extreme upper left-hand corner of the screen or in Windows95/98 by clicking once on the X in the upper right-hand corner.

THE PROTOTYPE DRAWING AND ITS USE IN THIS BOOK

Now that you have opened and saved the drawing Proto.dwg to a 3.5-inch disk it is time to tell you about some of the uses to which you can put the draw-ing in this book. This drawing is included with the CD-ROM accompanying the book so that you can use it in the exercises that follow each of the sections, though now that you have saved it to a 3.5-inch disk I would recommend that you work from that disk rather than the CD-ROM. You will start each of the exercises with the Proto.dwg drawing and then make modifications to it as you learn the AutoCAD commands. You can then save each of these exercises to the disk under the recommended name and compare them with the version of the same exercise already completed on the CD-ROM to see how you have done. This file has been designed so that it can be printed on most printers available today as a single sheet of paper. After you learn how to print from AutoCAD, you will be able to print out your copy of the exercise and then compare it directly with the copy of the completed exercise on the CD-ROM. Mistakes will be easier to see and you will then be able to go back through the exercise and figure out where you went wrong.

CREATING A NEW FILE OR DRAWING IN AUTOCAD

Any time that you open AutoCAD you automatically open in a new drawing called Unnamed in R12 and R13 or Drawing.dwg in R14. If you make any changes to that drawing you will be prompted before you can close the pro-gram to save it by giving it a name and location. If you are in an already exist-ing drawing and would like to create a new one, go to the pull down menu and click on File/New. A new drawing space will open. This new drawing will be based upon a sample drawing in the hard drive titled acad.dwg in R12 and R13 and is either based on Drawing.dwg or upon a template in R14. AutoCAD comes with these sample drawings already set up with certain units and limits. It is likely that these will be neither the units nor limits that you want for your drawing and you will need to modify them. You can also modify the sample drawing so that the drawing that opens when you open the program or click on File/New is closer to what you would desire.

SETTING DRAWING UNITS

When a new copy of AutoCAD first opens it has normally had the units set to Decimal and Decimal Degrees. These are not units that we normally use in theatre. We would usually work in Architectural Inches/Feet and Decimal Degrees. You must tell AutoCAD to use these units instead of its default. You can change the Units setting of AutoCAD for any drawing that you would like, but it is annoying to have to constantly change them each time that you start a new drawing. A little later in this section I will show you how to change the units so that AutoCAD will always open using the units that you desire.

To change the units for the drawing that is currently on the screen:

1. Click on Setting/Units Control in R12, Data/Units in R13, or Format/Units in R14.
2. The Units or Units Control dialogue box opens.
3. Put a dot in the circles next to Architectural and next to Decimal Degrees by clicking on them.
4. Click on OK.

SETTING DRAWING LIMITS

The next thing that you should do before you begin a drawing is establish your drawing limits and name the drawing. There are several ways to go about this. I will cover a couple here. I have given you a prototype drawing on your CD-ROM that already has drawing limits established for a 1/2-inch scale that will work on most printers. You can use this drawing, Proto.dwg, for most of the exercises in this book.

In establishing drawing limits without copying a prototype there are a number of things that you should take into consideration. Remember that in AutoCAD you are not drawing in any scale, you are actually drawing full size. So, for example, if you want to draw a symbol for a lighting instrument, you don't need to be concerned with what scale it will end up being, but only what size the real instrument is. However, in establishing drawing limits, you are planning ahead for when you will be printing or plotting the finished drawing. There you must consider both the scale that you want the drawing to be printed in and the limits of the printer/plotter that you will be using. If you

AutoCAD Command	Function
Limits	**Sets or modifies drawing limits.**

Keyboard Command	Pull Down Menu Path	Icon
LIMITS	R12 Settings/Drawing Limits R13 Data/Drawing Limits R14 Format/Drawing Limits	**None**

take these things into consideration when you establish your original drawing limits, you will not have to do a lot of moving things around and changing in your drawing in order to print/plot it.

Therefore, before establishing your drawing limits, decide in what scale you would like to print the final drawing—in theatre often 1/2 inch = 1 foot— and find out what the print/plot limits of your printer or plotter are. A typical printer's printing limits are 8 inches × 10 inches. In a 1/2 inch = 1 foot scale that would yield us a drawing representing 16 feet 0 inches × 20 feet 0 inches. These are the drawing limits that are set up on your prototype drawing. Here's another example for a plotter: Let's say that your plotter can handle a maximum paper size of 36 inches × 48 inches. You want the final drawing to plot out in a 1/2 inch =1 foot scale. Then the maximum size drawing space or limits that you could print out from AutoCAD would be 72 feet × 96 feet. In a 1/4 inch = 1 foot scale the maximum size drawing space or limits that you could print out would be 144 feet × 192 feet.

To establish drawing limits (limits) from the opening work space in AutoCAD or to modify the drawing limits of an existing file, the procedure is as follows:

1. To start a new drawing begin in the opening work space that appears when AutoCAD opens, or open the file that you want to modify.
2. Activate the limits command by one of the methods show in the Command Box.
3. The Command line will read: ON/OFF<Lower left Corner><0'0",0'0">.
4. This establishes the lower left corner of your drawing as your base point for measurements. Hit Enter.
5. The Command line will then read with whatever the existing drawing limit for the upper right corner of the drawing is.
6. To set a new drawing limit, type the new upper right corner limit in the following format: X,Y (i.e., X = horizontal limit, Y = vertical limit) and then hit Enter. For example, to establish 16 feet × 20 feet drawing limits, you would type 16',20' and then hit Enter.

MODIFYING THE OPENING DRAWING SPACE

When you first open AutoCAD you will open in a drawing space that has been set up by the program. If you want to create a new drawing space you will have to modify the limits and change a number of other items that will be covered later in the section of this book on settings (see page 66) and then you will have to save it to a file name. The initial limits, for example, are 1 feet × 9 inches, not a space size very suitable to many theatrical drawings. The initial drawing units are in an engineering scale rather than the architectural scale that we use in theatre. If you would like AutoCAD to open a drawing space that already has limits and other modifications that you desire, this is fairly simple to do. Remember that you can come back later and make more modifications to this opening drawing space as you discover them. You just have to make the changes in the initial opening screen and then follow the procedure outlined below.

R12 and R13

1. Open AutoCAD and work in the initial opening screen.
2. Make any modifications to the drawing space that you would like.
    A. Reset the Limits to a size you would commonly use.
    B. Reset the Units to values that you desire, usually Architectural Units and Decimal Degree Angles.
3. Attempt to save the drawing.
4. The Save As box will open.
5. In the File Name box, type acad.
6. Click on OK.

R14

1. Open AutoCAD and work in the initial opening screen.
2. Make any modifications to the drawing space that you would like.
    A. Reset the Limits to a size you would commonly use.
    B. Reset the Units to values that you desire, usually Architectural Units and Decimal Degree Angles.
3. Click on File/Save As. The Save Drawing As box opens.
    A. In the File Name box, type acad.
    B. In the Save as Type: box, select Drawing Template File (*.dwt).
4. Click on Save.
5. Click on File/New. The Create New Drawing box opens.
6. Click on the Use a Template button.
7. In the Select a Template window, click on Acad.dwt.
8. Click on OK.

Printing a Simple File

Printing or plotting with AutoCAD can be a rather complex process, but to help you work with the exercises following each section of this book, the following instructions will take you through printing a simple file on most regular printers. Depending upon your particular printer, some of the following may vary slightly, but the basics should be about the same. For the exercise following this section you will be using the drawing Proto.dwg that you saved earlier to a floppy disk. To be able to print, you will have had to already configured the program for a printer as per the section on Configuring the Program and Setting Preferences.

Using the Print/Plot Command (plot) with a Printer

1. Be sure that the printer is turned on and has paper in it.
2. Turn on the computer and monitor.
3. Open the Print Manager or Printer Setup program and check to see that your printer is set for Portrait mode. Close Print Manager or Printer Setup.
4. Enter AutoCAD. Open the file that you want to print.
5. Open the Plot Configuration box by using the print/plot (plot) command.
6. Check these details in the Plot Configuration box before starting to print: Each of the following is a part of the Plot Configuration box that you should always check before printing. When you are ready to print the box should look like the one shown in the figure labeled The Plot Configuration Box. The different versions of AutoCAD will display slight differences in the apprearance of the Plot Configuration box, but all of the elements that should be checked are the same.
   A. Device and Default Information section:
      1. Is the name you gave your printer during configuration the device selected?
      Note: For R14, this would usually be Default System Printer.
      2. If not, click once on Device and Default Selection bar.
      3. Click once on your printer name and then on OK.

THE PRINT/PLOT COMMAND

AutoCAD Command	Function
Print/Plot	**Opens Print/Plot Dialogue Box.**

Keyboard Command	Pull Down Menu Path	Icon	
PLOT	**File/Print/Plot**		R13 & 14: Standard

THE PLOT CONFIGURATION BOX

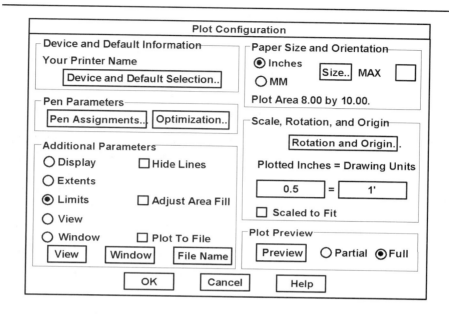

B. Pen Parameters section:

1. Click once on Pen Assignments bar to open box.
2. Setting Pen No.:
   a. Are all colors assigned to pen #1?
   b. If not, click once on any color number that is not. Pen number will appear by Pen: on the right side of the screen.
   c. Move the cursor to the right of the number in the box by Pen:, hit Backspace until that number is gone, then enter 1 on the keyboard.
   d. Move cursor to color number highlighted on the left side of screen and click once.
   e. Continue this procedure until all pen numbers for all colors are 1.
   f. Click once on OK.
   g. You can also change multiple pen numbers simultaneously by clicking on each color that you want to change and then entering the new number under Pen in the Modify Values box. After making the change in the Modify Values box you then click on each Color to establish that value.

Note: Depending upon the version of AutoCAD and the printer that you are using you may or may not be able to perform the following functions of the Pen Parameters box. If your version or printer does not allow you to do steps

4 and 5 below, you still should be able to set an overall pen width for the entire drawing in a **Pen Width:**____ area in the lower right-hand corner of the box.

    3. Setting **Linetype:** With some versions of AutoCAD and some printers, you can tell the printer to override the Linetype that you used in the drawing. When all **Linetypes** are set to **0** the printer will use the same Linetype as used in the drawing.

        a. Are all **Linetypes** assigned number 0?

        b. Follow the procedures in step 2 above (Setting Pen No.) to change all **Linetypes** to number **0** by making the changes under **Ltype** in the **Modify Values** box.

        c. To see the linetypes that are available with this printer you click on the **Feature Legend** box. These are the numbers that you would enter under **Linetype** to override a linetype that you were using in AutoCAD. For most of your drawings, the **Linetype** should be set to 0. This will then allow the printer to use the linetype that you used in the AutoCAD drawing.

    4. Setting **Pen Width:** With some version of AutoCAD and some printers, you can assign a different pen width to different layers of the drawing. With other versions and printers you can assign only a single pen width to all lines in the drawing.

        a. Are all **Pen Widths** assigned **0.010**?

        b. Follow the procedures in step 2 above (Setting Pen No.) to change all **Pen Widths** to **0.010** by making the changes under **Pen** in the **Modify Values** box.

        c. You can control the pen width of each **Layer Color** by changing the value through this procedure.

C. **Additional Parameters** section:

    1. Only the circle by **Limits** should have a dot in it.

    2. All other circles and boxes in the **Additional Parameters** section should be empty. Click in the circle to add or remove a dot.

Note: There are many other functions of this box that are covered in the plotting section later in this text (see page 155).

D. **Paper Size and Orientation** section:

    1. **Plot Area** should read **8.00 by 10.00** or something close to it depending upon the particular printer that you are using.

    2. If it does not, be sure there is a dot in the **Inches** circle and not in the MM circle.

    3. Click once on the **Size** button

    4. This opens the **Paper Size** box.

    5. If **MAX** is not highlighted, click once on **MAX**.

    6. Click once on **OK** to close box.

Note: You can set up the program to handle different paper sizes in this box by entering the effective plotting area of your printer in the right-hand side of the box under USER, USER1, etc. This will allow you to handle larger pieces of paper such as legal size. Check your printer's manual to find information on the effective plotting area for specific sizes of paper.

    E. Scale, Rotation and Origin section:
        1. Scaled to Fit box should not have an X in it.
        2. Plotted Inches = Drawing Units should be 0.5 = 1'.
           a. If not, move cursor to the right side of inappropriate figure and click once.
           b. Hit the Backspace key until figure is gone and then enter appropriate figure with keyboard.
        3. Rotation and Origin bar
           a. Click once on bar to open Plot Rotation and Origin box.
               1. Plot Rotation should be 0; click once on the circle by 0 if it is not.
               2. X Origin and Y Origin should both be 0.00; change them if they are not.
               3. click on OK to close box.

Note: The other functions of this box are covered in the plotting section later in this text (see page 155).

    F. Plot Preview section:
        1. It is a good idea to preview your plot before sending it to the printer to catch any problems.
        2. Click once on the circle by Full.
        3. Click once on the Preview bar.
        4. Examine preview carefully to see if there are any problems.
        5. Click once on End Preview bar to return to Plot Configuration box.
    G. To escape from Plot Configuration box without printing, click once on Cancel bar. *Any changes that you have made in the Plot Configuration box will be lost if you cancel printing.*
    H. To print from Plot Configuration box, click once on OK. *After printing, the Plot Configuration box will save any changes that you have made for the next time that it is opened.*
    I. Prompt will read: Press RETURN to continue or S to Stop for hardware setup:. Hit Enter and after the Vector Sort, printing will begin.
    J. Wait until the printer is finished printing to continue work in AutoCAD.

Note: Once you have clicked on OK to start printing, if you want to cancel printing, hit Ctrl-C in R12 or Esc in R13 and R14.

Exercise No. 1: Printing a Simple File

1. Open AutoCAD.
2. Reset your Units to Architectural Units and Decimal Degrees if they are not set as those.
3. Reset your Limits to a setting that would be realistic for many of your drawings.
4. Open the drawing Proto.dwg either from the CD-ROM or from the floppy disk that you saved it to earlier.
5. Save the drawing on a floppy disk (a: drive) as a new file name: Exer1.dwg.
6. Print a copy of your new file, Exer1.dwg, on your printer using the Print/Plot command in AutoCAD.
7. If it doesn't come out looking right, go back carefully through the steps outlined for setting up the Plot Configuration box and try to figure out where you went wrong.
8. Keep trying till you get it right.

VIEWING THE DRAWING

There are a variety of commands that allow you to move about in your view of the drawing you are working on in AutoCAD. The most important of these are pan, zoom, and dsviewer. Note that in some versions of AutoCAD Lite there is no DSViewer.

PAN (p)

The pan (PAN) command allows you to move the screen that you are viewing without changing screen size. Activate the pan command by using one of the methods shown in the pan Command Box.

THE PAN COMMAND

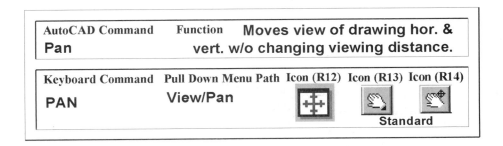

AutoCAD Command	Function	Moves view of drawing hor. &
Pan		vert. w/o changing viewing distance.

Keyboard Command	Pull Down Menu Path	Icon (R12)	Icon (R13)	Icon (R14)
PAN	View/Pan			Standard

R12

1. Activate the pan command.
2. At the Command line you will see: Command: PAN Displacement:.
3. Using the mouse, move the cursor to the point on the drawing that you want to move and click once.
4. The Command line will read: PAN Displacement: Second Point:. It is prompting you to move the mouse to the point to which you want to move the first point.
5. Using the mouse, move the cursor to the second point and click once.
6. Note that if Ortho is toggled on you can move only horizontally or vertically. If you want to move diagonally Ortho must be toggled off.

R13

In R13 you have many more options for panning than in previous versions. When the program is opened the first time the button on the Standard toolbar will be the Pan Point button, but notice that if you click and hold on that button, the following buttons will appear in a pop-up menu: Point, Left, Right, Up, Down, Up/Left, Up/Right, Down/Left, and Down/Right. These are also the options available under the pull down menu View/Pan. Point is the most useful of these options. The other options restrict you to panning in just the direction indicated in the title of the command. Point lets you pan in any direction that you would like and operates in the following manner.

1. Click on the Pan Point button.
2. At the Command line you will see: Command: PAN Displacement:.
3. Using the mouse, move the cursor to the point on the drawing that you want to move and click once.
4. The Command line will read: PAN Displacement: Second Point:. It is prompting you to move the mouse to the point to which you want to move the first point.
5. Using the mouse, move the cursor to the second point and click once.
6. Note that if Ortho is toggled on you can move only horizontally or vertically. If you want to move diagonally, Ortho must be toggled off.

R14

In R14 you have a different set of options for panning than in either of the other two versions. The icon button on the Standard toolbar is the pan realtime button. Under the pull down menu View/Pan there are other options available: Realtime, Point, Left, Right, Up, and Down. The Pan Point and directional options operate just like those commands in R13. The Pan Realtime function operates differently:

1. Click on the Pan Realtime button.
2. At the Command line you will see: Command: Pan.
3. Click and drag to move your view of the drawing. If you can't get to the view that you want in one click and drag, you can continue to click and drag until you have arrived at the view that you would like.
4. When you have arrived at the view of the drawing that you would like, you can hit Esc or Enter on the keyboard to exit the Pan Realtime function or you can right click on the mouse and then click on Exit on the pop-up menu that appears. In the pop-up menu, you also have the option of selecting the Zoom Realtime function by clicking on Zoom rather than exiting.

ZOOM (z)

R12

The zoom (zoom) command offers you many more options for moving about the screen. These options are All/Center/Dynamic/Extents/Left/Previous/Vmax/Windows. After you have activated the zoom command, the Command line will prompt you to choose one of the above options. Type the first letter of the option you desire and hit Enter. Then, depending upon the option chosen, the following will happen:

1. All: The screen will zoom to the limits that you have set for the drawing.
2. Center: The Command line will prompt you for the Center Point. Use the mouse and click once on the center of the window that you will be creating.
   A. The Command line then prompts you for Magnification or Height:.
   B. To ask for a Magnification of the drawing, type the magnification that you desire plus the letter X. For example, if you want to magnify around the center point you have chosen 2 times, type 2X. Then hit Enter.

THE ZOOM COMMAND

AutoCAD Command	Function	Changes the viewing distance
Zoom		to the drawing.

Keyboard Command	Pull Down Menu Path	Icon (R12)	Icon (R13 & 14)
Zoom	View/Zoom		See Illustrations for R13 & R14

    C. To ask for a **Height** around the center point you have chosen, type a height dimension in feet and/or inches. For example, to zoom to a box 10 feet high around the center point you have chosen, type **10'**. Then hit **Enter**.

3. **Dynamic:** This creates a window that you can move from side to side or make larger or smaller.

    A. Use the left mouse button to toggle between the **move** and **size** options. Then move the mouse to move the window or change its size.

    B. When you have the window sized and located where you want it, click on the right mouse button to zoom to the window.

4. **Extents:** The screen will zoom to the size of whatever you have already drawn. This is not to be confused with **Limits**. Your drawing is usually smaller than your limits.

5. **Left:** This option works exactly like **Center** except that the first Command line prompt is for the **Lower Left Corner** of the zoom field you are creating. After that, the **Magnification/Height** prompt works the same as in **Center**.

6. **Previous:** This option returns you to the screen view immediately previous to the one currently on the screen.

7. **Vmax:** This zooms out beyond the limits you have created to the largest possible view of your drawing.

8. **Window:** The Command line will prompt you for the **First Corner** of a rectangular window you want to define. Use the mouse to locate the first corner and click once.

    A. The Command line prompts you for the **Second Corner** of the window you want to create.

    B. Move the mouse diagonally to create a window, then click once.

    The **zoom** command is so useful that you may want to set up one or more buttons on the toolbar that have the options already written as the command for that button. **Zoom window**, for example, is an extremely useful command. You could set up a toolbar button that uses the character **Z** and for which the command is **zoom window**. Then when you clicked on that button you would automatically go to the zoom window option. Refer back to the earlier section on modifying the toolbar and toolbox for an explanation of how to do this (see page 25).

R13

The **zoom** command offers you many more options for moving about the screen than the **pan** command does. With zoom you can control the size of the view as well as its location. R13 offers the same options for zooming as R12

does plus some new ones. Review the options in R12 above so that you will understand them. The new options available in R13 are In, Out, and Scale. The icon buttons on the Standard toolbar are also different. In R13 from left to right as shown in the figure labeled The R13 Zoom Command Icons, there are buttons for zoom in, zoom out, and zoom window on the toolbar along with a pop-up button for all the other zoom options. The options that are new in R13 work in the following manner:

1. **Zoom In:** When activated, the zoom in command will automatically zoom closer to the center of the view by two times.

2. **Zoom Out:** When activated, the zoom out command will automatically zoom away from the center of the view by two times.

3. **Scale:** The scale command can be activated by keyboard or pull down menu. Type Z and hit Enter or click on View/Zoom/Scale.

    A. Prompt reads:
    All/Center/Dynamic/Extents/Left/Previous/VMax/Window/
    <Scale(X/XP)>:.

    B. Type in the zoom scale that you desire: 2X or 3X, for example, will zoom it in by those amounts; .5X or .75X will zoom it out by that amount.

    C. Hit Enter.

R14

In R14 you have the options available in R12 and R13 above, plus a new one: zoom realtime. Refer to the sections above on R12 and R13 for the other options. The button layout on the Standard toolbar is different from the layout in R13. In R14 there are three buttons, from left to right: Zoom Realtime, Zoom Window, above the pop-ups, and Zoom Previous. All of the other zoom options are available under the middle button of the three as pop-ups. Click and hold on the middle button and the pop-ups will appear. When you initially open R14, Zoom Window will be the middle button, but as you select other options, they will appear there in its place. Zoom realtime works in the following manner:

1. Activate the zoom realtime command.
2. Click and drag vertically on the screen to zoom in or zoom out.
3. Exit the zoom realtime command by hitting Esc or Enter on the keyboard or by right clicking the mouse to reveal a pop-up.
4. The pop-up offers you the options of Exit (exiting the command), Pan (switching to the pan realtime command), or Zoom (switching to the zoom realtime command). By working in this pop-up, you can switch between pan and zoom realtime to get exactly the view that you want, and then Exit.

Note: R14 also has a zoom tool box with icons for all Zoom commands.

DSViewer (dsviewer)

The DSViewer (dsviewer) Dynamic Screen Viewer in R12 or Aerial View in R13 and R14 creates a window within the AutoCAD window. This smaller window is set at your drawing limits and allows you to either pan or zoom from one part of the drawing to another. A warning about the DSViewer: you should close it before doing a Zoom/All on a complex drawing. In regenerating a full screen with the DSViewer open, AutoCAD will first regenerate the full screen and then also have to regenerate the DSViewer. This will double your screen regeneration time.

The DSViewer is not available in some versions of AutoCAD Lite. In R13, the Aerial Viewer may not be available depending upon your display driver.

Exercise No. 2: Viewing the Drawing

1. Open the drawing Proto.dwg from either the CD-ROM or from the floppy disk that you saved it to earlier.
2. Use the pan (R12) or pan point (R13 and R14) command to move the drawing to the center of your screen. Then move it back to where it was.
3. Use the zoom windows command to zoom down to just the word Prototype.

THE DSViewer COMMAND

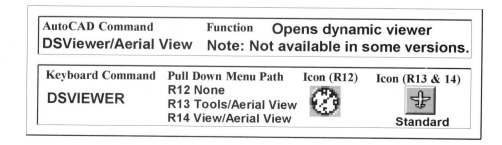

AutoCAD Command	Function	Opens dynamic viewer
DSViewer/Aerial View		Note: Not available in some versions.

Keyboard Command	Pull Down Menu Path	Icon (R12)	Icon (R13 & 14)
DSVIEWER	R12 None R13 Tools/Aerial View R14 View/Aerial View		Standard

4. Use the zoom all command to zoom back to the limits of the drawing.

5. Use the zoom extents command to zoom to the extents of the drawing. Note the difference between limits and extents.

6. Use the zoom previous command to zoom back to the limits from the extents.

7. Use the zoom vmax command to zoom way out from the drawing.

8. Use the zoom center command to zoom down into a closer view of the drawing.

9. Use the zoom left command to zoom down to a yet closer view of the drawing.

10. Return to the opening view by using the zoom all command.

11. If the Aerial or DSViewer is available, use the dsviewer command to move about the screen, zooming and panning to different views.

12. If you have R13 or R14, use the zoom in, zoom out, and zoom scale commands to move about the drawing.

13. If you have R14, use the pan and zoom realtime commands to move about the drawing. Use the right mouse button pop-up menus to switch between the pan and zoom realtime commands.

14. Exit the drawing, discarding any changes.

SAVING VIEWS, TRANSPARENT COMMANDS, AND MULTIPLE VIEWPORTS

AutoCAD also has options for saving a view of a drawing that you want to return to later; moving to a different view of a drawing in the middle of another command, so that, for example, you can select one end point of a line and then zoom down to a more detailed view of the drawing before selecting the other end point of the line; and dividing up your screen into sections so that you can have different views of the same drawing simultaneously.

THE VIEW COMMAND

AutoCAD Command	Function
View/Named View	**Names a view of a drawing for retrieval**

Keyboard Command	Pull Down Menu Path	Icon (R13 &14)
DDVIEW	R12 View/Set View/Named View R13 & 14 View/Named View	 **Standard**

View/Named View (ddview)

The View/Named View (ddview) command lets you save a view that you have been working in and would like to return to later. If you have panned or zoomed to a view of the drawing that you would like to save, you can do so by using this command. This command also lets you return to a view that you have named earlier.

1. Activate the command to open the View Control dialogue box.
   A. Click on New.
   B. Define New View box opens.
   C. Enter a name for the view in the New Name box and click on Save View.
   D. You are returned to the View Control dialogue box.
2. From the View Control dialogue box you can go to a view that has already been named by clicking on the name of the view, then on Restore, and then on OK.

Transparent Commands

The pan, zoom, view, and redraw commands all can be issued as what are known as transparent commands. This means that unlike most AutoCAD commands they can be issued while you are in the middle of another command. Say, for example, that you want to draw a line that connects two points that are on opposite sides of the screen. Start from a full view of the screen that lets you see both end points that you want for the line. In order to see the first point in detail you need to zoom down to one side of the screen. You start the line command and select the first point for it. You then issue a transparent zoom previous command and get into a full screen view, then issue a transparent zoom window command and get down to the detail that you want on the other side of the screen. Then you can finish the line command by selecting the second point. This can be especially useful when you are working in highly detailed drawings.

A transparent command is issued by placing an apostrophe (') before the command. After typing in the apostrophe you can either type in the command or use one of the buttons on the toolbar or toolbox or use a pull down menu command. *Do not hit* Enter *or the* space bar immediately after typing the apostrophe. To make the command transparent, the command must immediately follow the apostrophe. In the above example you would start the line command, select the first point of the line, hit the apostrophe, type Z and hit Enter, type P and hit Enter, hit the apostrophe again, activate the zoom window command, complete the zoom to the window that you want, and then select the second point of the line. Note that the zoom all (limits) and zoom extents commands are *not* available as transparent commands. Zoom previous will return you to a full drawing view *if* that is the view that you were in before you activated the zoom window command. In R14 both pan and zoom realtime can be issued as transparent commands.

MULTIPLE VIEWPORTS (mview) AND PAPER SPACE IN R12

Paper Space in R12

One of the additions that came about when AutoCAD moved into Windows from MS-DOS was the creation of paper space. The work space that you have been working in up to now is referred to as model space. In it you can set up multiple views that are tiled on top of one another. As you switch from one view to another you are switching from one layer, so to speak, to another. This is what you were doing in the ddview command. In paper space you can set up different views of a drawing right next to one another on the screen. This allows you to work on different parts of a drawing simultaneously. Later when you get into 3-D drawing you will be able to set up 2-D views of different sides of a 3-D drawing simultaneously by using paper space. In model space, however, you are able to look at a 3-D image of the drawing. Most of your work will be done in model space, but there are occasions when paper space is extremely useful.

Multiple Viewports in R12

One of the things that you can do while working in paper space is create multiple viewports (mview). Viewports are views of your drawing that can exist side by side or can be overlapped and whose boundaries can be edited and can be treated like an entity in themselves.

Note: The mview command does not work in some versions of AutoCAD Lite.

Entering Paper Space and Creating Viewports (mview) in R12

To enter paper space and create multiple viewports:

1. The Tilemode system must be set to 0 (off).
   A. Click on View, then on Tilemode. If there is a check by Tilemode, it is on. No check means that it is off. Click on it to toggle it on or off.
   B. Or, type tilemode and hit Enter. Then type 0 and hit Enter to turn off Tilemode and enter paper space. Type 1 and hit Enter to turn Tilemode on and exit paper space.
   C. The drawing will disappear until you create viewports.
   D. Note that the P button on the toolbar is lit when you are in paper space and not lit when you are in model space. You can use the P button on the toolbar to enter and exit paper space once Tilemode has been set to 0, but you cannot turn Tilemode on and off from there.

2. To create viewports:

    A. Click on View, then on Mview, and then on Create Viewport, or type mview and hit Enter.

    B. Prompt reads: ON/OFF/Hideplot/Fit/2/3/4/Restore/<First Point>:. This prompt offers you the following options:

        1. On: This makes all model space (drawing) entities in the selected viewport visible.

        2. Off: This makes all model space (drawing) entities in the selected viewport invisible.

        3. Hideplot: This allows you to select the viewports from which 3-D hidden lines are to be removed during plotting.

        4. Fit: This option creates a single viewport the size of the current paper space view.

        5. 2/3/4: These options create two, three, or four viewports. Note that when you create viewports with this option, they appear tiled, but you can move and stretch them as you desire.

        6. Restore: This allows you to recall a collection of viewports that you have saved using the vports command.

        7. First Point: This allows you to define the first corner of a new viewport, followed by Second Point, which lets you define the diagonally opposite corner of the new viewport.

    C. Choose the number of viewports that you would like: two, three, or four. Type in that number and hit Enter. For example, type 2 and hit Enter to create a total of two viewports.

    D. Prompt reads: Horizontal/<Vertical>:

Note: Other prompts will appear if you have chosen 3 or 4.

        • For 3, the prompts will read: Horizontal/Vertical/Above/Below/Left/<Right>:.

        • For 4, the prompt will read: Fit/<First Point>:.

These prompts let you chose the location and/or size of the two, three, or four new viewports relative to the one you have already created.

    E. For the two viewports prompt, type H or V and hit Enter to chose a horizontal or vertical division between the viewports.

    F. Prompt reads: Fit/<First Point>:.

    G. Type Fit and hit Enter to choose two viewports that will fill your screen, or you can determine the size of the viewports by clicking on the First Point—first corner—and then the Second Point—the diagonally opposite corner—of a rectangle that defines the combined size of the two new viewports. Fit is usually the best option.

H. The two new viewports will appear.

I. These same operations can be performed using the pull down menu under View: Click on View, then on MVIEW, then you can select Viewport ON, Viewport OFF, Hideplot, Fit Viewport, 2 Viewports, 3 Viewports, or 4 Viewports.

J. Note that at this point you are still in paper space.
   1. While in paper space you can move or stretch the viewports themselves by choosing the appropriate command and clicking on the edge of the viewport that you want to modify.
   2. To work in a viewport, however, you will have to get out of paper space and into model space. You can do this by either clicking on the P on the toolbar or by clicking on View and then on either Model Space or Paper Space.

K. To get out of the viewports that you have set up and return to the full-screen view toggle Tilemode to on (1).

L. To return to the viewports that you have set up toggle Tilemode to off (0).

MULTIPLE VIEWPORTS (mview) AND PAPER SPACE IN R13 AND R14

Paper Space and Floating Model Space in R13 and R14

One of the biggest changes that occurred with R13 and R14 in AutoCAD was the introduction of floating model space. Working with paper space in R12 could be extremely confusing. Floating model space lets you create multiple viewports using the mview command so that you can have different views of your drawing up on the screen simultaneously. Paper space still exists in R13 and R14, but now it is used primarily for layouts for printing. Everything has gotten much simpler for setting up multiple views.

Floating Model Space and the Multiple Viewport Command (mview) in R13 and R14

By switching to floating model space it is much simpler to set up multiple viewports in R13 and R14 than it is in R12. You can set up different views of the drawing in each of the viewports that you create and work in any of these views whenever you would like. To work in any of the viewports that you create using the mview command you simply move the cursor over that viewport and click with the mouse to activate the viewport.

To create multiple viewports, follow this procedure:

1. Turn on floating model space:
   A. R13: Use method 1 or 2 below:
      1. Pull Down Menu Path: Click on View/Floating Model Space.

**THE MULTIPLE
VIEWPORT
COMMAND
ICONS**

    2. Icon: Click on the Floating Model Space icon, which is located on the Standard toolbar in a pop-up menu with the Tiled Model Space icon and the Paper Space icon. The three icons shown above are stacked beneath one another in this pop-up. Click and hold on whichever icon is on top to see the other two. The top one displayed above is the Tiled Model Space icon. The middle icon is the Floating Model Space icon. The bottom one is the Paper Space icon.

    B. R14: Pull Down Menu Path: Click on View/Model Space (Floating).

2. When you turn on floating model space it will automatically activate the mview command and the prompt on the Command line will read: ON/OFF/Hideplot/Fit/2/3/4/Restore/<First Point>:. This prompt offers you the following options:

    A. **ON:** This option makes all model space entities in the selected viewport visible.

    B. **OFF:** This option makes all model space entities in the selected viewport invisible.

    C. **Hideplot:** This allows you to select the viewports from which 3-D hidden lines are to be removed during plotting.

    D. **Fit:** This option creates a single viewport the size of the current paper space view.

    E. **2/3/4:** These options create two, three, or four viewports. Note that when you create viewports with this option they appear tiled, but you can move and stretch them as you desire.

    F. **Restore:** This allows you to recall a collection of viewports that you have saved using the vports command.

    G. **First Point:** This allows you to define the first corner of a new viewport, followed by Second Point, which lets you define the other corner of the new viewport.

3. Choose the number of viewports that you would like: two, three, or four. Type in that number and hit Enter. For example, type 4 and hit Enter to create a total of four viewports. Prompt reads: Fit/</First Point>:.

4. Choose Fit:. Type F and hit Enter.

5. The four viewports will appear on the screen. If you had chosen 2 or 3 you would have gotten that number of viewports instead.

6. Move the cursor into each of the viewports that you have created and click. Notice that before you click, the cursor is represented as an arrow. After you click, the cursor is represented as crosshairs. The viewport where the cursor appears as crosshairs is the active viewport. You can perform any of the normal AutoCAD operations in the active viewport. You can make any viewport the active viewport by clicking in it.

7. You can switch between the full-screen drawing screen and the multiple-viewport drawing screen by clicking on

   A. View/Tiled Model Space in R13 or View/Model Space (Tiled) in R14 to get the full-screen drawing screen, or

   B. View/Floating Model Space in R13 or View/Model Space (Floating) in R14 to get the multiple-viewport drawing screen.

SAVING MULTIPLE VIEWPORT CONFIGURATIONS (**vports**)

The Multiple Viewport Configurations (vports) command can be used if you want to save a number of different viewport configurations. This command creates tiled viewports that you can switch between or you can return to a single viewport. With mview you can only switch between the single viewport and one set of viewports.

Type vports and hit Enter. Note that Tilemode must be set to 1 (on) to activate the vports command. Also note that the vports command operates only in model space. It does not operate in paper space, therefore you cannot use move and stretch to change the position or shape of the multiple viewports that you create using this command. Because the vports command operates in model space, however, it can be used to set up multiple 3-D views of 3-D drawings.

R12

To activate the vports command:

1. Keyboard: Type vports and hit Enter. Prompt reads: Save/Restore/Delete/Join/SIngle/?/2/3/4:. Type the capital letters or symbols to activate the command. The following options are available:

   A. Save: This option saves and names the current viewport configuration.

   B. Restore: Use this to redisplay any saved viewport configuration. Note: Enter a ? to display a list of saved configurations.

   C. Delete: This deletes a saved viewport configuration.

   D. Join: Use this option to combines the current configuration with a selected one that has already been saved.

E. SIngle: This function changes the screen to a single viewport.

F. ?: Enter a ? to display a list of saved configurations.

G. 2/3/4: Choose a number to create a viewport configuration that divides the screen into either two, three, or four sections.

2. Create the first viewport configuration that you want by using the 2/3/4 option.

A. Type 2 and hit Enter.

B. Prompt reads: Horizontal/<Vertical>:.

C. Type v for vertical or h for horizontal and hit Enter.

Note: In older versions of AutoCAD R12 you will proceed next to step D; in later ones you will skip directly to step F.

D. Prompt reads: Fit/<First Point>:.

E. Type fit and hit Enter.

F. The new viewport configuration will appear on the screen.

3. Type vports and hit Enter.

4. Prompt reads: Save/Restore/Delete/Join/SIngle/?/2/3/4:.

5. Type s and hit Enter.

6. Prompt reads: ?/Name for new viewport configuration:.

7. Type in a name and hit Enter.

8. Type vports and hit Enter.

9. Prompt reads: Save/Restore/Delete/Join/SIngle/?/2/3/4:.

10. Type si and hit Enter to return to the single viewport configuration. If you do not return to the single viewport configuration before creating new viewport configurations you will create multiple viewport configurations within the active viewport of the two that you have just created. By creating multiple viewport configurations within multiple viewport configurations, you can create a screen that contains up to sixteen multiple viewports.

11. Create the next viewport configuration that you want by using the 2/3/4 command.

12. Type vports and hit Enter.

13. Prompt reads: Save/Restore/Delete/Join/SIngle/?/2/3/4:.

14. Type s and hit Enter.

15. Prompt reads: ?/Name for new viewport configuration:.

16. Type in a name and hit Enter.

17. Repeat steps 8–14 above until you have all the viewport configurations that you want.

18. To switch from one viewport configuration to another, type vports and hit Enter.

19. Prompt reads: Save/Restore/Delete/Join/SIngle/?/2/3/4:.

20. Type r and hit Enter.

21. Prompt reads: Name of viewport configuration to restore:.

22. Type in the name of the viewport configuration to which you want to switch and hit Enter.

23. To switch to the single viewport at the Save/Restore/Delete/Join/SIngle/?/2/3/4: prompt, type si and hit Enter.

R13 and R14

To activate the vports command:

1. Pull Down Menu: R13 and R14: Click on View/Tiled Viewports/ and then on one of the following options.

   A. 1 Viewport: This will change the screen to a single viewport.

   B. 2 Viewports: This option creates a screen with two viewports.

   C. 3 Viewports: This creates a screen with three viewports.

   D. 4 Viewports: This creates a screen with four viewports.

   E. Restore: To redisplay a saved viewport configuration, use this function.

   F. Delete: To delete a saved viewport configuration, use this function.

   G. Join: This option combines the current viewport configuration with another that has already been saved.

   H. Save: Saves and names the current viewport configuration.

2. Click on 1, 2, 3, or 4 Viewport(s) to create a screen with that number of viewports.

3. After you have created a screen with one to four viewports you can then save it by clicking on: View/Tiled Viewports/Save:.

   A. The prompt will read: ?/Name for new viewport configuration:.

   B. Type in a name and hit Enter to name the configuration or type ? and hit Enter to see a list of already named viewport configurations.

4. After you have saved a viewport configuration you can then recall it by clicking on View/Tiled Viewports/Restore:.

   A. The prompt will read: ?/Name of viewport configuration to restore:.

   B. Type in a name and hit Enter to restore an already named configuration or type ? and hit Enter to see a list of already named viewport configurations.

5. Similarly, you can Delete or Join viewport configurations using the command.

Exercise No. 3: Using the View/Named View and Multiple Viewports Commands

1. While in AutoCAD, open the file Proto.dwg from either the CD-ROM or the floppy disk that you saved it to earlier.
2. Save this file as Exer3.dwg on a floppy disk (a: drive).
3. Zoom down to a view in which the word Prototype fits as much of the screen as possible.
4. Use the ddview command to save this view of the drawing as a view named Zoom1.
5. Use zoom all to zoom back to a full view of the screen.
6. Use the ddview command to save this view of the drawing as a view named All.
7. Use the ddview command to Restore the view Zoom1.
8. Use the ddview command to Restore the view All.

Note: If you are using AutoCAD Lite you will not be able to complete steps 9 and 10.

9. Create multiple viewports:
   A. If you have R12, use mview to create a screen with 4 Viewports, sized so that they Fit the available screen space.
   B. If you have R13 or R14, use floating model space to create a screen with 4 Viewports.
10. Save the work that you have just done as Exer3.dwg on a floppy disk.
11. If you have questions about how your Exer3.dwg should look, compare it with Projct3.dwg on the CD-ROM.

Exercise No. 4: Using the vports Command

1. Open the file Proto.dwg from either the CD-ROM or the floppy disk that you saved it to earlier.
2. Save this file as Exer4.dwg on a floppy disk (a: drive).
3. Use the vports command to create two different viewport configurations. The first viewport configuration should have 2 Viewports, sized to Fit the available screen space. Name this viewport configuration View2. The second viewport configuration should have 4 Viewports, sized so that they Fit the available screen space. Name this viewport configuration View4.
4. Return the screen to a SIngle viewport configuration.

5. Use the vports command to Restore View2.

6. Return the screen to a SIngle viewport configuration.

7. Use the vports command to Restore View4.

8. Return the screen to a SIngle viewport configuration.

9. Save the work that you have just done as Exer4.dwg on a floppy disk.

10. If you have questions about how your Exer4.dwg should look, compare it with Projct4.dwg on the CD-ROM.

USING SETTINGS AND CONTROL COMMANDS

Settings

There are many drawing aids and setups that can make the particular drawing you are working on easier to deal with. AutoCAD developers can't seem to make up their minds about where to place these commands. As you will see with each one, the way to get at the command varies greatly from one version of the program to another in terms of pull down menu path, icon, etc. Just about all of them, however, are available via the same keyboard command. You will find the keyboard command in the text in parentheses next to the name of the command. Note that these settings can be set up in your preferences and then saved so they will always be there when you open AutoCAD. Refer to the section on modifying the opening drawing space on page 23 for instructions. Some of the most important of them include the following.

DRAWING AIDS (ddrmodes)

This command opens the Drawing Aids box, which contains the following:

1. Modes

   A. Ortho (ortho): You can toggle ortho on and off either here or on the screen. When ortho is toggled on you can only draw or pan vertically or horizontally, but not diagonally.

THE DRAWING AIDS COMMAND

AutoCAD Command	Function
Drawing Aids	**Opens box w/settings for various aids.**

Keyboard Command	Pull Down Menu Path
DDRMODES	R12: Settings/Drawing Aids R13: Options/Drawing Aids R14: Tools/Drawing Aids

B. **Solid Fill** (fill): This must be on when you are using hatch or when you want to fill in a solid shape. I recommend leaving it off unless you are using hatch or fill, as it uses screen regeneration time.

C. **Quick Text** (qtext): Text takes up a lot of time in screen regeneration when you are working. Qtext substitutes rectangular blocks for large groups of text, saving you screen regeneration time.

D. **Blips**: This option leaves a small + where you have established a point. For example, there will be a + at each end of a line. You can get rid of them by doing a redraw. Many people find blips annoying and leave them turned off.

E. **Highlight** (highlight): Use this to indicate an object has been selected for an operation. For example, when you select an object to erase, it will turn it into a dotted line to indicate which object is going to be erased. This is a setting that you usually would like to have on.

2. **Snap, Grid, and Isometric Snap/Grid**: These boxes can be found in the **Drawing Aids** box and all are concerned with functions and operations of an imaginary or visible reference grid that can aid you in your drawing.

A. **Snap** (snap): This box lets you set up the X and Y dimensions for the snap command. The snap command can be toggled on or off here or on the S button on the toolbar. This box also lets you choose angled rather than horizontal and vertical snaps and lets you set up a base point for the snap command. Snap is an invisible grid template that controls the points that you select with your cursor. If you set snap to .5, for example, then you can only select points that fall on .5 unit increments.

B. **Grid** (grid): The command turns on or off a visible reference grid on the screen to help you with spacing in your drawing and allows you to control the size of the grid spacing. The grid by itself is just a visible reference. Only if you set snap to the same settings will you be able to use it for accurate snap points.

C. **Isometric Snap/Grid**: This command turns on or off an isometric drawing grid to aid you in isometric drawings. There will be more on isometric drawing later in the book.

OBJECT SNAP OR OSNAP (**ddosnap**)

This command opens the **Object Snap** box. Object snaps are covered in more detail in the section on draw commands (see page 74), because these are usually used with such commands, but the basic functions of the box are:

1. It allows you to set up a running snap to a particular entity such as an **Endpoint** or **Intersection**. When an object snap such as **Intersection** is selected here, AutoCAD will automatically look inside the snap apeture

**THE OBJECT
SNAP COMMAND**

AutoCAD Command	Function
Object Snap	**Allows you to "snap to" a selected object.**

Keyboard Command	Pull Down Menu Path
DDOSNAP	**R12: Settings/Object Snap** **R13: Options/Running Object Snap** **R14: Tools/Object Snap Settings**

for the intersection closest to the center of the crosshairs and snap the point that you are drawing, like the end of a line, to that intersection.

2. It also allows you to control the size of your Snap Apeture, which determines how big the box is around the center of the crosshairs to select an object for an object snap.

ENTITY MODES (ddmodify) IN R12 AND R13

The Entity Modes box lets you change various entity drawing modes. All of these changes can be made in other places, but when you are making a number of changes at once, this box can be useful. Note that for this box to be most useful you must have already loaded all of the linetypes and text styles that you are going to be using in the drawing.

In R14, this entire command has been discontinued and the Entity Modes box is replaced by the Object Properties toolbar.

1. Color: This option lets you change the color of a layer.
2. Layer: This option lets you change the current drawing layer.
3. Linetype: This option lets you change the linetype of a layer.
4. Text Style: This option lets you change the current text style.

**THE ENTITY
MODES
COMMAND**

AutoCAD Command	Function
Modify Entity/Properties	**Changes characteristics of an entity.**

Keyboard Command	Pull Down Menu Path	Icon (R12)	Icon (R13 & R14)
DDMODIFY	**R12: Modify/Entity** **R14: Modify/Properties**	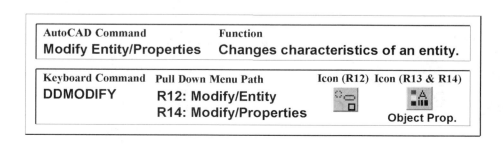	**Object Prop.**

**THE POINT
STYLE
COMMAND**

AutoCAD Command	Function
Point Style	**Sets the visual style of a Point.**

Keyboard Command	Pull Down Menu Path
DDPTYPE	**R12: Settings/Point Style** **R13: Options/Display/Point Style** **R14: Format/Point Style**

POINT STYLE (ddptype)

This command opens the box that lets you change the display style of a point or node. This is especially useful with the divide and measure commands so that you can see the points that a line has been divided or measured into.

UNITS CONTROL (ddunits)

This command opens the box that allows you to set the measurement units in which you will be working. Always check the Units Control before beginning a drawing.

1. Units: For most theatrical drawing we would use Architectural, which will give dimensions in feet and inches. This is one setting that I would definitely set up for the AutoCAD opening drawing space.
2. Angles: For most theatrical drawing we would use Decimal Degrees.

GRIPS (ddgrips)

The Grips dialogue box lets you adjust grips settings. A grip is a small square that appears at various places on an entity such as the quadrants of a circle or end points or midpoint of a line. You can use grips to stretch, move, rotate,

**THE UNITS
CONTROL
COMMAND**

AutoCAD Command	Function
Units	**Sets your drawing units.**

Keyboard Command	Pull Down Menu Path
DDUNITS	**R12: Settings/Units** **R13: Data/Units** **R14: Format/Units**

AutoCAD Command	Function
Grips	**Enables and sets sizes of Grips.**

Keyboard Command	Pull Down Menu Path
DDGRIPS	**R12: Settings/Grips** **R13: Options/Grips** **R14: Tools/Grips**

scale, and mirror selected objects. Be sure that there is a check in the box by Enable Grips. How to use grips will be covered under the drawing commands section (see page 74).

1. **Select Settings:** This allows you to enable or disable grips on entities or within blocks.
2. **Grip Colors:** This allows you to choose the colors of selected and unselected grips.
3. **Grip Size:** This allows you to change the size of the grips.

DRAWING LIMITS (limits)

This command allows you to set or reset your drawing limits.

Control Commands

There are a number of commands with which you should be familiar before you begin drawing. These are commands that can get you out of trouble in the middle of a mistake or after you have made one. This section is just to familiarize you with these commands. They will be covered in more detail later.

AutoCAD Command	Function	
Limits	**Sets or modifies drawing limits.**	

Keyboard Command	Pull Down Menu Path	Icon
LIMITS	**R12 Settings/Drawing Limits** **R13 Data/Drawing Limits** **R14 Format/Drawing Limits**	**None**

AutoCAD Command	Function	
Cancel	Cancels the command that you are in	

Keyboard Command	Pull Down Menu Path	Icon (R12)
R12: Control + C R13 & R14: Esc	R12:Assist/Cancel	^C

CANCEL

This command lets you escape from a command without completing it. If you are in the middle of executing a command and decide that you don't want to complete that command, use this command. In R12, hold down the Control key and hit the C key. If once doesn't work, do it twice. In R13 and R14, use the Esc key.

ERASE (erase)

This command erases an object that you have already drawn. For more details, see the modify commands section (see page 97).

After initiating the erase command:

1. You will be prompted: Select Objects:.
2. Click on object(s) to be erased; you may select more than one. You may also click outside of an object and drag the mouse to form a window. Click again to indicate the other corner of the window. Objects that are completely enclosed within the window will be selected for erasure.
3. Hit Enter or click on right mouse button to erase the object(s).
4. Undo Erase: If you have selected objects to be erased, but have not erased them yet, you can undo erase the selections by hitting the u key and then

AutoCAD Command	Function		
Erase	Erases selected entity/s		

Keyboard Command	Pull Down Menu Path	Icon (R12)	Icon (R13 & 14)
ERASE	R12: Modify/Erase R14: Modify/Erase		Modify

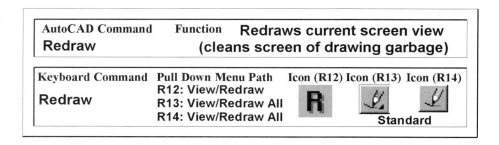

the Enter key. This will remove the last object selected for erasure from the **erase** command. Keep hitting the U key and the Enter key and it will remove items selected for erasure in the reverse order in which they were selected.

5. **Oops:** The **oops** command will undo the last erasure after it is completed. Type **oops** and hit the Enter key. Note that the regular **undo** command will do exactly the same thing, but will let you restore more than one erasure.

6. **Crossing Window:** Type **c** after activating the **erase** command and then hit Enter. A window formed by clicking on one corner and then clicking on the other corner is now a crossing window. Any object that is even partly within this window is selected for erasure. This is a very useful aspect of the **erase** command to remember.

REDRAW (r)

The **redraw (r)** command renews the screen to eliminate blips or check an erasure to see if it was complete.

UNDO (u)

The **undo (u)** command removes the effect of the last completed command. It can be repeated so that you can undo numerous steps back in your drawing.

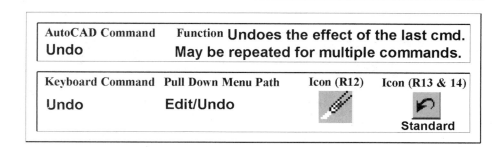

**THE REDO
COMMAND**

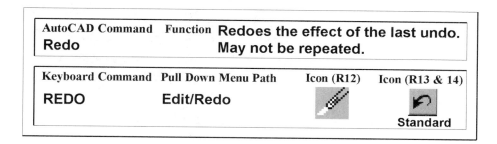

AutoCAD Command	Function	Redoes the effect of the last undo.
Redo		May not be repeated.

Keyboard Command	Pull Down Menu Path	Icon (R12)	Icon (R13 & 14)
REDO	Edit/Redo		
			Standard

REDO (redo)

The redo command removes the effect of the last undo command. Redo will *not* go back more than *one* step in undo.

TEXT WINDOW

The text window function allows you to review in text format all commands in your current session. It is only available on pull down menu. R12: Edit/Text Window. R13: Tools/Text Window. R14: View/Display/Text Window.

1. Activate the command
2. Use scroll bar on right side of window to scroll back commands.
3. Close text window by
   • clicking on X on AutoCAD text bar, or
   • double clicking on icon in left corner of AutoCAD text bar.

REPEATING A COMMAND

You can repeat the last completed command by either:
   • hitting Enter, or
   • clicking on the right mouse button.

Exercise No. 5: Using Settings and Control Commands

1. Open the file Proto.dwg from either the CD-ROM or the floppy disk that you saved it to earlier.
2. Erase the word Prototype.
3. Undo the erasure.
4. Erase the word Prototype using a crossing window.
5. Undo the erasure.

6. If blips is activated, deactivate it. If it is deactivated, activate it.

7. Do steps 2 through 5 again.

8. Begin an erasure, and then use the cancel command to get out of it.

9. Activate the grid with an X setting of 1'0" and a Y setting of 1'0".

10. Exit AutoCAD, discarding any changes.

Using Draw, Dimensioning, Object Snaps, Sketch, and Distance Commands

Most of the basic drawing tools for AutoCAD are located under the Draw pull down menu in R12 and R14 and/or on the Draw toolbox in R13 and R14. These are the commands that draw objects such as lines, arcs, circles, etc. If you are working in R13 or R14 be sure that the Draw and Modify toolbars are open on the screen before you continue with this section. For R13, this is done by clicking on Tools/Toolbars and then on the name of the toolbar. For R14, this is done by clicking on View/Toolbars to open the Toolbars dialogue box and then checking for an X in the box next to the name of the toolbar that you want to be open. For those commands without Command Boxes, remember that the keyboard command is shown in parentheses after the name of the command. Some of the most useful tools available are the following.

Line: (line)

Like most of the draw commands, line can be operated in a number of different ways. After activating the command you will see the prompt From Point: in the Command line. The command that I'm describing below is referred to in R12 as line segments and in R13 and 14 simply as line.

1. When prompted From Point:, simply click on the starting point of the line that you want to draw. You will then be prompted To Point:. Click on the end point. You can then go on and form another line segment that begins

THE LINE
COMMAND

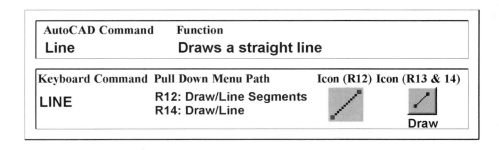

AutoCAD Command	Function		
Line	**Draws a straight line**		

Keyboard Command	Pull Down Menu Path	Icon (R12)	Icon (R13 & 14)
LINE	R12: Draw/Line Segments R14: Draw/Line		Draw

at the end point of the first line segment or click on the right mouse button to exit the command. By watching the coordinate display, you can achieve a line of approximately the length that you would like, but this method does not really allow you to be precise in line length, angle, etc. Remember that for horizontal or vertical lines you can toggle ortho on.

2. You can achieve much more precise positioning of lines by entering coordinates for the start point and end point of each line segment. When prompted From Point:, enter the X and Y coordinates of the point where you want the line to begin as X,Y in the drawing units from the origin. When prompted To Point, enter the X and Y coordinates of the point where you want that line segment to end as X,Y in the drawing units from the origin. For example, to draw a 2-foot-long horizontal line that begins at a point 8 feet left of the origin and 6 feet above the origin, you would do the following:

   A. Activate the line command. Prompt reads: From Point:.

   B. Type in the coordinates of the starting point of the line segment. For example, type 8',6' and hit Enter.

   C. Prompt reads: To Point:. Type in the coordinates of the ending point of the line segment. For example, type 10',6' and hit Enter.

   D. You can then draw a line segment that begins at that point and goes to the next coordinate that you type in, or you can terminate the command by hitting Enter again or clicking on the right mouse button.

3. In addition to entering points by coordinates or clicking on a point, you can also draw a line and most other draw commands by using relative coordinates. After activating the line command:

   A. Type in coordinates of the start point (X,Y) or click on the start point.

   B. Type @Distance<direction in degrees counterclockwise and hit Enter. For example, to draw a line 8 feet long straight to your right from the starting point, you would type: @8'<0 and hit Enter.

   C. Remember that in AutoCAD as you are looking at the screen,
      0 = horizontally to your right
     90 = straight up
    180 = horizontally to your left
    270 = straight down

4. Another way to establish points for drawing a line or other draw commands is to establish a grid and snap to the grid. If you are going to be drawing a lot of lines all of which can be determined by grid points, this can be a quick and easy method to use. See the settings section of this book (see page 66) for more information on grid and snap.

There are other line commands available.

One Segment in R12

This is available only in R12 by using a pull down menu. This works like segments, except it automatically terminates the command at the first end point. It is useful if you are drawing a lot of single line segments.

Double Lines in R12 (dline)

Use this command to draw double lines of a specified distance apart.

1. Click on Double Line under Draw or type dline and hit Enter.
2. Prompt will read: Break/Caps/Dragline/Offset/Snap/Undo/Width/ <start point>:.
3. Type first letter of option desired. For example, type w for width, and hit Enter.
4. You will be prompted for information on the option chosen. For example, the prompt New DLINE width<1'>: tells you that current width is 1 foot and asks you if you want to change it. If current width is desired, hit Enter. If not, type width desired and then hit Enter.
5. Break: This allows you to specify—by entering either on or off—whether you want to create a gap between intersecting lines.
6. Caps: This allows you to specify whether you want a cap joining the double lines at Both (both ends), End (last end), None (no caps), Start (beginning), or Auto (any open ends).
7. Dragline: This option lets you specify where the original line is placed in relation to the offset line. You can choose from Left, Center, or Right.
8. Offset: This lets you start a new double line at a specified distance from a specified base point.
9. Snap: Three options—On, Off, and Size—let you snap or not snap to an already existing object. Size lets you choose the area (in pixels) that will be searched for an object to snap to when you select a point.
10. Undo: This takes you back one operation when working within double line.
11. Width: This lets you specify the distance between the double lines.

Multiline (mline) in R14

Use the mline command to draw multiple lines of a desired width apart. Before you can use this command you must set and name a multiline style by using the mlstyle command. Type mlstyle and hit Enter. This opens the Multiline Styles dialogue box. There is one multiline style that has already been set, named Standard. This is a double line. If you would like to create a new multiline style, clear the Name box and enter a new name. This will be the name of your new style. Click on the Element Properties button. The Element Properties box will open. In the Elements section, the two lines of the Standard style will be defined by their offset distance from center. If you want to add a line, click on the Add button. A new line will be added at center. You can then redefine its position by highlighting it and then making a change in the Offset box. A line can be deleted by highlighting the line in the Elements section and then clicking on the Delete button. You can create a multiline style of up to sixteen lines in this manner. When you have the number of lines and their spacing set, click on OK to exit the Element Properties box and return to the Multiline Styles box. Next click on the Multiline Properties button to open the Multiline Properties box. Here you can add Caps to the End or Start points of the Lines, Outer Arc, or Inner Arc by checking the appropriate boxes. You can also select the options of showing the joints between multilines and of filling between multilines. Click on OK to return to the Multiline Styles box. By clicking on the down arrow next to the Current window you can also select which multiline style that you want to be currently active: Standard or the one that you just created and named. Click on OK to exit the box and save the new style that you just created and named. If you do not want to save the style that you just created click on Cancel.

Activate the multiline command:

1. Click on Multiline under Draw, type mline and hit Enter, or click on Draw toolbar icon shown in the figure labeled The Multiline Command Icon.

2. Prompt will read: Justification/Scale/STyle/<From Point>:. The following options are available:

   A. Justification: Type j and hit Enter.
      1. Prompt reads: Top/Zero/Bottom <top>:.
      2. This allows you to choose which one of the multiple lines you will be using as the baseline in drawing: the top line, the bottom line, or zero—the center between the two outside lines.
      3. Type T, Z, or B and hit Enter.

   B. STyle: Type st and hit Enter.
      1. Prompt reads: Mstyle name (or ?):
      2. Sets style for the multiline. If you have already named an mline style, type the name here and hit Enter. STANDARD, which is a double line, should already exist.

THE MULTILINE COMMAND ICON

3. If you want to see the names of mline styles already loaded, type ? and hit Enter. This will open a text box with a listing of mline styles. Close the text box by clicking on the X in the upper right-hand corner of the box.

C. Scale: Type s and hit Enter.
1. Prompt reads: Set Mline scale <1.00>:
2. Type in a value and hit Enter. This value will change the line width that has been set by the mline style. For example, entering a 2 here will double the width between the lines; entering a .5 here will divide the width between the lines in half.

D. If all of the above options have been adjusted to your liking, you can start a multiline just as you would a regular line by clicking with the mouse or entering coordinates. The command works just like Line in that it will continue drawing connected line segments until you terminate the command by right clicking the mouse or hitting Enter.

Ray (ray) in R13 and R14

The ray (ray) command allows you to draw a series of lines that emanate from a single point. This command can be activated in either R13 or R14 by typing ray and hitting Enter. In R13, it can be activated by clicking on the icon shown below on the pop-up that appears under the Line icon on the Draw toolbar. In R14, it can be activated by clicking on Draw/Ray on the pull down menu.

After the command has been activated:

1. Prompt reads: Ray from point:.
2. Select the point from which the rays will emanate either by clicking with the mouse or entering an X,Y coordinate value.
3. Prompt reads: Through point:.
4. Select a point through which a ray will be drawn from the origin point. You can click with the mouse or enter X,Y coordinates.
5. Prompt reads: Through point:.
6. Continue to select points until you have created all of the rays that you desire. When you are finished creating rays, hit Enter or right click to terminate the command.

THE RAY COMMAND ICON

**THE
CONSTRUCTION
LINE COMMAND
ICON**

CONSTRUCTION LINE (**xline**) IN R13 AND R14

This command creates infinite lines that pass through a selected point. These are most commonly used as construction lines, hence the name. This command can be activated in R13 or R14 by typing **xline** and hitting **Enter**. It can be activated in R14 by clicking on **Draw/Construction Line** on the pull down menu. It can be activated in R13 and R14 by clicking on the icon shown above on the **Draw** toolbar. In R13 this icon is part of the pop-up under the **Line** icon.

After the command has been activated:

1. Prompt reads: xline Hor/Ver/Ang/Bisect/Offset/<From Point>:.
   The options available are:
   A. **Hor:** This creates a horizontal line through the selected point.
   B. **Ver:** This creates a vertical line through the selected point.
   C. **Ang:** This creates a line through the selected point at a specified angle.
   D. **Bisect:** This creates a line that bisects an angle between two other lines.
   E. **Offset:** This creates a line that is offset at a specified distance from another line.

2. After you have selected your option by typing the capital letter, you will be prompted to continue with the information necessary for that option.

3. If you choose not to select one of the above options, select a point through which the construction line will pass by clicking with the mouse or entering X,Y coordinates.

4. Prompt reads: Through point:.

5. Select a second point through which the construction line will pass by clicking the mouse or entering X,Y coordinates.

6. Prompt reads: Through point:.

7. Select another point to create a second line that passes through the first point selected in step 3 above or hit **Enter** or right click to terminate the command.

ARC (**arc**)

This command lets you draw an arc by supplying three items of information either by keyboard—X,Y coordinates—or mouse. If you use the keyboard to activate this command you draw the arc by establishing three points—start, middle, and end. If you use the icon in R12 or R14 you draw the arc by

AutoCAD Command	Function
Arc	Draws an arc

Keyboard Command	Pull Down Menu Path	Icon (R12)	Icon (R13 & R14)
ARC	R12: Draw/Arc R14: Draw/Arc		Draw

establishing the same three points. If you use the icon in R13, there are a large number of pop-up options available for drawing the arc. If you use the pull down menu in R12 and R14, there are a large number of options available to you. Examine these options carefully to see which one is appropriate for the particular arc that you want to draw.

CIRCLE (circle)

This command lets you draw a circle by supplying the information required by the drawing option chosen. Note that you can use either keyboard, mouse, or some combination thereof when using this command. If you activate this command by keyboard you have a choice of first establishing the center of the circle and then giving its radius, establishing two points on the circle, establishing three points on the circle, or giving two tangents and a radius. If you use the icon in R12 or R14 you have the same three options available. Under the pull down menu in R12 and R14, you can also draw the circle by giving the center point and the diameter. If you use the icon in R13 the same options are available as pop-ups under the top icon.

AutoCAD Command	Function
Circle	Draws a circle

Keyboard Command	Pull Down Menu Path	Icon (R12)	Icon (R13 & R14)
CIRCLE	R12: Draw/Circle R14: Draw/Circle		Draw

**THE POINT
COMMAND**

AutoCAD Command	Function		
Point	**Establishes a single point on the screen.**		

Keyboard Command	Pull Down Menu Path	Icon (R12)	Icon (R13 & R14)
POINT	**R12: Draw/Point** **R14: Draw/Point**	✛	• Draw

POINT (point)

The point (point) command lets you establish a point on the drawing. This can be useful when you are laying out multiple points on coordinates to be connected later. This can be done with the keyboard—X,Y coordinates—or mouse.

Note: You may need to set a Point Style that you can see when using this command. Also remember when snapping to a Point to use the Node object snap.

POLYLINE (pline)

A polyline is a line whose width can be defined and that can be joined with other polylines to form a single entity. When you draw an object with regular lines, each line is a separate entity. With plines, the whole object can become one entity and can be erased, moved, copied, etc. as one entity. Plines will later become extremely important when we start creating 3-D entities. After you activate the command:

1. You will be prompted: From point: for the starting point. Enter coordinates or click on the starting point.

**THE POLYLINE
COMMAND**

AutoCAD Command	Function		
Polyline	**Draws a polyline.**		

Keyboard Command	Pull Down Menu Path	Icon (R12)	Icon (R13 & R14)
PLINE	**R12: Draw/Polyline** **R14: Draw/Polyline**	⌐	⌐ Draw

2. You will be prompted: Arc/Close/Halfwidth/Length/Undo/Width/<Endpoint of Line>:. Note that in AutoCAD when you are offered multiple options like this with one enclosed by < >, that one is the default option. In this case, if you click again, you have established the end point of that segment of the pline.

3. If you want to choose another option such as Arc, type the capitalized letter or letters of the option and hit Enter or click on the right mouse button.

4. When you have finished each segment of a pline you will be prompted again with your options. To finish the pline at that point hit Enter or click on the right mouse button.

5. Other pline options:

   A. Arc: This allows you to draw an arc by defining some combination of Points, Angle, Center, Direction, or Radius.

   B. Close: After you have drawn at least two pline segments, Close will automatically join the last end point to the first start point.

   C. Halfwidth: This allows you to draw a line one-half the width that you have chosen for your pline.

   D. Length: This allows you to specify a pline's length and AutoCAD will draw it for you automatically.

   E. Undo: This allows you undo your pline segment by segment.

   F. Width: This option defines the width of your pline.

DONUT (donut)

This command lets you draw two concentric circles defined as a solid entity or donut.

1. The first prompt will be: Inside Diameter:. Type in on keyboard and hit Enter.

2. The second prompt is for Outside Diameter:. Type in on keyboard and hit Enter.

THE DONUT COMMAND

AutoCAD Command	Function		
Donut	**Draws a 2D donut or torus**		

Keyboard Command	Pull Down Menu Path	Icon (R12)	Icon (R13)
DONUT	**R12: Draw/Donut** **R14: Draw/Donut**		 **Draw/Circle**

THE ELLIPSE COMMAND

AutoCAD Command	Function
Ellipse	**Draws an ellipse**

Keyboard Command	Pull Down Menu Path	Icon (R12)	Icon (R13 & R14)
ELLIPSE	**R12: Draw/Ellipse** **R14: Draw/Ellipse**		**Draw**

3. The third prompt is for Center of Circle:. Type in coordinates on keyboard and hit Enter, or click once with mouse at desired location.

4. You will be prompted again for Center of Circle:.

5. To finish donut, hit Enter or click right mouse button. If you enter a new location by using the keyboard or click on a location with the left mouse button, you will create a second donut. You can keep adding donuts until you hit Enter or click the right mouse button.

6. A donut is a solid object. Note the difference with Solid Fill toggled and untoggled.

ELLIPSE (ellipse)

This lets you draw an ellipse by defining a major axis and a minor axis. In R12 and R14 you can use the pull down menu for the other options shown below. In R13 there are pop-ups available under the icon for the other options. Use the mouse to define points, or enter them on the keyboard.

1. Axis, Eccentricity: This prompts you for the two end points of the major axis, then for the minor axis by distance or rotation.

2. Center, Axis, Axis: This prompts you for the center of the major axis, then one of its end points, then the minor axis by distance or rotation.

POLYGON (polygon)

This command lets you draw a polygon with multiple equal-length sides.

1. The first prompt is Number of Sides: Enter the number of sides you desire and hit Enter.

2. The second prompt is Edge/<Center of Polygon>:.

   A. You can establish the center of the polygon by entering coordinates and hitting Enter or by clicking with the mouse.

      1. You will be prompted whether you want it Inscribed in Circle/Circumscribed about Circle:.

THE POLYGON COMMAND

AutoCAD Command	Function	Draws a polygon w/a specified number of sides.
Polygon		

Keyboard Command	Pull Down Menu Path	Icon (R12)	Icon (R13 & R14)
POLYGON	R12: Draw/Polygon R14: Draw/Polygon	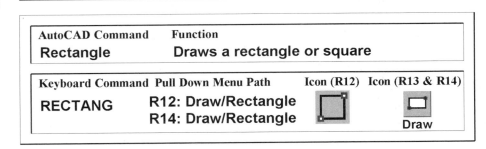	Draw

2. Enter i (inscribed) or c (circumscribed) and hit Enter.
3. Next prompt is for Radius of Circle:.
   a. If you enter the radius on the keyboard and hit Enter, it will establish a polygon based on a circle of that radius at an orientation of 0 degrees.
   b. Alternately, you can move the mouse and click on a point. This point will establish both the radius of the circle that defines the size of the polygon and its orientation simultaneously.
B. At the Edge/<Center of Polygon>: prompt, you can also chose Edge by typing the letter e and then hitting Enter.
   1. The next prompt is First Endpoint of Edge:. Enter on keyboard or with mouse.
   2. The next prompt is Second Endpoint of Edge:. Enter on keyboard or by dragging and clicking mouse.

Rectangle (rectang)

This lets you draw a rectangle or square by defining two corners with keyboard or mouse.

THE RECTANGLE COMMAND

AutoCAD Command	Function
Rectangle	Draws a rectangle or square

Keyboard Command	Pull Down Menu Path	Icon (R12)	Icon (R13 & R14)
RECTANG	R12: Draw/Rectangle R14: Draw/Rectangle		Draw

THE SPLINE COMMAND

SPLINE (spline) IN R13 AND R14

This command lets you create curves that would be much more difficult using just arcs or parts of circles and ellipses. The spline command creates curves by defining a series of points through which the curve must pass. The command can be activated in R13 or R14 by keyboard or the icon shown in the figure labeled The Spline Command. In R14 it can also be activated by clicking on Draw/Spline on the pull down menu. After the command is activated:

1. The first prompt reads: Object/<Enter First Point>:.
2. Select the first point for the curve with the keyboard or mouse.
3. The second prompt reads: Enter Point:.
4. Select the second point for the curve.
5. The next prompt reads: Close/Fit Tolerance/<Enter Point>:. Your options are:
   A. Close: (Type C and hit Enter.) Closes the curve by joining the start point and end point.
   B. Fit Tolerance: (Type F and hit Enter.) Changes how the curve is fitted to the selected points. If this option is chosen you can change the fit tolerance by moving the mouse and clicking when you see a curve that you like or entering a numerical value.
   C. Enter Points: You can also keep entering values on the keyboard or with the mouse to define more points on the curve. You can enter as many points as you would like.
6. When you have completed your curve, right click twice rapidly or hit Enter twice rapidly.
7. If you still are not satisfied with the curve, try using the grips (see next section) to modify it.

GRIPS

The grips in AutoCAD are small squares that will appear at various points on an entity when the entity is selected outside of a command (when the command line reads: Command:). If you click on the entity with nothing in the command line, the grips will appear. The grips will appear as small blue squares and the rest of the entity will be shown in dotted lines. If you click on one of these blue squares, it will turn red. Move your mouse to select a new location for the highlighted grip. Click the mouse again and the grip will move to the location selected. Hit Enter or click the right mouse button, and the grips will disappear. By doing this you can change the length of a line, the position of the corners of a rectangle or polygon, the center or diameter of a circle, or the vertices of a pline, spline, etc. Grips can be very handy tools to reshape something quickly and easily. Be sure that they are Enabled in the Grips dialogue box; type ddgrips and hit Enter to open the box.

DIMENSIONS (dim)

Use this command to add dimensions to objects that you have drawn. When first learning this command, you may find it is not easy to use through the keyboard. This is because you must be familiar with a large number of options in order to use this command. After you learn all of the options available, the keyboard may be the fastest way to use dimension. In R12 and R14 you have access to all of the dimension commands through pull down menus. R13 and R14 also have their own Dimension toolbar with individual icons for the various dimension commands.

DIMENSION SCALE

Even before you draw a dimension you need to set a dimension scale (dimscale) for the drawing you are working on. Dimensions are sized in a drawing relative to the scale in which the drawing will be printed out. This sizing is controlled by a dimscale formula. To understand the formula for dimscale you need to understand that in scale you are making one unit stand for a specified number of *other* units. For example, a common scale in theatre is 1/2 inch = 1 foot. The dimscale formula has to be stated so that 1 of *one unit* equals a specific number of the *same unit.* The 1/2 inch = 1 foot scale is stated in two different units.

THE DIMENSION COMMAND

AutoCAD Command	Function	Creates dimension lines.
Dimension		**Note: Must specify dimension type.**

Keyboard Command	Pull Down Menu Path	Icon (R12)	Icon (R13 & R14)
DIM	**R12: Draw/Dimensions** **R14: Dimension/**	⊢──⊣	See Dimension Toolbar

Another way of stating 1/2 inch = 1 foot is to state that 1 inch = 24 inches, or 1/24. Once you have stated it in this manner you must take the reciprocal and divide by two to arrive at the dimscale. For example, 24/2 = 12; the dimscale for 1/2 inch = 1 foot is 12. Remember that for 1/2 inch = 1 foot, the dimscale is 12 and for 1/4 inch = 1 foot, the dimscale is 24. You can set dimscale either by typing dimscale and hitting Enter, then entering your scale number or by going to the Feature Scaling box under Dimension Line under Dimension Style under the Settings menu. This same formula will later be used with linetype as ltscale to set up the look of various kinds of linetypes such as center line, dashed lines, etc.

DIMENSION STYLE

Before continuing on with actually doing dimensions, I want to remind you that there are other options in the Dimension Style box, which can be opened by typing ddim and hitting Enter. The Dimension Styles and Variables boxes let you create a specific dimension style to your own specifications that you can then name and recall. You do this by making choices in the Variables boxes and then naming and saving these choices in the Dimension Styles box. I would recommend that you start out using the options as they are set by AutoCAD until you become more familiar with the program. However, the Variables options that can be changed from the default settings are: Dimension Line, Extension Lines, Arrows, Text Location, Text Format, Features, and Colors.

DIMENSION TOOLBARS

The Dimension toolbars for R13 and R14 are each laid out differently. Here is the basic layout for each and what the buttons represent:

THE DIMENSION TOOLBAR: R13

From left to right the buttons are: Linear, Aligned, Radius, Angular, Ordinate, Baseline, Continue, Center, Leader, Tolerance, Home, and Dimension Style.

THE DIMENSION
TOOLBAR: R14

From left to right the buttons are: Linear, Aligned, Ordinate, Radius, Diameter, Angular, Baseline, Continue, Leader, Tolerance, Center, Dimension Edit, Dimension Text Edit, Dimension Style, and Dimension Update.

DIMENSIONING

In this description of how to dimension, you will work through the keyboard commands. The icons and pull down menus are shortcuts to these commands. In many cases after you learn the various keyboard commands you will find that it is actually faster to do your dimensioning that way.

1. To dimension an object, type dim and hit Enter. Here is a simple example of a linear dimension:
   A. To perform a linear dimension you must next type in one of the linear options: Horizontal (hor), Vertical (ve), Aligned (al), Rotated (ro), Baseline (b), or Continue (co).
   B. Your simplest choice for most dimensions usually is Aligned, since it will give you dimensions for a line that is horizontal, vertical, or at an angle. Type al and hit Enter.
      1. This prompt appears: First extension line origin or RETURN to select:.
      2. If you hit Return, a small pick box will appear at the cursor.
         a. Use it to click on the line that you want to dimension.
         b. Prompt is: Dimension Line Location:.
         c. Move the mouse and click to locate the dimension line.
         d. Prompt is: Dimension Text <7'6">: or whatever the length of the dimension is.
         e. Click on right mouse button or hit Enter to complete this dimension line, or
         f. at this point, you can enter a different text figure on the keyboard and hit Enter.
      3. Instead of hitting Return you can pick the beginning and end points of the dimension line (extension line origins). Usually these will be a point on a line such as an end point or intersection.
         a. At the prompt: First extension line origin or RETURN to select:, click on one end of line to be dimensioned or use an object snap such as end point or intersection to click on the point precisely.

b. The second prompt is: Second Extension Line Origin:. Click on the other end of line to be dimensioned.
c. The third prompt is: Dimension Line Location:. Move mouse to where you want dimension line to be located and click once.
d. The fourth prompt is: Dimension text <7'6">: or whatever the length of the dimension is.
e. Click on the right mouse button or hit Enter to complete the dimension line, or
f. at this point, you can enter a different text figure and hit Enter.

2. Most of the other options available under dimension work in a similar manner.

3. The following is a summary of the keyboard commands for dimensioning. Note that in all of the keyboard commands given below it is only necessary to type the letters in the parentheses and then hit Enter to activate the command.

First type dim and then hit Enter. The prompt that follows will read Dim:. Next type in the letters inside the parentheses below to activate that command.

A. Linear: This generates linear dimension lines. *Do not* type in linear, lin, etc.; type one of the commands in 1 through 6 immediately below.
  1. Horizontal (hor): This creates horizontal dimension lines.
  2. Vertical (ve): This creates vertical dimension lines.
  3. Aligned (al): This creates dimension lines parallel to the extension line origin points.
  4. Rotated (ro): This creates dimension lines at an angle that you specify.
  5. Baseline (b): This continues a linear dimension from the baseline of another linear dimension.
  6. Continue (co): This continues a linear dimension from the second extension line of another linear dimension.

B. Radial (rad): The dimensions a circle or arc. First type in rad and hit Enter, then type one of the commands below and hit Enter.
  1. Diameter (d): This dimensions the diameter of a circle or arc with an optional center mark or center lines.
  2. Radius (ra): This dimensions the radius of a circle or arc with an optional center mark or center lines.
  3. Center Mark (ce): This draws a center mark or center lines inside a circle or arc.

C. Ordinate (ord): This command dimensions coordinates of a feature. First type in ord and hit Enter, then type one of the commands below and hit Enter.

       1. **Automatic (or)**: This dimensions X and/or Y coordinates of a feature.

       2. **X-datum** (no keyboard entry): This dimensions X coordinate of a feature.

       3. **Y-datum** (no keyboard entry): This dimensions Y coordinate of a feature.

    D. **Angular (an)**: This creates dimension lines for an angle and generates a dimension arc and extension lines.

4. **Leader (l)** is another useful option under **Dimension**. This command lets you point at something with an arrow and then label what you have pointed at. To activate this command, type **dim**, hit **Enter**, type l, and hit **Enter** again.

    A. The first prompt is: _leader Leaderstart:. Click on the point you want the arrow to indicate.

    B. The second prompt is: **To point:**. Move the mouse and then click where you want the line that's coming from the back of the arrowhead to end.

    C. The third prompt is: **To point:**. You can continue as in step 2 to take your arrow around corners as many times as you like. When you arrive at the point you want the text label to be located, click on the right mouse button.

    D. Next prompt is: **Dimension text < >:**. Using the keyboard, enter the text you desire, and then hit **Enter**.

    E. The **default** for dimension text is always the length of the last dimension line drawn. You can, when drawing a dimension line, leave off the text and then add it with a leader.

Sketch (sketch)

The sketch (sketch) command is used for freehand drawing in AutoCAD. The freehand editor captures your drawing as a series of lines on which you can do some limited editing before it is entered into AutoCAD proper. After the lines have been entered into AutoCAD, the normal AutoCAD editing functions such as erase, move, etc. can be used.

Note: Sketch very quickly generates a large number of lines that occupy a lot of data space. Regeneration time and storage space limits can be exceeded very easily with heavy use of sketch. AutoCAD is really not a program designed for freehand drawing. If you plan on using a lot of freehand drawing there are programs much better suited for that operation than AutoCAD. It is much more efficient to do the freehand work in another program such as Painter or Photoshop and then import that drawing into AutoCAD.

THE SKETCH COMMAND

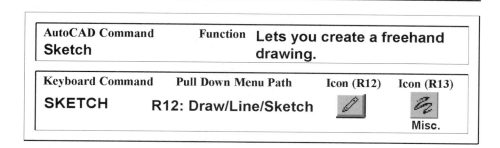

AutoCAD Command	Function	Lets you create a freehand
Sketch		**drawing.**

Keyboard Command	Pull Down Menu Path	Icon (R12)	Icon (R13)
SKETCH	R12: Draw/Line/Sketch		
			Misc.

USING THE SKETCH COMMAND

Use one of the methods in the Command Box to activate the **sketch** command.

1. Prompt reads: SKETCH Record increment <0'-0 1/8">:. AutoCAD is prompting you for the size of the line increment that you want to use in the sketch. The shorter the line increment that you specify the closer to a true curve you can achieve, but the more lines that will be created to achieve it. It will probably take some experimentation to determine what line increment works best for the particular sketching that you want to do.

    A. Type the line increment you desire, e.g., 1", and hit **Enter**, or

    B. just hit **Enter** to accept the default line increment inside the < >.

2. Prompt reads: Sketch: Pen/eXit/Quit/Record/Erase/Connect. When you enter **sketch** your "pen" is in the **up** position. (Think of it like the pen on a plotter.) To start sketching, move the cursor to where you want your line to begin and hit **p** on the keyboard. Do *not* hit **Enter**. This lowers the "pen" onto the "paper." Then as you move the mouse, AutoCAD will draw your sketch in a series of line segments each the length that you specified earlier in **Record increment**. When you have gotten to the end of the line you are sketching, stop moving the mouse and hit **p** on the keyboard to raise the "pen." At this point you can move the cursor to a different point and sketch another line by using the **p** key to lower and raise the "pen," or you can record the lines that you have already drawn into the main AutoCAD editor by hitting **Enter**.

3. Sketch subcommands: Note that the following subcommands only work while you are in **sketch**. You cannot use one of these commands on a sketch after it has been recorded into the main AutoCAD editor. Each is activated by a single keyboard key. Do *not* hit **Enter** after any of these commands until you are ready to record the sketching that you have done to the main AutoCAD editor and exit sketch.

    A. Pen Up/Down (p): This raises and lowers the "pen" for drawing or moving the cursor to a new location.

B. Line to Point (.): Hitting the **period key** (.) on the keyboard draws a straight line from the end point of the last sketched line to the current location of the cursor. Note that this command will only work when the pen is up.

C. Record (**r**): This records all the temporary lines that you have done in sketch to the AutoCAD editor without leaving sketch. Note that after you have hit the r key, you cannot edit these lines in sketch.

D. Record and Exit (**x**): This records all the temporary lines that you have done in sketch to the AutoCAD editor and exits you from sketch. Note that the **Spacebar** and **Enter** have the same effect.

E. Quit (**q**): This removes all the temporary lines that you have drawn in sketch and exits you from sketch.

F. Erase (**e**): The **e** command lets you erase from any point on the lines that you have drawn to the end of the lines. After hitting **e**:
1. Prompt reads: **Erase: Select end of delete**.
2. **E** automatically raises the pen if it is down.
3. Move the cursor to where you want the erasure to begin. AutoCAD blanks out the portion of the line that will be erased.
4. Hit the **p** key to erase the blanked-out portion of the line.
5. If you decide not to erase any portion of the line, hit the **e** key again and this will return you to the normal sketch prompt after displaying the message: **Erase aborted**.

G. Connect (**c**): The **c** command lets you rejoin a sketched line after you have raised the pen or erased some portion of the line you were working on. Note that you can only **connect** to the last end point of the last line that you were working on. This command also works only with the pen in the up position. To activate the command type **c**.
1. Prompt reads: **Connect: Move to endpoint of line**. Move the cursor to the end point of the last line you drew or erased part of. When you get to within one recorded increment of the end point, the pen will automatically be lowered, the sketch prompt appears, and you can resume sketching.
2. To terminate the **c** command without sketching, type **c** again. Prompt reads: **Connect Aborted**.

OBJECT SNAPS (**osnap**)

Object snaps (**osnap**) are commands that are used in conjunction with **draw** and other commands to designate a point precisely for AutoCAD. Usually you will click on the icon for one of these when AutoCAD prompts you for a point. A box will then be created at the crosshairs. Use the mouse to place any part of

**THE OBJECT
SNAPS**

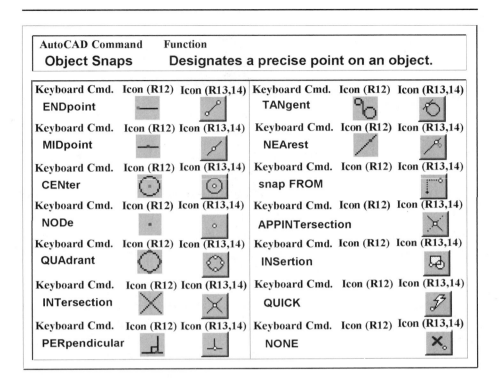

AutoCAD Command	Function				
Object Snaps	**Designates a precise point on an object.**				

Keyboard Cmd.	Icon (R12)	Icon (R13,14)	Keyboard Cmd.	Icon (R12)	Icon (R13,14)
ENDpoint			TANgent		
MIDpoint			NEArest		
CENter			snap FROM		
NODe			APPINTersection		
QUAdrant			INSertion		
INTersection			QUICK		
PERpendicular			NONE		

this box over the point desired and click once. AutoCAD will automatically snap to the kind of point that you designated within the box. Be sure that only one point of the kind you have chosen is within the box before you click. Object snaps can also be selected using the keyboard in any of the versions. When AutoCAD prompts you for a point in the middle of a command type the letters in parentheses from the following list and hit **Enter** or click on the icon for the object snap. In R12, object snaps are also available under the pull down menu **Assist**. R13 and R14 both have toolbars specifically for object snaps. R14 also has the object snaps available in a pop-up menu on the **Standard** toolbar. Useful object snaps are:

1. Endpoint (end): This snaps to the end of a line or arc.
2. Midpoint (mid): This snaps to the middle of a line or arc.
3. Center (cen): This snaps to the center of a circle or arc.
4. Node (nod): This snaps to the nearest point entity (dimension definition point).
5. Quadrant (qua): This snaps to quadrant point of arc or circle.
6. Intersection (int): This snaps to intersection of lines, arcs, or circles.

7. **Perpendicular (per):** This snaps perpendicular to line, arc, or circle.

8. **Tangent (tan):** This snaps tangent to arc or circle.

9. **Nearest (nea):** This snaps to nearest point on line, arc, circle, or point.

10. **Snap from (from):** This is used with other object snaps to establish a temporary reference point.

11. **Appintersection (appint):** This snaps to point that may look like an intersection, but isn't.

12. **Insertion (ins):** This snaps to the insertion point of text, block, shape, or attribute.

13. **Quick (qui):** This snaps to first find, not closest.

14. **None (non):** This overrides a running object snap.

A running object snap can be a very useful device in AutoCAD when you know that you will be using a lot of snaps to the same kind of point. When you set up a running object snap, AutoCAD will always look for the nearest point of the type that you specify, such as intersection, and go to that point with the start of a line, etc. You can also set up a running object snap by typing **osnap** and hitting **Enter**. This opens the **Object Snap** dialogue box.

In R12 you can set a running object snap by clicking on **Setting/Object Snap**. In R13, click on **Options/Running Object Snap**. In R14, click on **Tools/ Object Snap Settings**. In R13 and R14, there is an icon in the **Object Snap** toolbar that will open the **Object Snap** dialogue box.

Running object snaps remain in force until changed or canceled at the **Object Snap** dialogue box, though they can be overridden by clicking on or entering on the keyboard a different object snap. Typing **non** also temporarily cancels a running object snap.

INQUIRY

An extremely useful area of AutoCAD is the **Inquiry** submenu available in some of the versions. Here you can get the coordinates of a point on the drawing, determine the distance from one point to another, or calculate the area and perimeter of a closed figure. In R12 all of the commands below can be activated by clicking on the **Assist/Inquiry** pull down menu. In R13 they can be accessed from a pop-up menu under the last button on the right on the **Object Properties** toolbar. In R14 they can be accessed from the pull down menu **Tools/Inquiry** or from the **Inquiry** toolbar. All of these commands can also be activated by typing the term enclosed in parentheses below and hitting **Enter**. The units that are involved in each of the commands will depend upon what settings you have established under the **units** command—architectural, metric, etc.

1. Area (area): The area command calculates the area and perimeter that is enclosed by a sequence of points that you enter or that are defined by a specified circle or polyline. You can keep a running total of measured areas, and you can ask AutoCAD to add or subtract subsequent areas from the total.

   A. Prompt reads: <First point>/Entity/Add/Subtract: Enter a point.

   B. Click on the first point.

   C. Prompt reads: Next Point: Enter a point.

   D. Continue clicking on points until the area that you want is defined.

   E. When all points necessary to define the area are selected, hit Enter or click on the right mouse button to calculate the area and perimeter.

   F. The other options available at the first prompt are Entity/Add/Subtract. By typing the first letter of any of these three options at this prompt and hitting Enter or right mouse button you can:

      1. compute the area of a selected circle or polyline, with entity;

      2. add the area to the running total, with add; or

      3. subtract the area from the running total, with subtract.

   G. The area command will take you through the prompts above after you have selected the Entity/Add/Subtract options and then perform the chosen function.

2. Distance (dist): If you would like to measure an actual distance on the drawing you can use the distance command. When you use this command in combination with object snaps such as end point or intersection you can find the exact distance between any two points on the drawing quickly and easily. By using the command with the ortho command turned on you can also measure the horizontal or vertical spacing between two points rather than the straight line distance between two points.

   A. Prompt reads: '_dist First Point:. Click on the first point of measurement. For accuracy it is usually best to use an object snap such as end point, midpoint, or intersection when you click on measurement points.

   B. Prompt reads: '_dist First Point: Second Point:. Click on the end point of the measurement and it will give you the distance between the two points.

   C. If the ortho command is turned on, you will get the horizontal or vertical distance between the points rather than the straight-line distance.

3. ID Point (id): This displays the coordinates of a specified point. Click on the point of which you want the coordinates. It is usually desirable to use one of your object snaps to specify the point precisely.

Calculator (cal)

To use the calculator function of AutoCAD in R12, click on Calculator under the Assist pull down menu or type cal and hit Enter. In R13 and R14, type cal and hit Enter.

1. For standard mathematical expressions, use the number pad section of the keyboard; NumLock must be on. Do not use the numbers or expressions on the regular keyboard.

2. You can enter the calculator transparently by typing an apostrophe (') before typing cal and hitting Enter.

3. The AutoCAD calculator will also perform a number of specialized geometric functions dealing with points, vectors, and AutoCAD geometry. Refer to the Help section of AutoCAD under cal for a list of these functions.

Exercise No. 6: Using Draw, Dimensioning, Object Snaps, Sketch, and Distance Commands

1. Open the file Proto.dwg from either the CD-ROM or the floppy disk that you had previously saved it to.

2. Save this file as Exer6.dwg on a floppy disk.

3. Work in Exer6.dwg.

   A. Erase the word Prototype.

   B. Draw a line from 2'0", 18'0" to 14'0",18'0".

   C. Draw an arc from one end of the line you just drew to the other, with the center of the arc 1' below the midpoint of the line.

   D. If you have R13 or R14, establish a point and draw three rays emanating from that point.

   E. If you have R13 or R14, enclose a square area with four construction lines.

   F. Draw a square using a double line with a width of 2.5".

      • If you have R14, also draw a square using a triple line multiline with a spacing of 1" between each of the lines.

   G. Draw a circle with a 1' radius.

   H. Establish three points on the page that are easily seen and connect all three with an arc.

   I. Using pline, draw a *closed* square 2' on a side.

   J. Draw an ellipse with a major axis of 2' and a minor axis of 6".

   K. Draw a hexagon that is 2' wide point to point.

L. Without measuring, draw a rectangle, using the rectangle command and the mouse.

M. Set your dimscale for a printout of 1/2 inch = 1 foot.

N. Dimension one side of your pline square, the radius of your circle, and the major axis of your ellipse.

O. Use a leader to label your hexagon.

P. Use the distance command to measure the lengths of the wide and narrow sides of your rectangle.

Q. Sketch a simple freehand figure.

R. Using plot, print Exer6.dwg from your floppy disk. Also print Projct6.dwg from the CD-ROM.

S. Compare these two drawings and try to figure out why there may be differences. Note that Projct6.dwg is in R12 format and thus will not have D, E, or the second part of F on it.

Using Modify Commands

There are a number of commands useful in creating a drawing that allow you to modify or change other drawing elements. These commands are often those that make the drawing process faster or simpler or allow the drawing to be used in a wider variety of applications. In R12 and R14, most of these can be found under the Modify pull down menu. In R13 and R14, most of these can be found on the Modify toolbar. They can also be activated by typing the letters inside the parentheses below and hitting Enter.

Entity or Properties (ddmodify)

The modify entity or modify properties (ddmodify) command is an editing command that opens a box with information about the selected entity. It also allows you to make a wide variety of changes in the selected entity.

THE MODIFY ENTITY/ PROPERTIES COMMAND

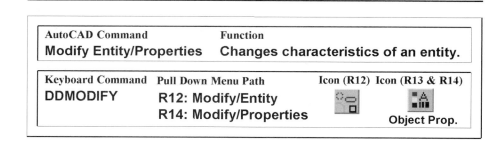

AutoCAD Command		Function		
Modify Entity/Properties		**Changes characteristics of an entity.**		

Keyboard Command	Pull Down Menu Path		Icon (R12)	Icon (R13 & R14)
DDMODIFY	**R12: Modify/Entity**			
	R14: Modify/Properties			**Object Prop.**

1. Activate the modify entity command.

2. Once you have entered ddmodify you will be prompted to select the entity that you would like to modify by clicking on it.

3. When you click on the entity to be modified a Modify dialogue box will open. The particular dialogue box opened will depend upon the entity that you have selected and its attributes. If you have a number of changes to make to an entity, the ddmodify command can be a quick way to make them all at once. This is a command that becomes more useful the more complex that the drawing becomes. You may not have use of all of its capabilities right away, but as you get better at AutoCAD, you will.

4. For example, if the entity selected is a circle, you could change the Layer, Color, Linetype, Center, Coordinates, Radius, Diameter, Circumference, or Area. If the entity selected is text you could change the Layer, Color, Text, Origin, Justification, Style, Height, Rotation, Width, or Obliquing.

ERASE (erase)

There are several options available with the erase command that were not discussed earlier as well as several ways to activate the command as shown in the Command Box.

Erase can be activated by any of the methods shown in the Command Box. After the command has been activated a number of options are available. To use one of these options, simply type the letters in parentheses for the option and hit Enter after you have activated erase.

1. Select/Window (w): This is the default option for erase. You do not have to hit the w to activate this option. You can either select an object by using the pick box that appears at the cursor and clicking on it or you can click outside of the object to be erased and then drag the mouse to form a window. A second click completes the window. Erase will then select all objects completely enclosed by the window. Hitting Enter or the right mouse switch completes the erasure.

THE ERASE COMMAND

AutoCAD Command	Function		
Erase	**Erases selected entity/s**		

Keyboard Command	Pull Down Menu Path	Icon (R12)	Icon (R13 & 14)
ERASE	**R12: Modify/Erase** **R14: Modify/Erase**		Modify

2. Crossing (c): This works similar to the window option except that it will erase any object the window crosses in addition to any object inside it.

3. Add/Remove (a/r): These functions allow you to add or remove objects to or from the group picked to be erased. It must be activated before you have completed the erasure.

4. Undo (u): Do not confuse this undo with the larger undo command. This undo is activated by typing u and hitting Enter after you have selected several objects to be erased. It will remove objects from the group to be erased in the reverse order from which they were selected.

5. Last (last): This function automatically erases the last object drawn when activated.

6. Oops (oops): The oops command automatically restores the last object erased when activated. You cannot repeat this command and restore objects erased earlier.

BREAK (break)

The break (break) command will erase a portion of an object by breaking it into parts and then erasing the part selected. This command is very useful for such things as erasing the portion of an electric pipe inside a lighting instrument. There are two methods for using the break command, plus a way to break an object into parts without erasing part of it. In R12 if you use the pull down menu you can choose a method by picking one of the subcategories under the break command. In R13 there are pop-up buttons under the Break button for choosing methods. If you use the keyboard command or R14 follow the procedures outlined below.

1. One-Step Method:
   A. Prompt reads: Break Select Object:.
   B. Click on the object you want to break at the point on the object where you want the break to begin. **Note:** This is usually a good place to use an object snap to locate this point precisely.

THE BREAK COMMAND

AutoCAD Command	Function		
Break	Breaks a single line into two pieces		

Keyboard Command	Pull Down Menu Path	Icon (R12)	Icon (R13 & R14)
BREAK	R12: Modify/Break R14: Modify/Break		Modify

C. Prompt reads: Enter second point (or F for first point):.

D. Click on the point on the object where you want the break to end.

Note: If you are working your way across an electric pipe, breaking the pipe inside instruments, this would be a good place to use a running object snap like intersection.

2. Two-Step Method:
    A. Prompt reads: Break Select Object:.
    B. Click anywhere on the object you want to break.
    C. Prompt reads: Enter second point (or F for first point):.
    D. Type F and hit Enter.
    E. Prompt reads: Enter first point:.
    F. Click on the already selected object at the point where you want to begin the break. You may want to use an object snap to locate this point precisely
    G. Prompt reads: Enter second point:.
    H. Click on the already selected object at the point where you want to end the break.

3. **Break at Selected Point:** You can use this method to break an object into two parts. You can activate it on the R12 pull down menu by clicking on **Break** and then on **At Selected Point**, or activate it on the R13 pop-up by clicking on the button labeled **1 Point**. Then click on the point on the object where you want the break to occur.

    If you want to break at a single point by using the typed or R14 command, use the following procedure.
    A. Prompt reads: Break Select Object:.
    B. Click on the object you'd like to break at the point of the break. It is a good idea to use an object snap to locate this point precisely.
    C. Prompt reads: Enter second point (or F for first point):.
    D. Click on the object at the same point that you did in part B. If you used an object snap, use the same object snap again.

EXTEND (**extend**)

The **extend** (extend) command lets you extend a line or arc to meet another line or arc.

1. Prompt reads: Select boundary edge(s) . . . Select objects:.
2. Click on line or arc that you want to be met by another line or arc.

THE EXTEND COMMAND

AutoCAD Command	Function
Extend	**Extends a line/s to another line/s**

Keyboard Command	Pull Down Menu Path	Icon (R12)	Icon (R13 & R14)
EXTEND	**R12: Modify/Extend** **R14: Modify/Extend**		**Modify**

3. Prompt reads: Select objects:. Either select a second boundary or click on right mouse button.
4. Prompt reads: <Select object to extend>/Undo:.
5. Click on line or arc you want to extend. At this point you can also extend another line to the same boundary or boundaries or click on right mouse button to complete command. Note that you can extend a line in two directions as part of the same operation by selecting two boundary lines and then clicking on the line to be extended twice, once closer to the first boundary line and then closer to the second boundary line.

Trim (trim)

You can use the trim (trim) command to cut off lines, arcs, or circles that cross other lines, arcs, or circles.

1. Prompt reads: Select cutting edge . . . Select objects:. Click on the object(s) that will serve as the edge(s) of your trim(s).
2. Prompt reads: Select objects:. Click on right mouse button.
3. Prompt reads: <Select object to trim>/Undo:. Click on part of line(s) to be removed. Then click on the right mouse button to complete command.

THE TRIM COMMAND

AutoCAD Command	Function	**Uses one line to trim the**
Trim		**length of another.**

Keyboard Command	Pull Down Menu Path	Icon (R12)	Icon (R13 & R14)
TRIM	**R12: Modify/Trim** **R14: Modify/Trim**		**Modify**

AutoCAD Command	Function
Move	**Moves an object/s to a new location.**

Keyboard Command	Pull Down Menu Path	Icon (R12)	Icon (R13 & R14)
MOVE	R12: Modify/Move R14: Modify/Move		**Modify**

MOVE (move)

Use this command to move one or more objects to another part of the drawing.

1. Prompt reads: Select objects:.
2. Click on object(s) you want to move, then click on the right mouse button.
3. Prompt reads: Base point or displacement:. Click on a point on or near the object that will serve as the point from which the object will be moved.
4. Prompt reads: Second point of displacement:. Drag the selected object with the mouse and click on the point at which you want to insert the object.

Note: For more precision in moving objects, use an object snap in both steps 3 and 4 above.

ROTATE (rotate)

Use this command to rotate an object around a selected point.

1. Prompt reads: Select objects:. Click on object(s) you'd like to rotate, then click on the right mouse button.
2. Prompt reads: Base point:. Click on the point around which the object should be rotated. This point can be on or outside of the object.

AutoCAD Command	Function	**Rotates selected object/s by**
Rotate		**degrees desired counterclockwise.**

Keyboard Command	Pull Down Menu Path	Icon (R12)	Icon (R13 & R14)
ROTATE	R12: Modify/Rotate R14: Modify/Rotate		**Modify**

3. Prompt reads: <Rotation Angle>/Reference:. You have two choices here. You can:
- drag the mouse until the object is rotated to where you want and then click on that location, or
- type a number in degrees counterclockwise that the object is to be rotated and hit Enter.

SCALE (scale)

This command is used to change the size of objects proportionally. It does not affect the scale of your drawing in any way.

1. Prompt reads: **Select objects:**. Click on object(s) you want to scale and then click on right mouse button.
2. Prompt reads: **Base point:**. Click on the point that you want to stay stationary while the object is shrinking or enlarging.
3. Prompt reads: <Scale factor>/Reference:. At this point there are three methods that you can use to determine the new size of the object.
   A. Move the mouse until the object is the size you want and click once.
   B. Enter a **Scale Factor Number:**
      1. Type a number that indicates how much you want to enlarge or shrink the object proportionately and hit **Enter**. For example, .5 will shrink the object to half its size; 5 will increase the object to five times its size.
   C. Use the **reference** method:
      1. Type **r** and hit **Enter** to activate the reference method.
      2. Prompt reads: **Reference length <1>:**.
      3. Type in a known length on the object for which you have determined how much you want to increase or decrease and hit **Enter**. For example: If you know that one side of an object is 5 feet long and you want to increase it to 7 feet long, type in 5' and hit **Enter**.

THE SCALE COMMAND

AutoCAD Command	Function	Increases or decreases size of
Scale		selected object/s.

Keyboard Command	Pull Down Menu Path	Icon (R12)	Icon (R13 & R14)
SCALE	R12: Modify/Scale R14: Modify/Scale		Modify

**THE STRETCH
COMMAND**

AutoCAD Command	Function	**Lengthens or shortens one side of selected object/s.**
Stretch		

Keyboard Command	Pull Down Menu Path	Icon (R12)	Icon (R13 & R14)
STRETCH	**R12: Modify/Stretch** **R14: Modify/Stretch**		 **Modify**

4. Prompt reads: New length:. Type in the new size that you want the reference length to become and hit Enter. In the example we're using, you would now type in 7' and hit Enter.

STRETCH (stretch)

This command allows you to stretch an object in one direction only, either horizontally or vertically.

1. Prompt reads: Select objects to stretch by window or polygon Select objects:. In selecting the parts of the drawing to stretch, you must leave at least one end unselected to serve as the stationary point to be stretched from. This can be done by selecting individual pieces of the drawing one at a time or by using a crossing window.
2. To use a crossing window, type c and hit Enter.
3. Prompt reads: First Corner:. Click on the first corner of your crossing window and drag the mouse to include all objects that you want to stretch.
4. Prompt reads: Other Corner:. Click on the other corner of your crossing window.
5. Prompt reads: Select objects:. AutoCAD will stretch everything that appears with a dotted outline. At this point you can use the add or delete commands to select other objects or unselect objects that you don't want to be stretched. When everything you want to stretch is selected, hit Enter.
6. Prompt reads: Base point or displacement:. Click on a point that you want to use as a "handle" to drag the objects to be stretched.
7. Prompt reads: Second point of displacement:. Use the mouse to drag the objects to be stretched to their new location and click once to complete command.

LENGTHEN (lengthen) IN R13 AND R14

The lengthen (lengthen) command lets you change the length of a line or arc. It will not work with a closed entity such as a circle, rectangle, or pline. This command is only available in R13 and R14.

THE LENGTHEN COMMAND

AutoCAD Command	Function	Lengthens or shortens lines or arcs.
Lengthen		

Keyboard Command	Pull Down Menu Path	Icon (R13 & R14)
R13 & 14: LENGTHEN	**R14: Modify/Lengthen**	Modify

Activate the lengthen command.

1. Prompt reads: DElta/Percent/Total/DYnamic/<Select Object>:. Your options include the following:
    A. **DElta:** This option changes the length of a line by a specified amount or changes the length of an arc by changing the angle.
    B. **Percent:** This feature changes the length of a line or arc by a specified percentage.
    C. **Total:** With this option, you can change the length of a line by specifying a new total length or change an arc by specifying a new angle.
    D. **Dynamic:** You can use this feature to change the length of a line or arc by dragging the end point of the object.

2. For example, say that you typed t for total at the initial prompt and then hit Enter.
    A. Prompt reads: Angle/<Enter total length (0'-1")>:.
    B. Type in a new angle if you are going to change an arc or the new length for a line that you want to change. For example, type 1'6" for a line and hit Enter.
    C. Prompt reads: <Select Object to Change>/Undo:. Click on the line or arc that you want to lengthen. It will lengthen by the amount that you specified.
    D. Prompt reads: <Select Object to Change>/Undo:. If you don't like the change that just occurred, type u for undo and hit Enter. If you like the change, hit Enter or click the right mouse button.

CHANGE PROPERTIES (**ddchprop** IN R12), (**ai_propchk** IN R13 AND R14)

This command opens the Change Properties box that allows you to simultaneously change a number of different properties of an entity such as color, layer, linetype, thickness, location of end points, etc. The specific properties you can change will vary with the entity selected. You can activate the command by typing ddchprop in R12 or ai_propchk in R13 and R14 and hitting

THE EXPLODE COMMAND

AutoCAD Command	Function	Separates block or polyline
Explode		**into component entities.**

Keyboard Command	Pull Down Menu Path	Icon (R12)	Icon (R13 & R14)
EXPLODE	R12: Modify/Explode		
	R14: Modify/Explode		Modify

Enter. In R12 you can also activate it by clicking on Modify, then on Change, then on Properties. In R13 and R14 this command is the same as the ddmodify command. See the section on the ddmodify command (see page 68) for pull down menu path and icons for R13 and R14.

1. Prompt reads: Select Objects:.
2. Click on the entity you want to change.
3. Prompt reads: Select Objects: 1 found Select Objects:.
4. Select more entities and the same prompt will appear again. When you have selected all the entities that you want to change you can activate the command by hitting Enter or clicking on the right mouse button.
5. Remember that while it is possible to select more than one entity using the change properties command, the changes that you make will be made to *all* entities selected.
6. Once you have selected all the entities of which you want to change properties, a dialogue box in which you can make the changes will open.

EXPLODE (**explode**)

The explode command will break an object into its component parts. It can do this to either a polyline, a dimension, or a block.

1. Prompt reads: Select Objects:.
2. Click on the object or objects you want to explode.
3. Prompt reads: Select Objects:.
4. Click on the right mouse button or hit Enter when you have picked all the objects that you want to explode.
5. This will complete the command.

POLYLINE EDIT (**pedit**)

This command is used to change a line to a polyline and to edit or make changes in a polyline.

THE POLYLINE
EDIT COMMAND

AutoCAD Command	Function
Polyline Edit	**Allows you to edit a polyline.**

Keyboard Command	Pull Down Menu Path	Icon (R12) Icon (R13 & R14)
PEDIT	R12: Modify/Pedit R14: Modify/Object/Polyline	Modify Modify II

1. To change a line to a polyline:
   A. Activate the command.
   B. Prompt reads: Select polyline:.
   C. Click on the line to be changed.
   D. Prompt reads: Entity selected is not a polyline. Do you want to turn it into one? <Y>:. Hit Enter.
   E. You will now get the opening pedit prompt that you would have gotten if you had selected a polyline to begin with.

2. Pedit Options: You can use pedit to make a wide variety of changes to a polyline, including changing a straight line to a curved one. Select your option at the pedit prompt by typing the letter in parentheses for the option and hitting Enter.
   A. Open/Close (o/c): These allow you to open a closed polyline or close an open one.
   B. Join (j): This joins polyline segments into a single polyline.
   C. Width (w): This option changes the width of a polyline.
   D. Edit Vertex (e): Use this to move or insert polyline vertices. A vertex is a point where two polyline segments meet. Edit vertex gives you another series of options. When you enter e, an X will appear at one of the vertices. In using the edit vertex commands you work your way around the polyline from vertex to vertex. The edit vertex options include the following:
      1. Next (n): This advances the X to the next vertex.
      2. Previous (p): This option moves the X back to the previous vertex.
      3. Break (b): Use this to break a segment out of the polyline. The highlighted vertex will be the beginning of the break.
      4. Insert (i): This function adds a new vertex. Click with the mouse to locate the new vertex.
      5. Move (m): Use this to move a vertex to a new location. Click with the mouse to pick the new location.

6. Regen (r): This regenerates the screen.
7. Straighten (s): This option straightens the segment between two vertices.
8. Tangent (t): This indicates a tangent direction to a vertex for curve fit. Click with mouse to set tangent direction.
9. Width (w): Use this to change the width of a segment.
10. Exit (x): This gets you out of edit vertex and returns you to pedit.

E. Fit Curve (f): This changes a straight polyline to a curved one by fitting the curve to the vertices.
F. Spline Curve (s): This option changes a straight polyline to a curved one by averaging out differences between vertices.
G. Decurve (d): Use this to change a curved line back to its original shape.
H. Undo (u): This command undoes pedit commands one step at a time.
I. Exit (x): This gets you out of pedit.

EDIT DIMENSIONS (dim IN R12), (dimedit IN R13 AND R14)

You can use the edit dimensions command to change the content or appearance of dimensions after they have been made. There are several options under edit dimensions.

R12

In R12, the following commands can be entered by clicking on Modify, then on Edit Dimensions, then on the appropriate command: Dimension Text (Change Text, Home Position, Move Text, Rotate Text), Oblique Dimensions, or Update Dimensions. They can also be entered by typing dim, then hitting Enter, then typing the appropriate text for one of the following commands and hitting Enter. The appropriate text for each command is given inside the parentheses below.

1. Dimension Text:
   A. Change Text (n): This command changes the text in a dimension.
      1. Prompt reads: Enter new dimension text:.
      2. Type in new dimension or text desired.
      3. Hit Enter or click right mouse button.
      4. Prompt reads: Select objects:.
      5. Click on dimension you want to change.
      6. Prompt reads: Select objects:.
      7. Hit Enter or click right mouse button to change selected text.
   B. Home Position (hom): This option returns moved or stretched dimension text to its original location.
      1. Prompt reads: Select objects:.

      2. Click on the text you want to return to its home position.

      3. Prompt reads: Select objects:.

      4. Hit Enter or click right mouse button.

  C. Move Text (te): This controls placement and orientation of dimension text.

      1. Prompt reads: Select objects:.

      2. Click on dimension you'd like to move.

      3. Prompt reads: Enter text location (Left/Right/Home/Angle):.

      4. Either move the text to the new location with the mouse and click the left mouse button or enter the desired prompt and hit Enter. The prompt options are:

        a. Left (l): This will move the text to the left.

        b. Right (r): This will move the text to the right.

        c. Home (h): This will move text to the home position.

        d. Angle (a):

          1. Prompt reads: Enter text angle:.

          2. Type angle counterclockwise to which you would like text to be rotated and hit Enter.

  D. Rotate Text (tr): Use this to set orientation of dimension text.

      1. Prompt reads: Enter text angle:.

      2. Type angle counterclockwise to which you would like text to be rotated and hit Enter.

      3. Prompt reads: Select objects:.

      4. Click on text(s) you would like to rotate to the chosen angle.

      5. Prompt reads: Select objects:.

      6. Click the right mouse button or hit Enter.

2. Oblique Dimension (oblique): This command offsets a dimension at an angle of your choosing.

  A. Prompt reads: Select objects:.

  B. Click on the dimension(s) you want to oblique.

  C. Prompt reads: Select objects:.

  D. Click right mouse button or hit Enter.

  E. Prompt reads: Enter obliquing angle (Return for none):.

  F. Type in angle desired (clockwise) and hit Enter; or, use mouse to establish an angle by clicking on two points.

3. Update Dimension (update): If you change your dimensioning variables in the middle of a drawing (e.g., dimscale), this command will update the dimensions selected.

  A. Prompt reads: Select objects:.

  B. Click on dimension(s) you want to update.

C. Prompt reads: **Select objects:**.

D. Hit **Enter** or click the right mouse button.

R13

In R13 the **edit dimensions** command can be activated by typing **dimedit** and hitting **Enter** or through the icons on the **Dimension** toolbar (see figure labeled The Dimensions Toolbar). The first group of icons, working from top to bottom, represent the commands: **Home**, **Rotate**, **Left**, **Center**, and **Right**. These are all available underneath one another on the Dimension toolbar as pop-ups. The last icon (see figure labeled The Oblique Dimension Button) is the **Oblique** icon. It is available as a pop-up on the button to the right of the last group. If you type **dimedit** and hit **Enter** you will get the following prompt: **Home/New/Rotate/Oblique <Home>:**. These are the options available. Type the first letter of the command and hit **Enter** to activate that command. (The icon-activated commands work in the same manner.)

1. **Home:** The **home** command returns moved or stretched dimension text to its original location.

    A. Prompt reads: **Select objects:**.

    B. Click on the text that you want to return to its home position.

    C. Prompt reads: **Select objects:**.

    D. Hit **Enter** or click right mouse button.

2. **New:** This changes the text in a dimension.

    A. Prompt reads: **Enter new dimension text:**.

    B. Type in new dimension or text desired.

    C. Hit **Enter** or click right mouse button.

    D. Prompt reads: **Select objects:**.

**THE
DIMENSIONS
TOOLBAR**

E. Click on dimension you'd like to change.

    F. Prompt reads: Select objects:.

    G. Hit Enter or click right mouse button to change selected text.

3. Rotate: Use this to set orientation of dimension text.

    A. Prompt reads: Enter text angle:.

    B. Type angle (counterclockwise) to which you would like text to be rotated and hit Enter.

    C. Prompt reads: Select objects:.

    D. Click on text(s) you would like to rotate to the chosen angle.

    E. Prompt reads: Select objects:.

    F. Click on right mouse button or hit Enter.

4. Oblique: This offsets dimension at an angle of your choosing.

    A. Prompt reads: Select objects:.

    B. Click on the dimension(s) you want to oblique.

    C. Prompt reads: Select objects:.

    D. Click right mouse button or hit Enter.

    E. Prompt reads: Enter obliquing angle (Return for none):.

    F. Type in angle desired clockwise and hit Enter; or, use mouse to establish an angle by clicking on two points.

5. The Left, Center, and Right icons very simply will shift any selected dimension to the left, center, or right sides between the dimension arrows.

R14

In R14, the edit dimensions command can be activated by typing dimedit and hitting Enter, by opening the pull down menu Dimension, or by clicking the icons on the Dimension toolbar (see the corresponding figures). The three icons are ways to activate the dimension edit (dimedit) command, the dimension text (dimtedit) command, and the dimension update (update) command.

1. Dimension Edit (dimedit): When the dimension edit command is activated, the following prompt appears: Home/New/Rotate/Oblique <Home>:. These are the options available. Type the first letter of the command and hit Enter to activate that command.

**THE DIMEDIT
COMMAND**

    A. Home: Use this to return moved or stretched dimension text to its original location.
      1. Prompt reads: Select objects:.
      2. Click on the text that you want to return to home position.
      3. Prompt reads: Select objects:.
      4. Hit Enter or click right mouse button.

    B. New: This changes the text in a dimension.
      1. Prompt reads: Enter new dimension text:.
      2. Type in new dimension or text desired.
      3. Hit Enter or click right mouse button.
      4. Prompt reads: Select objects:.
      5. Click on dimension you want to change.
      6. Prompt reads: Select objects:.
      7. Hit Enter or click right mouse button to change selected text.

    C. Rotate: This sets orientation of dimension text.
      1. Prompt reads: Enter text angle:.
      2. Type angle counterclockwise to which you would like text to be rotated and hit Enter.
      3. Prompt reads: Select objects:.
      4. Click on text(s) you would like to rotate to the chosen angle.
      5. Prompt reads: Select objects:.
      6. Click on right mouse button or hit Enter.

    D. Oblique: This command offsets dimension at an angle of your choosing.
      1. Prompt reads: Select objects:.
      2. Click on the dimension(s) you'd like to oblique.
      3. Prompt reads: Select objects:.
      4. Click right mouse button or hit Enter.
      5. Prompt reads: Enter obliquing angle (Return for none):.
      6. Type in angle desired clockwise and hit Enter; or, use mouse to establish an angle by clicking on two points.

2. Dimension Text (dimtedit): This command allows you to shift the position of the dimension text between the dimensioning arrows. The prompt reads: Left/Right/Home/Angle <Home>:. Type the first letter of the option that you desire and hit Enter to activate that option.
    A. Left or Right: This will shift the text to the left or the right side.

**THE DIMTEDIT
COMMAND**

**THE UPDATE
COMMAND**

B. **Home:** This option returns the text to the center position.

C. **Angle:** This rotates the text to the angle specified in degrees counter-clockwise.

3. **Update Dimension (update):** If you change your dimensioning variables in the middle of a drawing (e.g., dimscale) this command will update the dimensions selected.

A. Prompt reads: **Select objects:**.

B. Click on dimension(s) you want to update.

C. Prompt reads: **Select objects:**.

D. Hit **Enter** or click on right mouse button.

Exercise No. 7: Using Modify Commands

1. Open the file **Proto.dwg** from either the CD-ROM or the floppy disk to which you had previously saved it.

2. Save this file as **Exer7.dwg** on a floppy disk.

3. Work in **Exer7.dwg**.

A. **Erase** the word **Prototype** using the **crossing** option of **erase**.

B. Draw a circle with its center at (X,Y) 2',16'9" and a radius of 1'. Using the **modify entity/properties (ddmodify)** command, modify the circle so that its center is at 13'6",17' and it has a radius of 1'6".

C. Draw a line with a rectangle over it.

1. Use the **break** command to erase the line inside the rectangle. **Note:** Sometimes if you use the intersection object snap to try to simultaneously select your first point and the object you want to break, AutoCAD will pick the wrong object to break when using the one-step method. If this happens, cancel the **break** command and start over using the two-step method.

D. Draw two lines, one of which is perpendicular to the other but does not touch it. Using the **Extend** command, extend the perpendicular line so that it touches the other line.

E. Draw a line crossed by two other lines. Trim the first line so that no part of it extends past the other two.

F. Draw two lines and move them from one side of the drawing to the other.

G. Draw a vertical line and then rotate it 30 degrees.

H. Draw a 1 foot square and then scale it to 18 inches on each side.

I. Draw a square and then change it into a rectangle using the stretch command.

J. In R13 and R14 only, draw a line that is 1 foot long. Use the lengthen command to change it into a line that is 18 inches long.

K. Draw two parallel lines and then using the change/points command, force them to converge at a single point.

L. Use the rectangle command to draw a rectangle. Erase it. Notice when erasing that it is a single entity. Draw the rectangle again using the same command. Now explode the rectangle. Erase the rectangle again. Notice that now it consists of four separate entities. Draw the rectangle again and explode it.

M. Draw two polylines that cross one another. Then use the trim command to form a corner. Using pedit:
1. Join the two polylines to make a single polyline.
2. Change the width of the joined polyline to .5 mm.

N. Draw a rectangle and dimension one side. Move the text to the left side. Note that if the text is too large, this command will not work. There has to be room available for it to move. It is best to initially create a rectangle with a side that has an even length such as 2 feet rather than a long text figure such as 4 feet 9/16 inches.

O. Draw a rectangle and dimension one side. Using the oblique command, oblique the dimension 45 degrees.

P. Draw a circle with its center at (X,Y) 4',16'9" and a radius of 1'. Use the change properties command to change the circle so that its center is at 11'6",17' and it has a radius of 1'6". Compare this process with what you did using the ddmodify command in B above.

Q. Print the work you have done using the print/plot command, save the work to a floppy disk as Exer7.dwg and then print the file Projct7.dwg from the CD-ROM. Compare the two printouts. Note: The projct7.dwg file from the CD-ROM will not have the lengthen command (step J) illustrated on it because it was done in R12 and that command only exists in R13 and R14.

Using Modify/Construct Commands

This is a group of commands that take already existing entities and perform a variety of operations on them.

Array (array)

The array command makes multiple copies of selected objects, in a rectangular or circular pattern. In R12 and R14 the prompts below will appear exactly as you see them because both the polar and the rectangular array are activated by the same command. In R13 you select either the polar or rectangular array by the icon you click, then the prompts will follow the ones detailed below for either the polar or rectangular array.

1. Prompt reads: Select objects:.
2. Click on the objects that you want to include in the array.
3. Prompt reads: Select objects:.
4. Click on the right mouse button or hit Enter when all of the objects have been selected.
5. Prompt reads: Rectangular or Polar array (R/P):.
6. Type r or p and hit Enter.
   A. Rectangular Array: AutoCAD will prompt you for the number of columns and rows and the spacing between them. The array is built along a baseline defined by the current snap rotation angle set by the snap rotate command.
   B. Polar or Circular Array: First you must supply a center point. Then you must supply two of the following three parameters:
      • the number of items in the array
      • the number of degrees to fill
      • the angle between items in the array
      You can also rotate the items as the polar array is drawn.

THE ARRAY
COMMAND

AutoCAD Command	Function
Array	**Duplicates objects in a geometric array**

Keyboard Command	Pull Down Menu Path	Icon (R12)	Icon (R13)	Icon (R14)
ARRAY	R12: Construct/Array R14: Modify/Array			Modify

AutoCAD Command	Function	Creates a similar object/s at a
Offset		**specified distance and direction.**

Keyboard Command	Pull Down Menu Path	Icon (R12)	Icon (R13 & R14)
OFFSET	**R12: Construct/Offset** **R14: Modify/Offset**		Modify

OFFSET (offset)

The offset (offset) command lets you copy an object at a specific distance from the object or create a smaller or larger version of a closed object. You will find this to be one of the most useful drawing commands in all of AutoCAD. By using offset you can quickly lay out a ground plan precisely without doing a lot of calculations or figuring of points. Become very familiar with the use of offset; it is one of the best friends that the theatrical draftsman has in this program.

1. Activate the offset command.
2. Prompt reads: Offset distance or Through < >:. You can create your offset by either using the through method or by specifying an offset distance.
   A. The Through Method: At the above prompt, select through by typing t and hitting Enter.
      1. Prompt reads: Select object to offset:. Click on the object you want to offset.
      2. Prompt reads: Through point:. Click on a point at the distance from the old object at which you want to create the new object.
      3. Prompt reads: Select object to offset:. Click on right mouse button to complete command.
   B. Offset Distance Method: At the above prompt, type a distance from the old object at which you want the new object created and hit Enter.
      1. Prompt reads: Select object to offset:. Click on the object to be offset.
      2. Prompt reads: Side to offset?. Click on the side of the old object that the new object is to be offset from.
      3. Prompt reads: Select object to offset:. Click on the right mouse button to complete command.
3. When you use offset with a closed object you can either offset inside or outside the object to decrease or increase its size by the offset distance.

**THE COPY
COMMAND**

AutoCAD Command	Function
Copy	Makes copy/s of an entity/s

Keyboard Command	Pull Down Menu Path	Icon (R12)	Icon (R13 & R14)
COPY	R12: Construct/Copy R14: Modify/Copy		Modify

Copy (copy)

The copy (copy) command allows you to create a duplicate of one or more objects at a new location. There is also an option that lets you make multiple copies.

1. Activate the copy command.
2. Prompt reads: Select objects:. Click on object(s) you'd like to copy.
3. Prompt reads: Select objects:. Click on right mouse button.
4. Prompt reads: <Base point of displacement>/Multiple:. Click at a point on or near the old object that will become a reference point for inserting the new object.
5. Prompt reads: Second point of displacement: Click on the point where you want to insert a copy of the old object.
6. If you want to make multiple copies of the object, type m at the <Basepoint of displacement>/Multiple: prompt and hit Enter.
7. Prompt reads: Base Point:. Click at a point on or near the old object that you want to be a reference point for inserting the new object.
8. Prompt reads: Second point of displacement:. Click on the point where you want to insert the new object.
9. Continue to click at each new location that you want to insert a copy of the old object until you have created all the copies you want, then click on the right mouse button to complete the command.

Mirror (mirror)

The mirror (mirror) command allows you to create a mirror image of an object on the opposite side of a line that you establish.

1. Activate the mirror command.
2. Prompt reads: Select objects:. Click on the object(s) you want to mirror.

AutoCAD Command	Function	Creates a mirror image of an object/s on the other side of a centerline.
Mirror		

Keyboard Command	Pull Down Menu Path	Icon (R12)	Icon (R13 & R14)
MIRROR	**R12: Construct/Mirror** **R14: Modify/Mirror**		Modify

3. Prompt reads: Select objects:. Click on right mouse button.

4. Prompt reads: First point of mirror line:. Click on a point that establishes one end of the mirror line. The object will be mirrored on the opposite side of the mirror line.

5. Prompt reads: Second point:. Click on a point that establishes the other end of the mirror line.

6. Prompt reads: Delete old object <N>: Type y for yes or n for no and hit Enter. The object will appear on the opposite side of and the same distance away from the mirror line.

CHAMFER (chamfer)

Chamfer takes a sharp point off of a corner and replaces it with a bevel.

1. Activate the chamfer command. Before you can actually chamfer you must first use the command to set up the distances from the corner where you want the chamfer to happen.

2. Prompt reads: Polyline/Distances<Select first line>:. Type d for Distances and hit Enter.

3. Prompt reads: Enter first chamfer distance <0'0">:. Type the first chamfer distance and hit Enter.

AutoCAD Command	Function
Chamfer	**Bevels corner at preset distance**

Keyboard Command	Pull Down Menu Path	Icon (R12)	Icon (R13 & R14)
CHAMFER	**R12: Construct/Chamfer** **R14: Modify/Chamfer**		Modify

**THE FILLET
COMMAND**

AutoCAD Command **Fillet**	Function **Creates a fillet of a specified diameter at a corner.**		
Keyboard Command **FILLET**	Pull Down Menu Path **R12: Construct/Fillet** **R14: Modify/Fillet**	Icon (R12)	Icon (R13 & R14) **Modify**

4. Prompt reads: Enter second chamfer distance <0'0">:. Type the second chamfer distance and hit Enter.

5. Prompt reads: Command:. Hit the Chamfer button again or hit Enter again.

6. Prompt reads: Polyline/Distances/<Select first line>:. Click on the line you want to use the first chamfer distance on.

7. Prompt reads: Select second line:. Click on the second line.

FILLET (fillet)

Fillet connects two lines with an arc or rounds off a corner.

1. Activate the fillet command.

2. Prompt reads: Polyline/Radius/<select first object>:. Before you can fillet you must first set up a distance. In this case you are setting up the fillet radius. Select Radius by typing r and hitting Enter.

3. Prompt reads: Enter fillet radius<0'0">:. Type the fillet radius desired and hit Enter.

4. Prompt reads: Command:. Click on Fillet button again or hit Enter again.

5. Prompt reads: Polyline/Radius/<Select first object>:. Click on the first of the two lines to be filleted.

6. Prompt reads: Select second object:. Click on the second line to be filleted.

DIVIDE (divide) AND MEASURE (measure)

Divide divides an object into the number of divisions you specify. Measure divides an object into divisions of a specific length. Before you can use either of these commands, however, you will need to specify a point style. The default point style in AutoCAD is a dot. This will not be visible in the middle of a line. You will need a point style that is more visible to mark the division points for you. Open the Point Style box by typing ddptype. In R12, go to

THE DIVIDE COMMAND

AutoCAD Command	Function
Divide	**Divides a line into a specified # of parts**

Keyboard Command	Pull Down Menu Path	Icon (R12)	Icon (R13)
DIVIDE	**R12: Construct/Divide** **R14: Draw/Point/Divide**	🄰	✏️ **Draw/Point**

Setting/Point Style; in R13, go to Options/Display/Point Style; in R14, go to Format/Point Style. Select a point style that you want to use and click on it. Then proceed with either the divide or measure command. You can also use the divide and measure commands to insert a block that is currently defined within the drawing at each of the division or measure points.

1. Divide: Activate the divide command.
   A. Prompt reads: Select object to divide:. Click on the object you want to divide.
   B. Prompt reads: <Number of segments>/Block:. Type the number of divisions that you want the object divided into and hit Enter.
2. Measure: Activate the measure command.
   A. Prompt reads: Select object to measure:. Click on the object to be measured.
   B. Prompt reads: <Segment length>/Block:. Type the measurement length that you want to divide the object by and hit Enter.
   C. Note that measure starts dividing lines/objects into segments working from the end of the line/object back to the start. Any leftover segments will be at the start of the line/object.
3. Divide and Measure Points: Note that the points that an object is divided or measured into are nodes. In order to snap to these points you must use the node object snap.

THE MEASURE COMMAND

AutoCAD Command	Function
Measure	**Divides a line into specific lengths.**

Keyboard Command	Pull Down Menu Path	Icon (R12)	Icon (R13)
MEASURE	**R12: Construct/Measure** **R14: Draw/Point/Measure**	📏	📐 **Draw/Point**

4. Block: If you type b at the initial prompt for either divide or measure, at the next prompt you can specify a block to be inserted at the division or measure points. This must be a block that is defined within the drawing. You cannot insert a block from outside the drawing using this command. After you have specified a block for insertion, the command will continue as above prompting you to specify the number of division and measure points. For more information on Blocks see the section on Working with Blocks starting on page 143.

Exercise No. 8: Using Modify/Construct Commands

1. Open the file Proto.dwg from either the CD-ROM or the one that earlier was copied to a floppy disk.

2. Save this file as Exer8.dwg on a floppy disk.

3. Work in Exer8.dwg.

   A. Draw a small rectangle. Form a polar array of five of these rectangles that have not been rotated.

   B. Draw two lines perpendicular to one another. Then use offset and trim to turn them into a square with 1-foot sides.

   C. Draw an arc and then mirror the arc.

   D. Draw an ellipse and then copy it five times.

   E. Draw a square. Then form a 6-inch chamfer between two lines that meet at a corner.

   F. Working on the same square, form a 6-inch radius fillet between two other lines that meet at a corner.
   Note: For parts E and F, be sure that you create a corner where two lines meet, not one formed by two pline segments or one where two lines do not quite meet or cross.

   G. Copy the square with the chamfer and fillet. Mirror the square with the chamfer and fillet.

   H. Draw a line and then divide it into five equal parts. Be sure you select a point style so that the divisions are easily seen.

   I. Draw a line and then measure it into 1-foot segments.

   J. Draw a line that connects one of the division points on the line that you divided in part G to one of the measured points on the line that you measured in part H.

   K. Print out your Exer8.dwg. Print out Projct8.dwg from the CD-ROM. Carefully examine the differences between these two printouts.

CREATING TEXT, LINETYPES, AND LAYERS

DYNAMIC TEXT: (dtext)

Dynamic text allows you to add text to your drawing in a variety of styles, sizes, and orientations. In many ways the dtext command works like a simple word processor.

   The initial prompt reads: dtext Justify/Style/<start point>:. From this prompt you can simply click on the location where you want the text to begin and start writing. AutoCAD will give you the default options of left justify and standard text style automatically. It will ask you two important questions after you click on the start point: what height and angle rotation you desire.

1. Prompt reads: Height< >:. Type in the height you want your text to be and hit Enter.

2. Prompt reads: Rotation angle <0>:. If you want your text rotated 0 degrees, hit Enter. If you want another rotation angle, type it in degrees counter-clockwise and hit Enter.

3. Prompt reads: Text:, and a box appears on the screen where the text will begin in the height you specified for the text. Now you can start typing your text. The Enter and Backspace keys now work just like on a type-writer. When you have finished this block of text and want to exit dtext, hit Enter twice. Note that each line of text becomes a separate entity for commands like erase, move, copy, etc.

4. Other Text Options: At the initial prompt Justify/Style/<Start point>:, you may chose other text options. You can pick one of the Justify options by typing j and hitting Enter, or you can set a different Style by typing s and hitting Enter.

   A. Justify Options: Prompt reads:
      Align/Fit/Center/Middle/Right/TL/TC/TR/ML/MC/BL/BC/BR:. Type the capital letter(s) of the option and hit Enter to choose that option.

THE DYNAMIC TEXT COMMAND

AutoCAD Command	Function		
Dynamic Text	**Creates text for your drawing.**		

Keyboard Command	Pull Down Menu Path	Icon (R12)	Icon (R13)
DTEXT	**R12: Draw/Text** **R14: Draw/Text/Single Line**	**A**	**A▯** **Draw**

1. **Align:** This lets you set up a line at any angle you desire. The text will then follow that alignment. You are prompted for a First text line point and then for a Second text line point. Click on each to establish your text line. The First text line point is also the start point for your text.

2. **Fit:** This lets you click on the start and end points of your text and automatically adjusts the size of the text to fit the space you have chosen.

   a. Prompt reads: First text line point:. Click where you want your text to begin.

   b. Prompt reads: Second text line point:. Click where you want your text to end.

   c. Prompt reads: Height<1'0">:. Type a height that you think is close to the size the text will end up being and hit Enter. This is *not* the size your text will end up being; this is just to give you a size to work with while you are typing.

   d. Prompt reads: Text:. Type in the text that you want to fit between the two points you have chosen and hit Enter twice. The text will be adjusted in height to fit the chosen space. Note that this adjustment does not take place until after you have hit Enter twice.

3. **Center:** Use this to align your block of text to be centered and above the point that you chose. Prompt reads: Centerpoint:. Click on the point you want the text to be centered on and above. Proceed as in the regular dtext command. The alignment will not happen until after you have hit Enter twice.

4. **Middle:** Use this command to align your block of text to be centered vertically and horizontally around the point you chose.

5. **Right:** Use this function to align your block of text to be above and to the left of the point you chose.

6. **Horizontal Text Alignment Options:** The following options are only for horizontal text alignment. They align the first line of your text to the point chosen. Subsequent lines of text will be below the first line and justified left, right, or center.

   TL: top left
   TC: top center
   TR: top right
   ML: middle left
   MC: middle center
   MR: middle right
   BL: bottom left
   BC: bottom center
   BR: bottom right

MULTILINE TEXT (mtext) IN R13 AND R14

Although dynamic text is still available in both R13 and R14, the primary method of creating text for your drawing in these two versions of the program is a new command called multiline text or mtext. It works in very different ways from the dynamic text command. The first major difference is, as the name implies, the creation of multiple lines of text as a single entity. Remember that in dtext, every line of text is a separate entity. In mtext, when you create multiple lines of text they come into AutoCAD as a single entity and can be erased, modified, etc. as one unit. The mtext command is activated in one of the manners described below. Note that mtext works slightly differently in R13 and R14.

R13

The initial prompt reads: mtext Attach/Rotation/Style/Height/Direction/<Insertion Point>:. The options available are:

1. **Attach:** Selecting this option opens another set of options that allow you to select the alignment at the insertion point of the text. These options work exactly like the top right, top center, top left, etc. options in dtext.

2. **Rotation:** Selecting this option allows you to enter a rotation angle in degrees counterclockwise for the text.

3. **Style:** This option allows you to specify a style for the text. To use this option you must know the names of the text styles. See the text style command (see page 129) later in this section for how to create new text styles.

4. **Height:** You are immediately prompted for the height of the text when you choose this option.

5. **Direction:** This allows you to chose horizontal or vertical text.

6. **Insertion Point:** This is the default option, the one that you will use the most often with mtext. You can click anywhere in the drawing space to select the insertion point of the text or enter X,Y coordinates on the keyboard and hit Enter.

THE MULTILINE TEXT COMMAND

AutoCAD Command	Function	
Multiline Text	**Creates text for your drawing.**	

Keyboard Command	Pull Down Menu Path	Icon (R13 & R14)
R13 & R14: **MTEXT**	**R14: Draw/Text/Multiline Text**	**A** Draw

A. Prompt reads: Attach/Rotation/Style/Height/Direction/Width/2 points/ <Other corner>:. Again, you are offered the same options as before plus three new ones:
   1. Width: This allows you to give a width for the text.
   2. 2 points: This lets you specify two points that will form the corners of a window enclosing a typical letter. This specifies both the height and width of the text simultaneously. The two points can be entered on the keyboard or by clicking with the mouse.
   3. Other Corner: Once again, this is the default option. You can click anywhere in the drawing space or enter coordinates on the keyboard to select the other corner of a window. The first corner of the window was defined by Insertion Point back in step 6 above. This second corner will define both the height and the width of the text simultaneously.

B. Once you have specified the height and width of the text through one of the three methods outlined above, then the Edit Mtext box will open. In this box you will be able to change several aspects of the text by doing the following operations:
   1. Click on the Properties button to change style, height, and direction.
   2. Click on the Browse button to select a different font.
   3. Click in the Overline or Underline boxes to have a line drawn over or under the text.
   4. Double click to the right of the number in the Height window and then enter a new figure on the keyboard to change the height of the text.

C. Once you have made the changes you want to the properties of the text you can start to type text in the Edit Mtext box. This text will appear in the upper window of the box. You can enter as many lines of text as you would like in the box, but remember that once you have clicked on the OK button, all of the text will be entered into the drawing as a single entity. While you are still in the box you can edit the text that you have already typed by clicking at a point in the text and then using the Backspace key, etc. After you have entered all the text that you want, click on the OK button.

R14

The initial prompt reads: mtext Current text style: STANDARD. Text height: 3/16" Specify first corner:.

1. Click on the point in the drawing space where you would like the text to begin or specify a beginning point by entering coordinates on the keyboard.

2. Prompt reads: Specify opposite corner or [Height/Justify/Rotation/Style/Width]:. You can immediately define a window by clicking on the opposite diagonal corner of the window, and this will simultaneously specify both the height and width of the text. If you go with this default option you will immediately open the Multiline Text Editor and can modify and create text. However, you also have the following options available to you before you specify the opposite corner.

A. Height: This function prompts you for a height for the text.

B. Justify: This function prompts you for a justification for the text such as top left, etc.

C. Rotation: This prompts you for a rotation angle for the text.

D. Style: This option prompts you for a text style. You must know these styles by name to use this command. See the text style command later in this section (see page 129) for information on creating new text styles.

E. Width: This option prompts you for a width for the text.

All of these options will return you to the Specify opposite corner: prompt when you have finished with them. Click on the point in the drawing space that defines the diagonal corner of a window for text size, and the Multiline Text Editor box will open.

3. Multiline Text Editor box: With this box you can make the following adjustments to the text:

A. Character tab: Click on the Character tab just under the title of the box to reveal these options:

1. Font: The first down arrow that you see on the left allows you to choose the font. Unlike R12 and R13, which have limited fonts available, R14 offers many of the same fonts that already exist on your computer. As you add new fonts to your computer many of them will also become available in AutoCAD.

2. Height: The window to the right of the Font Window lets you change the height of the text. Click to the right of the number in the window and type in a new height.

3. B, I, U buttons: If the font that you have chosen has bold, italic, or underline options available, you can click on these buttons to utilize them.

4. You can also choose the color of the text and some symbols on this tab.

B. Properties tab: Click on the Properties tab to reveal these options:

1. Style: Enter a standard AutoCAD text style by name in this window.

2. Justification: Click on the down arrow to enter a justification.

3. Width: Double click to the right of the width given here to highlight the current number and enter a new width using the keyboard.

4. Rotation: Enter a rotation angle in degrees counterclockwise in this window.

C. Find/Replace tab: This tab lets you search for specified text strings and replace them with new text.

1. In the Find window, type in the text that you would like to replace.

2. Click on the Find button next to the Find window to search for this text. The icon looks like binoculars.

3. In the Replace with window, type in the text that you would like to replace the above text.

4. Click on the Replace button next to the Replace with window to replace the selected text with the new text. The icon looks like a small a and b with an arrow.

D. Import Text button: Click on this button to import text from another source. AutoCAD will accept a text file in either .txt (ASCII) or .rtf formats.

E. Type in new text in the main text window that appears just below the tabs. When you have completed all of the text that you want, click on OK to bring it all into the drawing as a single entity.

QUICK TEXT (qtext)

The quick text (qtext) command speeds up your screen regeneration time by substituting a rectangle for a large block of text. Qtext is either on or off. Type the command qtext and hit Enter, then type on or off and hit Enter.

CHANGE TEXT (change) IN R12

The change command lets you make changes in text position, style, height, or rotation angle or the text itself. You can enter the change command through the keyboard or through the pull down menu. This command only works on text in R12.

Click on Modify, then on Change, then on Points, or type change and hit Enter.

1. Prompt reads: Select objects:.

2. Click on the line or lines of text you want to change. You must click on each line of text separately or select several lines with a window.

3. Prompt reads: Select objects:. Click on the right mouse button or hit Enter.

4. Prompt reads: Properties/<change point>:. If you want to move the position of the text, click on the new position of the text. If you do not want to

move the position of the text, click twice with the right mouse button or hit Enter twice.

5. Prompt reads: Text style: STANDARD (or whatever the current style is) New Style or RETURN for no change:. If you want to change the text style, type in the new style name and hit Enter. If you do not want to change the text style, hit Enter.

6. Prompt reads: New height<current ht.>:. If you want to change the height, type in the new height and hit Enter. If not, just hit Enter.

7. Prompt reads: New rotation angle<old rotation angle>:. If you want to change the rotation angle, type in the new rotation angle in degrees counterclockwise and hit Enter. If not, just hit Enter.

8. Prompt reads: Text<old text>:. If you want to change the text, type in the new text and hit Enter. If not, just hit Enter.

EDIT TEXT (ddedit)

In R12, the ddedit command is another way to change a single line of text. It is faster than using the change command if all you want to do is change the content of the text line. It will not, however, allow you to make the other modifications that are possible with the change command such as position, text style, height, and rotation angle. In R13 and R14, the ddedit command will activate the Edit Mtext box or the Multiline Text Editor box for the text that you have selected and allow you to change any of the options available in these boxes.

Note: This command can also be used to edit the contents (attdef) of attributes in blocks such as changing an instrument number or gel color.

Activate the ddedit command. In R12 the prompt reads: <select a TEXT or ATTDEF object>/UNDO:.

1. Click on the text that you want to change.

2. Edit Text box opens with a blinking cursor. Use your arrow keys on the keyboard or the mouse to move the cursor and use the keyboard to edit

THE EDIT TEXT COMMAND

AutoCAD Command	Function		
Edit Text	**Edits already existing text.**		

Keyboard Command	Pull Down Menu Path	Icon (R12)	Icon (R13 & R14)
DDEDIT	**R14: Modify/Object/Text**		
			Modify Modify II

the text as you desire. When you have the new text the way that you want it, click on the OK button.

3. Prompt reads: <select a TEXT or ATTDEF object>/UNDO:.

4. If at this point you decide that you do not want to make the changes that you just made, then type u on the keyboard and hit Enter.

5. If you want to change another line of text, click on it.

6. When you have made all the changes that you want to make and are ready to record them, hit Enter.

In R13 and R14 you will be prompted to select an object. Click on the text that you would like to edit and the editing box will open.

Modify Text (ddmodify)

The ddmodify command opens a dialogue box that allows you to simultaneously change many aspects of the text. The Modify Text box that opens offers these options: Layer, Color, Origin, Height, Rotation, Width, Obliquing, Justify, Style, Upside down, Backward, and Text. The command is entered by typing ddmodify and hitting Enter. In R12, you can also click on Modify/Entity on the pull down menu.

1. Prompt reads: Select object to modify:.

2. Click on the text line you want to change.

3. This opens the Modify Text box.

4. Make the changes that you want in this box and click on OK.

Text Style (textstyle) in R12

The text style (textstyle) command changes the font or styles of text that you are currently using. The default text style for AutoCAD is Standard. There are about 38 other text styles available to you, however.

1. When you begin a drawing in AutoCAD the only text style available is Standard. To open one or more of the other text styles, go to the pull down menu.

   A. Click on Draw, then on Text, then on Set Style.

   B. This opens the Select Text Font box. Here you can view examples of all of the fonts available.

   Caution: Do not open fonts unless you want to use them. Fonts use up a lot of active RAM. Taking up a lot of RAM for something you will not use can slow down your working process.

C. To select a font, either click on the list of names on the left or on the box on the right with the sample of the font. Then click on **OK**.

D. When you open a font, AutoCAD will ask you a number of questions about options for that particular font. If you enter a value for one of these options, that option is locked in until you change it by reopening the font from the **Select Text Font** box. For most of your use, you should enter the default option when opening a font. Options are:

   1. **Height<0'0">**: Hit **Enter**. This default will let you choose your height each time you activate **dtext**.

   2. **Width Factor<1.000>**: Hit **Enter** unless you want fat or skinny letters. This default will give you normally proportioned letters. Entering a value of less than 1 will give you skinny letters, while more than 1 produces fat ones.

   3. **Obliquing angle<0>**: Hit **Enter** unless you want all your letters obliqued. This default gives you vertical letters. Entering a positive (+) or negative (–) number of degrees here will angle your text forward or backward by that amount.

   4. **Backwards<N>**: Hit **Enter**. This default gives you forward-facing letters. If you enter a **Y** for yes here you will get backward-facing letters.

   5. **Upside-down<N>**: Hit **Enter**. This default gives you right side–up letters. If you enter a **Y** for yes here you will get upside-down letters.

   6. **Vertical?<N>**: Hit **Enter**. This default gives you letters that follow one another horizontally. If you enter a **Y** for yes here you will get letters that follow one another vertically.

This completes opening this particular font. It also sets it as the current text style.

2. You now have two fonts open: Standard and the one you just opened. If you want to open another font you must return to the **Select Text Font** box. Now, however, with two fonts open, you can switch between them by using the **textstyle** command without having to return to the **Select Text Font** box. You can also change the text style in any of the other commands already discussed whenever the Justify/Style/<Start point>: prompt appears by typing **s**, hitting **Enter**, and then typing in the name of the new text style and hitting **Enter**. To use the **textstyle** command to change the current text style to another one that is also open:

A. Type **textstyle** and hit **Enter**.

B. Prompt reads: New value for Textstyle<STANDARD>:. The name inside the default arrows is the current text style. Type the name of the text style that you want to switch to and hit **Enter**. For example, type **romand**. Remember that you must have already opened a text style in order to switch to it this way.

TEXT STYLE (style) IN R13 AND R14

This command opens the Text Style box, where you can change many aspects of the current style of text as well as create new text styles. You should not be currently working with a text command when you open this box. The next time that you use a text command, however, the changes that you made in this box will be applied. Type style and hit Enter to activate this command. In R13, you can also use the pull down menu Data/Text Style. In R14, the pull down menu is Format/Text Style. Any of these methods will open the Text Style box, where you can make the following changes to the current text style or create new ones.

R13

1. Styles: This area lets you create a new text style from a font that exists in your computer. Once you have created a style name, the text style can be selected anytime that you have a Style prompt in a text command. First enter a new name in the window next to New. Then click on the New button. Next select a font in the Font area and make any changes that you would like in the Effects area. Click on the Apply button to apply all of these to the new name that you entered earlier.

   After you have created a new text style, it will be available to you simply by opening the Text Style box and clicking on the list that appears in the window underneath the New window. You can also select the text style by typing its name after selecting the Style prompt during the dtext or mtext command.

2. Font: This area of the box lets you select a new font from those available. To select a new Font:
   A. Click on the Browse button next to Font File or Bigfont.
   B. The Select Font File box opens. You will have to locate on your hard drive the main directory for AutoCAD 13. Then under the main directory for AutoCAD 13, you will have to locate the folder com and the subfolder fonts. When you have opened the subfolder fonts, you will be able to select from among the files available. After you have selected a file and opened it, it will appear in the Preview window.

3. Effects: This area lets you select the following changes to the font.
   A. Upside Down: Check here for text to appear upside down.
   B. Backwards: Check here for text to appear backwards.
   C. Height: Set the height of the font here.
   D. Width factor: Enter a new value here to change width.
   E. Oblique Angle: Enter a new value for obliquing the text here.

4. Preview: The preview area of the box shows you what the changes you made look like.

R14

1. Style Name: This area lets you create a new text style from a font that exists in your computer. Once you have created a style name, the text style can be selected anytime that you have selected the Style prompt in a text command. First pick a new font in the Font area and make any other changes that you would like in the Font or Effects areas. Note that as you scroll down through the available fonts, the AutoCAD-specific fonts will have an AutoCAD icon next to them rather than a True Type icon. If you are going to be saving your drawing in any format other than R14 you should be using the AutoCAD fonts. Then click on the New button in the Style Name area. The New Text Style box will open. Enter a name for the new text style and click OK. Close the Text Style box to use the new text style.

   After you have created a new text style, it will be available to you simply by opening the Text Style box and clicking on the down arrow next to the Style Name window. You will also be able to select it by entering its name after selecting the Style option in any of the text commands.

2. Font: This area of the box lets you select the following:

   A. Font Name: Pick a new font.

   B. Font Style: Select regular, italic, or bold.

   C. Height: Set the height of the font.

3. Effects: This area of the box lets you select the following options:

   A. Upside Down: Check here for text to appear upside down.

   B. Backwards: Check here for text to appear backwards.

   C. Width Factor: Enter a new value here to change width.

   D. Oblique Angle: Enter a new value for obliquing the text here.

4. Preview: The Preview area of the box shows you how the changes that you made look. Click on the Preview button after making any changes to see them.

LINETYPE (linetype)

There are a large number of linetypes (linetype) available to you with AutoCAD. However, only one of these linetypes is open when you begin a drawing: Continuous. In order to use one of the other linetypes, you must load it first. As with text styles, you do not want to load a linetype unless you intend to use it because of the active RAM that it occupies. For theatrical drawings the most useful linetypes other than Continuous are Center and Hidden1, Hidden2, Dashed1, or Dashed2. Once a linetype has been loaded it still has to be assigned to a layer before it can be used in the drawing. This process will be covered in the next section on layers (see page 136). Each layer can have one linetype assigned to it. Anything drawn in that layer will have that linetype.

R12

To view the linetypes available and load them:

1. Type linetype and hit Enter.
2. Prompt reads: ?/Create/Load/Set:. Type ? and hit Enter.
3. This opens Select Linetype File box. Click on the OK button.
4. This opens the AutoCAD Text file: c:\ACAD\SUPPORT\ACAD.lin, which contains the available linetypes. Look at the linetypes available and write down the exact names of the ones you want to use—you will need to know them later. Note that there is a second page to this file and you must hit Enter in order to view it. After you look at the second page, the prompt reads: ?/Create/Load/Set:.
5. Type l and hit Enter to load linetypes.
6. Prompt reads: Linetype(s) to load:.
7. Type the correct name of the linetype that you want to load, e.g. Center, and hit Enter.
8. The Select Linetype File box will appear, click on OK.
9. Prompt reads: Linetype CENTER loaded ?/Create/Load/Set:. If you want to load another linetype, repeat steps 5 through 8. If you want to draw with the linetype that you have loaded, you will have to associate it with a layer. Layers will be the next subject covered in this book, and then you'll learn how to associate a linetype with a layer. Before you can do that or anything else, however, you must first escape from the AutoCAD text screen that you are in. To do this hit Enter. Prompt should read: Command:. If it does not, hit Enter again.
10. Look at the top of your screen. You should see two title bars. The top one is the title bar for the drawing you are working in. Below it is the title bar AutoCAD Text-UNNAMED. On the right side of that title bar is an X. Click on the X on the AutoCAD Text-UNNAMED title bar. This returns you to your drawing screen.

Note: Sometimes at this point you will find that you cannot type an entry on the command line. This is because AutoCAD has been trapped in a loop and you have to regenerate the screen. To do this, activate the zoom all command.

11. Ltscale (ltscale): Before you can use one of the new linetypes you have loaded there is one more thing that you must do. You must set the ltscale factor to the size of the drawing you are working in. Ltscale is a proportional formula based on the scale that you will be viewing and/or printing. For theatre this is usually 1/2 inch = 1 foot or 1/4 inch = 1 foot.

To determine your ltscale factor you first must work out your viewing/printing scale to a proportion of 1" = X". For a 1/2 inch = 1 foot scale, it would be 1 inch = 24 inches. For the 1/4 inch = 1 foot scale it would be 1 inch = 48 inches. To get your ltscale factor, divide X by two. So, for the 1/2 inch = 1 foot scale you have an ltscale factor of 24/2 = 12. For the 1/4 inch = 1 foot scale you have an ltscale factor of 48/2 = 24.

To set the ltscale factor:

A. Type ltscale and hit Enter.
B. Prompt reads: New scale factor<1.0000>:.
C. Type the ltscale factor that you have worked out—12 for 1/2 inch = 1 foot or 24 for 1/4 inch = 1 foot—and hit Enter.

R13

To view the linetypes available and load them:

1. Click on the icon in the middle of the Object Properties toolbar (see figure labeled The Linetype Button, R13) or type linetype and hit Enter.
2. This opens the Select Linetype dialogue box. Here you can
    *   see which linetypes have already been loaded in the Loaded Linetypes area
    *   change the Linetype Scale (see step 4 below), and
    *   click on the Load button to select other linetypes, opening the Load or Reload Linetypes box
        A. Scroll up and down to see the linetypes that are available.
        B. Click on the name of a linetype to select it.
        C. Click on OK to load it into the Select Linetype box. It is now available for use in your drawing.
3. When you are finished loading new linetypes click on the OK button to close the box. I do not recommend selecting linetypes any other way than by layer for the time being. After you get more familiar with AutoCAD you may want to select linetypes in other ways. For now, be sure that the window next to Linetype: says BYLAYER.
4. Ltscale (ltscale): Before you can use one of the new linetypes you have loaded there is one more thing that you must do. You must set the ltscale factor to the size of the drawing you are working in. Ltscale is a proportional formula based on the scale that you will be viewing and/or printing.

For theatre this is usually 1/2 inch = 1 foot or 1/4 inch = 1 foot. To determine your ltscale factor you first must work out your viewing/printing scale to a proportion of 1" = X". For a 1/2 inch = 1 foot scale, it would be 1 inch = 24 inches. For a 1/4 inch = 1 foot scale it would be 1 inch = 48 inches. To get your ltscale factor, divide X by two. So, for 1/2 inch = 1 foot scale you have an ltscale factor of 24/2 = 12. For the 1/4 inch = 1 foot scale you have an ltscale factor of 48/2 = 24.

To set the Ltscale factor:

A. Type ltscale and hit Enter.

B. Prompt reads: New scale factor<1.0000>:.

C. Type the ltscale factor that you have worked out—12 for 1/2 inch = 1 foot or 24 for 1/4 inch = 1 foot—and hit Enter.

D. You can also enter the ltscale in the Linetype Scale area of the Select Linetype dialogue box.

R14

To view the linetypes available and load them:

1. Click on the icon in the middle of the Object Properties toolbar (see figure labeled The Linetype Button, R14) or type linetype and hit Enter.

2. This opens the Layer and Linetypes Properties box. If it is not already selected, click on the tab labeled Linetype.

    Here you can:

    • see which linetypes have already been loaded in the main window of box, and

    • click on the Load button to select other linetypes, opening the Load or Reload Linetypes box

        A. Scroll up and down to see the linetypes that are available.

        B. Click on the name of a linetype to select it.

        C. Click on OK to load it into the Select Linetype box. It is now available for use in your drawing.

3. When you are finished loading new linetypes, click on the OK button to close the box. I do not recommend selecting linetypes any other way than by layer for the time being. After you get more familiar with AutoCAD you may want to select linetypes in other ways. For now, be sure that the window next to Current: says BYLAYER.

**THE LINETYPE
BUTTON, R14**

4. **Ltscale (ltscale):** Before you can use one of the new linetypes you have loaded there is one more thing that you must do. You must set the ltscale factor to the size of the drawing you are working in. Ltscale is a proportional formula based on the scale that you will be viewing and/or printing. For theatre this is usually 1/2 inch = 1 foot or 1/4 inch = 1 foot. To determine your ltscale factor you first must work out your viewing/printing scale to a proportion of 1" = X". For the 1/2 inch = 1 foot scale, it would be 1 inch = 24 inches. For the 1/4 inch = 1 foot scale it would be 1 inch = 48 inches. To get your ltscale factor, divide X by two. So, for the 1/2 inch = 1 foot scale you have an ltscale factor of 24/2 = 12. For the 1/4 inch = 1 foot scale you have an ltscale factor of 48/2 = 24. To set the ltscale factor:

A. Type **ltscale** and hit **Enter.**

B. Prompt reads: **New scale factor<1.0000>:.**

C. Type the ltscale factor that you have worked out—**12** for 1/2 inch = 1 foot or **24** for 1/4 inch = 1 foot—and hit **Enter.**

Layers

One of the most important features of AutoCAD is its use of **layers.** You already know that one use of layers is to give you different linetypes in your drawing. Once you have set a linetype for a layer, everything drawn in that layer will have that linetype. However, layers have many other uses. Layers allow you to separate different elements of your drawing from one another. You can then choose to view or not view and print or not print different layers as you desire, by turning a layer on or off. This gives you a large variety in the kind of printed drawing that you can produce from one AutoCAD drawing and much more flexibility in what you are viewing on your screen at any given time. You can also associate different colors with different layers so it is easier to tell them apart on the drawing screen, and when printing you can tell your plotter to print different layers in different pens to enhance the printout. All of this is determined from the settings you make in the **Layer Control** box—in R12 and R13—or **Layer Properties** box in R14.

R12 and R13: The Layer Control Box

There are three ways to open the **Layer Control** box. The simplest is to click on the **Layer** button at the far left of the toolbar. Another is to click on **Layer Control** on the pull down menu under **Settings** in R12 or on **Layer** on the pull down menu under **Data** in R13. The last is to type **layer** and hit **Enter.** The Layer Control box lets you create new layers, rename old ones, turn them on and off, freeze and thaw them, lock and unlock them, and change the color and linetype associated with them.

1. To create a new layer:
    A. When you open the **Layer Control** box you will notice a blinking cursor in the rectangle under **New**. If it is not there take your mouse and move the cursor to the rectangle and click once. The blinking cursor will appear at the beginning of the rectangle.
    B. Type the name of the new layer that you want to create in this rectangle. For example, say you want to create a layer for your center line on the drawing. Type **center line** and then click on the **New** button.
    C. The information on your new layer will appear in the **Layer Name** box. All new layers are created with a color of white and a linetype of **Continuous**. You will have to change these to what you want.
2. To change the color of a layer:
    A. Click on the name of the layer in the **Layer Name** box. The layer you have chosen will be highlighted.
    B. Click on the **Set Color** bar. The **Set Color** box opens.
    C. Click on the color you want from the **Standard Colors, Gray Shades,** and **Full Color Palettes.**
    D. Click on **OK.**
3. To change the linetype of a layer:
    A. Click on the layer name in the **Layer Name** box.
    B. Click on the **Set Ltype** bar. The **Select Linetype** box opens.
    C. Click on the linetype that you want.
    D. Click on **OK.**

    Note: Only the linetypes that you have previously loaded will appear in the **Select Linetype** box.

4. To rename a layer:
    A. Click on the layer name in the **Layer Name** box.
    B. Move the cursor to the right of the current name of the layer in the rectangle under the **New, Current,** and **Rename** buttons and click once. Hit the **Backspace** key until the name in the rectangle is gone and you are left with a blinking cursor. Type the new name of the layer. Click on the **Rename** button.
5. On/Off, Thaw/Freeze, Lock/Unlock:
    A. To activate any of these functions:
        1. Click on the layer name in the **Layer Name** box.
        2. Click on the appropriate button in the upper right corner of the **Layer Control** box.

B. On/Off: When a layer is off, it is not visible on the screen and it cannot be printed. AutoCAD still takes it into consideration in screen regeneration and other functions, however.

C. Thaw/Freeze: When a layer is frozen it is not visible on the screen and it cannot be printed. When a layer is frozen, AutoCAD ignores it in screen regeneration and other functions. This can save you time in drawing. For theatrical drawing purposes it is usually best to use Thaw/Freeze rather than On/Off.

D. Lock/Unlock: When a layer is locked it is still visible on the screen, but it cannot be changed.

6. To exit the Layer Control box:

A. To exit the Layer Control box and *keep the changes you have made,* click on the OK button.

B. To exit the Layer Control box *without making any changes,* click on the Cancel button.

7. To change the layer you are working in from the drawing screen:

R12: The far left rectangle on the toolbar displays the color of the layer you are currently in. The rectangle to the right of the Layer button displays the name of the layer you are currently in. To change layers click on the down arrow to the right of the layer name and then on the name of the layer.

R13: The left window on the Object Properties toolbar displays the color and the property icons of the layer you are currently in. To change layers, click on the down arrow to the right of this window.

A. This opens a box with the names of the currently available layers in it. The currently active layer is highlighted.

B. To switch to another layer, click once on the name of the layer you want to make active.

C. You can only draw in one layer at a time, so when working it is usually best to get as much as possible done in one layer before switching to another one.

8. To change the layer of an entity in R12: If you should discover that you have drawn an entity in the wrong layer or just decide that you want to rearrange the layers of various entities in a drawing you can do that by using the Change Properties command (ddchprop). Type ddchprop and hit Enter or click on the Modify pull down menu, then on Change, and then on Properties:

A. Prompt reads: Select objects:.

B. Click on the entity or entities of which you want to change the layer.

C. Prompt reads: Select objects:.

D. Click the right mouse button or hit Enter.

    E. Change Properties box opens.
       1. Click on Layer.
       2. Select Layer box opens.
       3. Click on the name of the layer that you want the entity to be in.
       4. Click on OK.
       5. Change Properties box opens.
       6. Click on OK.

9. To change the layer of an entity in R13: If you should discover that you have drawn an entity in the wrong layer or just decide that you want to rearrange the layers of various entities in a drawing, you can do so by using the Change Properties command (ai_propchk). Type ai_propchk and hit Enter or click on the Edit pull down menu, and then on Properties.

    A. Prompt reads: Select objects:.
    B. Click on the entity or entities of which you want to change the layer.
    C. Prompt reads: Select objects:.
    D. Click the right mouse button or hit Enter.
    E. Modify box opens.
       1. Click on Layer.
       2. Select Layer box opens.
       3. Click on the name of the layer that you want the entity to be in.
       4. Click on OK.
       5. Change Properties box opens.
       6. Click on OK.

R14: The Layer Properties Box

There are three ways to open the Layer Properties box. The simplest is to click on the Layers button that is second from the left on the Object Properties tool-bar. Another is to click on Layer on the pull down menu under Format. The last is to type layer and hit Enter.

    The Layer Properties box lets you create new layers, rename old ones, turn them on and off, freeze and thaw them, lock and unlock them, and change the color and linetype associated with them.

1. To create a new layer:

    A. When you open the Layer Properties box, you will notice a button labeled New.
    B. Click on the New button.
    C. The information on your new layer will appear in the main window. A name such as Layer1 will appear highlighted in a box. To give your new layer a name, simply type in the name that you would like and hit Enter. All new layers are created with a color of white, which looks

like black, and a linetype of Continuous. You will have to change these to what you want.

2. To change the color of a layer:
   A. Click on the name of the layer in the Layer Properties box window. The layer you have chosen will be highlighted.
   B. Click on the colored or black square for the layer under C in the window.
   C. Click on the color you want from the Select Color box.
   D. Click on OK.

3. To change the linetype of a layer:
   A. Click on the name of the layer in the Layer Properties box window. The layer you have chosen will be highlighted.
   B. Click on the name of the linetype under the Linetype column in the window. The Select Linetype box opens.
   C. Click on the linetype that you want.
   D. Click on OK.

   Note: Only the linetypes that you have previously loaded will appear in the Select Linetype box.

4. To rename a layer:
   A. Click on the name of the layer in the Layer Properties box window. The layer you have chosen will be highlighted. Move the cursor away from the name of the layer. Move the cursor back to the name of the layer and click on it again. Move the cursor away from the name of the layer. The box surrounding the name of the layer will expand and a blinking cursor will appear behind the name. Type in the new name that you would like and hit Enter.

5. ON/OFF, Thaw/Freeze, Lock/Unlock:
   A. To activate any of these functions:
      1. Click on the layer name in the Layer Name box.
      2. Move the cursor across the icons that appear in the Layer Properties box window to the right of the name of the layer. The name of the function of each of these icons will appear. Click on the icon to toggle that function on or off.
   B. On/Off: When a layer is off, it is not visible on the screen and it cannot be printed. AutoCAD still takes it into consideration in screen regeneration and other functions, however.
   C. Thaw/Freeze in All Viewports: When a layer is frozen it is not visible on the screen and it cannot be printed. When a layer is frozen AutoCAD ignores it in screen regeneration and other functions. This can save

you time in drawing. For theatrical drawing purposes it is usually best to use Thaw/Freeze rather than On/Off. This button thaws or freezes the layer in all of the viewports of a multiple viewport screen.

D. Thaw/Freeze in Current Viewport: This button thaws or freezes the layer in only the currently active viewport of a multiple viewport screen.

E. Thaw/Freeze in New Viewports: This button thaws or freezes the layer in any new viewports that you might create.

F. Lock/Unlock: When a layer is locked it is still visible on the screen, but it cannot be changed.

6. To exit the Layer Properties box:

A. To exit the Layer Properties box and *keep the changes you have made,* click on the OK button.

B. To exit the Layer Properties box *without making any changes,* click on the Cancel button.

7. To change the layer in which you are working from the drawing screen: On the Object Properties toolbar the left window displays the name of the currently active layer. To change layers click on the down arrow to the right of the window.

A. This opens a box with the names of the currently available layers. The currently active layer is highlighted.

B. To switch to another layer, click once on the name of the layer you want to make active.

C. You can only draw in one layer at a time, so when working it is usually best to get as much as possible done in one layer before switching to another one.

8. To change the layer of an entity: If you should discover that you have drawn an entity in the wrong layer or just decide that you want to rearrange the layers of various entities in a drawing, you can do so by using the change properties command (ai_propchk). Type ai_propchk and hit Enter or click on the Modify pull down menu, and then on Properties.

A. Prompt reads: Select objects:.

B. Click on the entity or entities of which you want to change the layer.

C. Prompt reads: Select objects:.

D. Click the right mouse button or hit Enter.

E. Modify box opens.
   1. Click on Layer.
   2. Select Layer box opens.
   3. Click on the name of the layer that you want the entity to be in.

4. Click on OK.
5. Change Properties box opens.
6. Click on OK.

Exercise No. 9: Using Text, Linetype, and Layer Commands

1. Open the file Proto.dwg from either the CD-ROM or the one that you copied earlier to a floppy disk.
2. Save this file as Exer9.dwg on a floppy disk.
3. Work in drawing a:\Exer9.dwg.
   A. Draw a line in Center linetype and label it as a center line. Make the layer that you are using for Center linetype blue in color. Be sure that you set ltscale properly for a scale of 1/2 inch = 1 foot.
   B. Draw a rectangle in Hidden2 linetype. Make the layer that you are using for Hidden2 linetype red in color.
   C. Erase the word Prototype.
   D. Use the Standard text style to label the drawing Exercise 9 in letters 1 foot high.
   E. Use the Script Simplex text style to put your name in the lower right-hand corner in letters 10 inches high.
   F. Use the Standard text style to enter the word ROTATED rotated to a 30-degree angle.
   G. Use the Standard text style and the align option under justify or Justification to enter the word DOWNHILL aligned so that the end of the word is lower than the beginning.
   H. Use the Standard text style and the fit option under justify or Justification to enter the word SQUEEZED so that the height of the letters are 1 foot high and the word fits into a space 18 inches in length.
   I. Use the Standard text style and the center option under justify or Justification to enter the word centered so that it is aligned with a + mark that you have drawn.
   J. Use the Standard text style and the right option under justify or Justification to enter the word RIGHT so that it is aligned with a + mark that you have drawn.
   K. Copy the text RIGHT that you have just drawn and move it to the other side of the + mark that it is aligned with. Then, using the command ddedit, change it to the word LEFT.

   L. Create a layer called Text. Make its color dark gray and linetype Continuous. Change all of the text in the drawing to the new layer Text.

  M. Save Exer9.dwg to a floppy disk. Print out a copy of Exer9.dwg. Print out a copy of Projct9.dwg from the CD-ROM. Compare the two carefully.

Exercise No. 10: Working with Edit, Construct, and Modify Commands

1. Print out the file Projct10.dwg from the CD-ROM in 1/2 inch = 1 foot scale.

2. Save the file Proto.dwg as Exer10.dwg on a 3.5-inch disk.

3. Do your best to duplicate this drawing by working in AutoCAD in the file Exer10.dwg.

Note: This project was designed not so much to test your drawing skills as your ability to understand and work with the edit, construct, and modify commands. If you really understand how to use such commands as offset, copy, move, mirror, rotate, and the use of object snaps, this drawing becomes much simpler.

The simple flat can be done with double line or by using single line and offset. The corner blocks and keystones are a good exercise in copy and rotate. All of those strange dimensions in the chevron are derived from offsetting by an even figure. Think carefully about the geometry of the chevron drawing and you should be able to figure out the quickest and easiest way to do it.

Hint: Start with the curved line of the chevron closest to the center line. Don't think of it as an arc yet, though. Think of it as a straight line from its top point to its bottom point. Draw that line. Offset that line. The midpoint of the offset line then becomes the middle point of the arc.

Remember too that you only have to draw half of a symmetrical figure—the other half can be mirrored. The basic parquet for the table is a simple exercise in offset and then becomes a more complex exercise in the use of copy and object snaps. Don't forget the multiple option in copy.

To efficiently use AutoCAD it is just as important to understand basic geometry as it is to remember all the commands.

DRAWING AN INSTRUMENT AND WORKING WITH BLOCKS

In the last exercise you drew a simple flat and some more complex items as well. To practice using the block command, you will draw a lighting symbol for a light plot. In the next exercises you will learn how to form that drawing into a block and how to insert that block into a drawing, thus forming the beginning of a light plot. The block technique used in AutoCAD can also be useful to the scenic designer. Anytime that you have a drawing element that gets repeated, a block can be a good way to do it. If you turn something into a block the first time that you draw it, then anytime that you need it again it can be inserted into the drawing and does not have to be redrawn.

Exercise No. 11: Drawing an Instrument

1. First print out the file Projct11.dwg from the CD-ROM. When you print this drawing, unlike the last prints that you have made, make the scale 3 inches = 1 foot. This is a drawing of a Leko symbol that is used on lighting plots. I have given it to you in 3 inches = 1 foot scale so that you can make more accurate measurements by using the larger scale. Using a scale ruler to measure the drawing, you will be able to take accurate measurements for the drawing that you are about to make. Remember that you are going to be drawing full size in AutoCAD.

   Next start with a drawing space that has a format suitable for drawing a lighting instrument. The drawing Proto.dwg found on the CD-ROM fits these qualifications. Save Proto.dwg as Exer11.dwg on a floppy disk. Erase everything already in the drawing such as the border, title, etc. You need an absolutely clean space to begin your drawing of the instrument, which will later become a block.

2. Draw a vertical line approximately 3 feet long in the center of your limits; this will be the center line of your instrument.

3. Draw a horizontal line approximately 2 feet long centered on the vertical line and near the top of it. This will be the front of your instrument.

4. Working from these two lines, use primarily your edit commands to draw the instrument pictured in the printout of Project11.dwg. You can draw 90 percent of your instrument just using offset and trim. Mirror will also be a useful command to keep in mind. You will need to use a few draw commands such as arc and possibly circle, but try to keep the use of line to an absolute minimum.

5. Pay close attention to all measurements and proportions on the printout from Projct11.dwg. Be sure that all lines that appear to meet do actually meet.

6. When the instrument itself is complete, add the circuit/dimmer circle, channel hex, and connecting lines.

7. Do not erase the center line in the drawing. You will be using it to create the insertion point of your block.

8. Save this drawing as Exer11.dwg on the floppy disk.

Working with Blocks

The wblock (wblock) or write block to disk command is the AutoCAD tool that really makes doing a lighting plot a realistic endeavor. Without this tool, every time you wanted a symbol for a lighting instrument you would have to draw it. Wblock saves a drawing that you have made to a permanent file in the AutoCAD directory of your hard drive so that you can call it up later via the insert command and use that drawing again and again. By wblocking an instrument library to a permanent file on hard or floppy disk you can reuse the same instrument drawings again and again when drawing different light plots. Wblock is very similar to the block (block) command. They both turn all or part of a drawing into a file that can be called up later with the insert (insert) command, but wblock saves the file to a permanent disk or floppy disk, while block only saves it in the drawing file in which you are currently working.

In order to insert the information that is around the instrument along with the instrument, you must use the attribute definition (attdef) command. Attdef allows you to create what AutoCAD calls attributes. These attributes are categories of values associated with the block. When you insert the block you will be prompted to enter values into the categories. For example, if you create an attribute called Color when creating a block, then when you insert that block you will be prompted for a value to enter for Color. The value that you entered when you inserted it—say R37 for Roscolux 37—will appear on the drawing in the location that you put the attribute Color. Other commands are used to insert the block in the drawing or minsert (minsert) multiple copies of the same block. In this lesson I am going to take you step by step through the process of creating a block and using it in a drawing. Then I will cover other commands that are useful in working with blocks.

Exercise No. 12: Creating a Block

1. The first step in building your instrument block inventory is to make a drawing of the instruments that you want to save as part of a permanent file. You should already have one of these in your file Exer11.dwg. Open the file Exer11.dwg and save it as file Block.dwg.

2. Now we want to add the attributes we would like to associate with the block we are going to create. Attributes can contain any kind of information you would like and be given any name you choose, but the ones that you will be creating here are the standard USITT Graphics Recommended Practice instrument information in the locations specified. Print out the file Projct12.dwg in 1 1/2 inches = 1 foot scale from the CD-ROM for the information that you will need on the location and size of the attributes to be added. Next open the file Block.dwg. Let's start at the front of the

instrument and work our way to the back. The first attribute we will create is focus. I will talk you through each step on creating the first attribute, then it will be up to you to add Color, Inst. Type, Location, Inst. No., Wattage, Circuit, Dimmer, and Channel on your own.

3. In R12:

A. The command for creating an attribute is attdef. This can be typed on the keyboard and followed by Enter to activate it. You can also use the pull down menu Draw/Text/Attributes/Define.

B. Prompt reads: Attribute modes Invisible:N Constant:N Verify:N Preset: N Enter (ICVP) to change, RETURN when done:. Each of these is an attribute mode that you can toggle between yes and no at this prompt by typing the first letter of the mode you want to change and hitting Enter. If the mode is already toggled to the choice you want, do not type the letter. Here are your options:

1. Invisible: When on, this tells AutoCAD not to display or print anything with this attribute.

2. Constant: This tells AutoCAD that the value of this attribute will never change.

3. Verify: This mode tells AutoCAD to issue an extra prompt to verify a proper value.

4. Preset: This option tells AutoCAD not to prompt for this attribute during block insertion.

5. For lighting instruments, the Verify and Preset modes should always be N. Occasionally you will have a Constant or Invisible attribute, but not in the case of Focus. For the attribute Focus we want all of these modes set in N. Therefore, do not enter any letters at this prompt, just hit Enter.

C. Prompt reads: Attribute Tag:. This identifies the information in the attribute. It is important to use the same attribute tag for the same information on all instruments when creating blocks so that this information can later be accessed by a uniform label. In this case let's use the tag Focus. Type Focus and hit Enter.

D. Prompt reads: Attribute Prompt:. This is the prompt that AutoCAD will use when you insert the block to ask you for this information. Type Focus again and hit Enter.

E. Prompt reads: Default Attribute Value:. If there is a constant value or default value for this attribute you would enter it here. If you enter a Default Attribute Value that value will initially appear when the Block is inserted into a drawing. You can still change that value later, however. If you do not want to assign a constant or default value then just hit Enter.

F. Prompt reads: Justify/Style<start point>: This is your standard dtext opening prompt. This allows you to determine where the value of the attribute will be displayed next to the instrument. All of the dtext commands can be utilized here in positioning the attribute value text. Remember, you are *not* entering an attribute value in response to this prompt; you are setting up how the text of the attribute value will be displayed when you do enter a value during Insertion. I recommend that you use one of the justify commands, usually bc (bottom center) to center the actual value that will appear in this location when you insert the instrument.

   1. Type j and hit Enter.
   2. Type bc and hit Enter.
   3. Click on the location of the bottom center of the attribute value.
   4. Prompt reads: Height < >:. For most lighting instrument attributes, 2 inches is a good text height to use. Type 2" and hit Enter.
   5. Prompt reads: Rotation angle <0>:. If you want the text to be rotated, enter a figure in degrees counterclockwise and hit Enter. If you want the default value given, just hit Enter.

G. You have just created your first attribute to accompany this instrument when you wblock it. At this point take a look at the position of the attribute relative to the instrument. If you want to reposition the attribute use the move command to get it located precisely where you want it.

H. Continue with the creation and positioning of all other attributes in the same manner. Use the printout from the file Projct12.dwg to determine position and attribute tag and prompt. None of these attributes will have a default value. Wattage, Location, and Inst.Type should all be set in Invisible mode.

4. In R13 and R14:

A. The command for creating an attribute is attdef. This can be typed on the keyboard and followed by Enter to activate it. In R13 it can also be activated from the Attribute toolbar by clicking on the Define Attribute icon. In R14 it can also be activated by clicking on the pull down menu Draw/Block/Define Attributes. This opens the Attribute Definition dialogue box.

B. When the Attribute Definition dialogue box opens you will be able to work in the following areas in the box:

   1. Mode: This area allows you to define the modes of the attribute. These can be toggled on by clicking in the box next to the name of the mode. When the mode is toggled on an X will appear in the box. The functions of the modes are as follows:

a. Invisible: This tells AutoCAD not to display or print this attribute.
b. Constant: This mode tells AutoCAD that the value of this attribute will never change.
c. Verify: This tells AutoCAD to issue an extra prompt to verify a proper value.
d. Preset: Use this to tell AutoCAD not to prompt for this attribute during block insertion.

For lighting instruments the Verify and Preset modes should always be toggled off. Occasionally you will have a Constant or Invisible attribute, but not in the case of Focus. For the attribute Focus, you want all of these modes set to off, meaning there is no X in the box.

2. Attribute: This area lets you set the tag, prompt, and a preset value for the attribute.
   a. Tag: This is the name of the attribute. Enter Focus in the window.
   b. Prompt: This is the prompt that AutoCAD will use to ask you for the information on this attribute when you insert the block. Type Focus? in the window.
   c. Value: If you wanted to have a starting value for a default value for the attribute you could enter it here. Do not enter anything in this window for the Focus attribute.

3. Text Options: This area controls how the text of the attribute will appear in the drawing.
   a. Justification: The justification is like a text command justification. It controls how the value of the attribute will be displayed next to the instrument. Remember that you are *not* entering a value for an attribute here, you are determining how the text will be justified when it does appear. For Focus, select bottom center by clicking on the arrow next to the Justification window and then on Bottom Center.
   b. Text Style: This lets you select the text style that you would like the attribute to appear in on the screen. For Focus, select Standard.
   c. Height: Type in a height figure for the display of the attribute in this window. For most lighting instrument attributes, 2 inches is a good text height to use. Enter 2" in the window.
   d. Rotation: You can enter a figure in degrees counterclockwise in this window to make the value of the attribute in the drawing appear rotated. Enter a figure of 0 for the Focus attribute.

4. Align below previous attribute: If you check this box, the attribute on which you are currently working will have the same text options as the previous attribute and will be aligned directly below it. Do not check this box for Focus.

5. Insertion Point: This area lets you select where the attribute will be inserted into the drawing. You can enter X, Y, and Z coordinates, but for most of your work you will probably prefer the Pick Point option.

   a. Click on the Pick Point button. You are returned to the drawing with the command prompt: Start point:.

   b. Click at the point in the drawing where you would like the bottom center of the Focus attribute to appear relative to the lighting instrument. You will then be returned to the Attribute Definition box.

   c. Click on OK.

C. You have just created your first attribute to accompany this instrument when you wblock it. At this point take a look at the position of the attribute relative to the instrument. If you want to reposition the attribute use the move command to get it located precisely where you want it.

D. Continue with the creation and positioning of all other attributes in the same manner. Use the printout from the file Projct12.dwg to determine position and attribute tag and prompt. None of these attributes will have a default value. Wattage, Location, and Inst.Type should all be set in Invisible mode.

5. Now that all the attributes are added you are almost ready to create the block. There is one more thing to be concerned about before you can do this: the insertion point of the block. As part of creating a block you are asked to define an Insertion Point. This is a point on or near the block that will become the point where the block itself is inserted into the drawing. You will need to define this precisely. The insertion point that you pick for the block and the insertion point that you pick on the drawing will determine how the block fits with the rest of the drawing. Usually, to make inserting the block more uniform you want the insertion point of the block to be at the center of the instrument. Most instrument symbols do not have a line or other entity at their center that will help you establish this point, so you need to add one and then remove it as part of the creation of the block. This creates a precise insertion point at an otherwise difficult-to-define point in space.

   If you have not used a center line in drawing the block then draw a line from the center of the line at the back of the instrument to the center of the line at the front of the instrument.

6. Now we are ready to create a block in a permanent file by using the wblock command. You will be using wblock rather than block for the lighting instrument so that you can control the location of the file to which the

block is saved. Remember, the **wblock** command lets you save the block to a file anywhere that you would like so that it can be used in a later drawing. The **block** command only saves the block for later use in the current drawing.

A. Activate the **wblock** command by typing **wblock** and hitting **Enter**.

B. Prompt reads: **Wblock**, and the **Create Drawing File** box opens.

1. This is where you would tell AutoCAD to save your block for later use. If you are creating an instrument block for use with later lighting plots you would want to save this file to your main AutoCAD directory or folder. For now, though, save this file to the floppy disk from which you are working.

2. In the **Create Drawing File** box, enter the file name in the box under **File Name:**. Name this file **6x9leko.dwg**.

a. Click on the down arrow in the rectangle under **Drives** or next to **Save In:**.

b. Click on the **a:** (floppy) drive icon.

c. Click on **OK** or **Save**.

C. Prompt reads: **Block name:**. Hit **Enter**.

D. Prompt reads: **Insertion base point:**. Click on **Midpoint** and then on the line through the center of the instrument.

E. Prompt reads: **Select objects:**. Click on a point outside of the drawing and attributes and drag the mouse to create a window that includes the entire drawing and all of its attributes. Click again.

F. Prompt reads: **Select objects:**. Type r for **Remove** and hit **Enter**.

G. Prompt reads: **Remove objects:**. Click on the center line created earlier to remove it from the block you are creating.

H. Prompt reads: **Remove objects:**. Hit **Enter** or click on right mouse button. All of the instrument and attributes should disappear except for the center line that you removed from the block. You have just created the block **6x9leko.dwg** and saved it to your 3.5-inch disk. If you had specified the c: drive—your hard drive—and the main AutoCAD directory in step 6B above, it would be a part of your permanent AutoCAD directory and could be used in any drawing.

I. Exit AutoCAD. When you exit AutoCAD it will ask you whether you want to save the changes to the drawing or discard them. Click on **Discard Changes**. This will also save your drawing **Exer11.dwg** as you drew it in Exercise No. 11.

Exercise No. 13: Inserting a Block

Reenter AutoCAD and open Proto.dwg from the 3.5-inch disk you saved it to earlier. This must be the same disk that you saved the block 6x9leko.dwg to earlier. Save this drawing to your 3.5-inch disk as Exer13.dwg. Erase anything in the drawing and set it up for a block insertion by drawing a line from left to right that will act as an electric pipe.

1. You must use the insert command to insert a block from a file into a drawing.
2. Activate the insert command.
    A. Prompt reads: Insert Block name (or ?) < >:. Type the name and path of the block you want to insert—a:\6x9leko—and hit Enter.

Note: If this block were in your main AutoCAD directory on the hard drive all you would have to type is just the name of the block—6x9leko.

    B. Prompt reads: Insertion point:. Click on the point in the drawing where you want to insert the block. You must use an object snap such as nearest to be sure that the block is inserted on the electric pipe line or you will have trouble breaking the line later on.
    C. Prompt reads: X scale factor <1>/Corner/XYZ:. Here you could insert a scale factor to increase or decrease the size of the block. Just hit Enter.
    D. Prompt reads: Y scale factor (default = X):. Hit Enter.
    E. Prompt reads: Rotation Angle <0>:. If you want to rotate the block on insertion, type a figure in degrees counterclockwise and hit Enter. Otherwise just hit Enter.
    F. Prompt reads: Enter attribute values:.
        Now you will enter the values for all of the attributes you created earlier. Type in the appropriate value at the appropriate prompt and

THE INSERT COMMAND

AutoCAD Command	Function		
Insert	**Inserts a block into a drawing.**		

Keyboard Command	Pull Down Menu Path	Icon (R12)	Icon (R13 & R14)
INSERT	**R12: Draw/Insert** **R14: Insert/Block**		Draw

hit **Enter**. After the last value is entered, the instrument will appear with attributes.

Use these values for this drawing:

Focus: A
Color: R54
Inst.Type: 6X9LEKO
Location: 1ELECT
Inst.No.: 1
Wattage: 750
Circuit: do not enter a value
Dimmer: 5
Channel: 5

G. **Break** the electric pipe line inside the instrument.
   1. Activate the **break** command.
   2. Prompt reads: **Select object:**. Click on **Intersection** on the toolbox and then click on one of the intersections between the instrument and the electric pipe.
   3. Prompt reads: **Enter second point (or F for first point):**. Click on **Intersection** on the toolbox and then on the second intersection between the instrument and the electric pipe.

H. Save the work to your floppy disk as **Exer13.dwg**. Compare this to **Projct13.dwg** on the CD-ROM.

I. Note that when you have finished a complete library of all instrument symbols with blocks you should save all of these blocks in your main AutoCAD directory. When you are working to create a light plot you should be working in your main AutoCAD directory or one of its subdirectories. Then when you are ready to insert a block all you will need to type is the name of the block, e.g., **6x9leko**, after the **insert** command. You will not need to type the path.

J. If you are going to be creating a lot of blocks I would recommend that you establish a **Wblock** button on the toolbar. This will make the job easier. If you are a lighting designer working in R12 and will be inserting a lot of blocks then I would also recommend that you establish an **Insert** button on the toolbar.

K. See the instrument library section of this book (see page 230) for information on the complete lighting instrument library that is available for your use on the CD-ROM that accompanies this book.

Using Other Commands That Are Helpful with Blocks

Explode (**explode**)

Explode is a command that is useful with blocks, but also with any drawing entity composed of segments. Explode breaks up an entity into its component parts. When you explode a block, for example, all of its attributes become visible by their attribute tags. Anytime something is inserted, it is inserted as a single entity. To erase or change part of it you must first Explode it. Also when you draw with the polygon or rectangle commands you're creating single entities. To erase or change a side you must explode the entire polygon or rectangle.

You will also find explode useful when creating a legend or key for your lighting plot. For example, when creating a key, you can use the block for an instrument. Don't enter any values in the attribute prompts. Explode the block. Erase the attribute names, and you will be left with your basic symbol for the key, to which you can add text.

Multiple Insert (**minsert**)

Multiple Insert (minsert) lets you insert the same block in a succession of places. It is not usually a very useful command for a lighting designer because in the case of instrument blocks it would insert not just the same block, but the same attribute values including the instrument number in all locations. However, you could then use the **ddatte** command to edit the values of the attributes in those blocks.

For the set designer or technical director, the minsert command could be extremely useful for any item that is repeated. Turning the item into a block and then using minsert could save a lot of time. In all three AutoCAD releases, you can access this command via the keyboard. In R13 there is also an icon on the Miscellaneous toolbar.

Purge (**purge**)

Purge rids your drawing of all blocks, layers, linetypes, shapes, and styles that you aren't using. This saves memory space. If you have changed a block but

THE EXPLODE COMMAND

AutoCAD Command	Function	Separates block or polyline
Explode		into component entities.

Keyboard Command	Pull Down Menu Path	Icon (R12)	Icon (R13 & R14)
EXPLODE	R12: Modify/Explode R14: Modify/Explode		
			Modify

kept the same name for it, you will not be able to insert the new block until you have purged the old one.

R12

Purge will only work if it is the *first* command given upon opening a drawing.

1. Type purge and hit Enter immediately upon opening the drawing.
2. Prompt reads: Purge unused Blocks/Dimstyles/LAyers/LTypes/SHapes/ STyles/All:. Type the capital letters of the items you want to consider for purging and hit Enter.
3. AutoCAD will list the items and ask you if you want to purge them. For example, Prompt reads: Purge Block TESTLEKO ? <N>:.
4. The default is always <N> for no. If you *do not* want to purge the item just hit Enter. If you *do* want to purge the item type y for yes and then hit Enter.

R13 and R14

Purge can be used at any time when the program is open. R13 access is via the keyboard or pull down menu Data/Purge. R14 access is via the keyboard or pull down menu File/Drawing Utilities/Purge. Then you will be able to select the following options to be purged:

- Layers
- Linetypes
- Multiline Styles
- Dimension Styles
- Shapes
- Blocks
- All

TEXT EDIT (ddedit)

See the section on text, page 122, for an introduction to text commands. The ddedit command can be used to edit the values of attributes in blocks. If you only

THE EDIT TEXT COMMAND

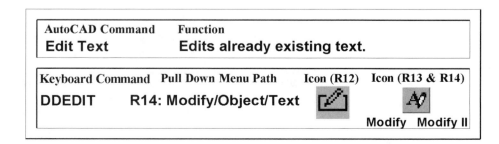

AutoCAD Command	Function		
Edit Text	**Edits already existing text.**		

Keyboard Command	Pull Down Menu Path	Icon (R12)	Icon (R13 & R14)
DDEDIT	**R14: Modify/Object/Text**		
			Modify Modify II

THE EDIT ATTRIBUTE COMMAND

AutoCAD Command	Function
Edit Attributes	**Edits values of all attributes in a block.**

Keyboard Command	Pull Down Menu Path	Icon (R13 & R14)
DDATTE	**R12: Draw/Text/Attributes/Edit** **R14: Modify/Object/Attribute**	**Attribute Modify II**

want to change the content of *one* attribute, this is a good command to use. If, however, you have several attributes in a single block that you want to change the content of, you can do so more rapidly using the **ddatte** command.

1. Activate the **ddedit** command.
2. Prompt reads: Select Text:.
3. Click on the text line you want to edit.
4. Edit Text box opens with a blinking cursor. Use the keyboard and mouse to edit the line of text that you want to change.
5. Click on OK to record the changes.

EDIT ATTRIBUTE (**ddatte**)

This command allows you to edit all of the attribute values in a block at one time. If you want to change the values entered for several attributes in a block such as Color, Focus, Location, etc. at once, this is the command to use.

1. Activate the **ddatte** command.
2. Prompt reads: Select Block:.
3. Click on the block you want to edit.
4. Edit Attributes box opens with a blinking cursor. Use the keyboard and mouse to edit all of the attribute values that you want to change.
5. Click on OK to record the changes.

PLOTTING

In many of the exercises so far in this book you have been using the Print/Plot command along with your regular printer. Most standard printers, however, are limited in the paper size that they can handle to 8.5 inches × 11 inches or 8.5 inches × 17 inches. If you want to print out a 1/2 inch scale theatrical drawing you will need a larger piece of paper than that. That is what a plotter is designed to do—produce a printout on a large piece of paper or vellum. Using plotters with AutoCAD is somewhat more complicated than printing. Every plotter has its own requirements and its own software driver. There would not be enough room in this book to give you complete information on every plotter manufactured so I will have to assume that your plotter has been properly installed and configured to AutoCAD. Specifics on your particular plotter will have to come from the business where it was purchased and the manufacturer. However, I will try to explain to you the basic information that AutoCAD is going to need to set up a plot with a properly installed and configured plotter.

If you do not own a plotter, it doesn't mean that you can't get full-size plots from your AutoCAD drawings. Most commercial blueline/blueprint operations now run plots from AutoCAD for their customers. They will usually have a large, high-speed commercial plotter with a number of options that are not available on smaller plotters that you might purchase for yourself. Before you bring a disk for plotting to a business, you must find out how your machine must be configured for your .plt disks to work on its machine. If the employees tell you, for example, to set up your plots for a HP7585—a common commercial configuration—then you will have to go into your configuration menu and add HP7585 to the list of plotters and printers that are a part of your configuration. Refer to the section in this book on configuring (see page 15) for instructions on how to do this. Also check with you local plotting business about any features that its machine might have that could be useful. Many commercial machines, for example, may be able to apply a "pattern" to a pen. This is a sort of greyscale that can give you the line width that you want, but

THE PLOT CONFIGURATION BOX

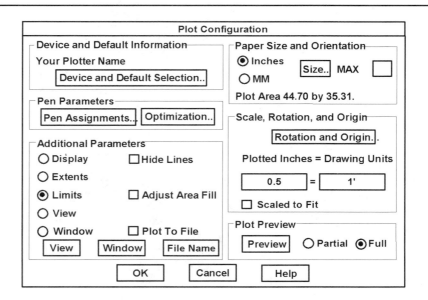

Paper Size					
Size	**Width**	**Height**	**Size**	**Width**	**Height**
A	10.50	8.00			
B	16.00	10.00	USER:		
C	21.00	16.00			
D	33.00	21.00	USER1:		
E	43.00	33.00			
MAX	44.70	35.31	USER2:		
			USER3:		
			USER4:		

Orientation is landscape ☐

[OK]   [Cancel]

with a shading to it so that it is not as dark. Most of them can also run colors for you as well. The employees will usually be happy to talk to you about the details of the features that are available on their machine and what you need to do to prepare a disk for their use.

WORKING WITH YOUR OWN PLOTTER

Once your plotter has been installed and configured properly, you can begin by opening the Print/Plot box just as you would for printing with a printer. You must go through each of the sections of the Plot Configuration box carefully to be certain that all of the settings in that area are correct.

1. Plot Configuration box elements:
   A. Device and Default Selection section: Select the name that you gave your plotter when it was configured by clicking on the Device and Default Selection bar and then clicking on your plotter's name.
   B. Paper Size and Orientation section:
      1. Place a dot in the Inches circle. Then click on the Size bar. This will open the Paper Size box.
      2. In the Paper Size box, select the size paper that you want in the box on the left labeled Size Height Width by clicking on it. The names given to the paper sizes will vary with each plotter, but it should look something like what you see in the figure labeled The Paper Size Box, with selections like A, B, MAX, etc. You should select a paper size that is just slightly larger than the plot that you are going to be running.
      3. Click on OK to exit the Paper Size box.

```
┌─────────────────────────────────────────────┐
│          Plot Rotation and Origin            │
│ ┌─Plot Rotation───────────────────────────┐  │
│ │  ⊙ 0      ○ 90      ○ 180      ○ 270     │  │
│ └─────────────────────────────────────────┘  │
│ ┌─Plot Origin─────────────────────────────┐  │
│ │  X Origin│ 0.00 │    Y Origin│ 0.00 │    │  │
│ └─────────────────────────────────────────┘  │
│        ┌─────────┐      ┌──────────┐          │
│        │   OK    │      │  Cancel  │          │
│        └─────────┘      └──────────┘          │
└─────────────────────────────────────────────┘
```

    4. When you return to the Plot Configuration box, the size paper and plot area that you selected should be reflected in the Paper Size and Orientation section.

C. Scale, Rotation, and Origin section:

    1. Click on the Rotation and Origin bar. The Plot Rotation and Origin box will open.

    2. The usual selection here is a Plot Rotation of 0 and X and Y Origins of 0.00. If when you do a Full Preview, the rotation is incorrect, come back here to correct it. If you have moved the origin point of your drawing from the lower left-hand corner elsewhere in the drawing, you will need to find the location of that origin point and make corrections here as well. Click on OK to exit this box and return to the Plot Configuration box.

    3. Plotted Inches = Drawing Units. For most theatrical plots it would be:

       a. 0.5 = 1' or

       b. 0.25 = 1' as desired.

       Click in the appropriate box and use the Backspace and the keyboard to enter the proper values.

    4. Do not place an X in the Scaled to Fit box. You can click in the box to toggle the X on and off. If the Scaled to Fit box is checked, AutoCAD will automatically fit your drawing into the size of paper that you have selected, thus printing out at whatever scale is necessary for this to occur.

D. Additional Parameters section: You will usually have a dot in Limits only. There are other options available in this section that you may want to explore. Different options will be available with different plotters, however. With some plotters Extents will not be available, for example.

    1. Display: This lets you print out only what is displayed on the screen.

    2. Extents: Remember the difference between extents and limits? Extents only covers the area where there is actual drawing. Limits could be smaller or larger than this.

3. Limits: This prints out to the limits that you have set for your drawing.
4. View: With this you can select a view that you have named using the view command. This is only available when there are named views in the current drawing. First select View, then click on the View button at the bottom of the box to select the one desired.
5. Window: This lets you select a window to be plotted by defining a rectangular area using X and Y coordinates. First select Window, then click on the Window button at the bottom of the screen to define the X and Y coordinates.
6. Hide Lines: Later in this book you will learn about the hide command, which is used to eliminate what would be hidden lines in a perspective view. This option does the same thing when plotting and printing.
7. Adjust Area Fill: If you have filled solids or wide polylines in your drawing, this option will automatically adjust pen width for them.
8. Plot To File: You can use this to create a .plt file when you are going to use a plotter that isn't connected to your computer such as one at a commercial plotting business. This will be covered in more detail later.
9. File Name Button: Use this in combination with Plot To File to create a .plt file on a disk.

E. Pen Parameters box: Plotters control line width by using different pen widths. By clicking on the Pen Assignments button, you can instruct your plotter to use certain pens for certain layers of your drawing. It is usually a good idea to write these assignments down before leaving the Pen Assignments box. Depending upon your

THE PEN ASSIGNMENTS BOX

Color	Pen No.	Linetype	Speed	Pen Width	Modify Values
1	1	0	36	0.010	Color:
2	2	0	36	0.010	
3	3	0	36	0.010	Pen:
4	4	0	36	0.010	
5	5	0	36	0.010	Ltype:
6	6	0	36	0.010	
7	7	0	36	0.010	Speed:
8	8	0	36	0.010	
9	9	0	36	0.010	Width:
10	10	0	36	0.010	

Feature Legend

Pen Width:

OK Cancel

plotter you may have to physically change pens at prompts from AutoCAD during the plotting process or you may have to program the plotter's pen assignments as part of the setup procedure for each plot. Read the instruction manual that comes with your plotter carefully to see how this is done.

1. The first thing to understand about the **Pen Assignments** box is that **Color** in this box refers to the color of a layer in an AutoCAD drawing. If more than one layer has been given the same color in the **Layer Control** box, all of those layers will have to be assigned to the same **Pen No.** If you want layers to be assigned to different numbers they will have to be given different colors in the Layer Control box. Pen numbers control the width of the line being drawn by the plotter, so if you want different line widths—"line weights" as we refer to them in theatre—then you must assign different colors to the layers with different line widths in the Layer Control box.

2. To make changes in the **Pen Assignments** box:

    a. Click in the box on the left side on the line with a **Color**, **Pen No.**, etc. that you want to change.

    b. The **Color**, **Pen**, **Ltype**, etc. will appear in the **Modify Values** box on the right.

    c. Click in the box to the right of the value that you want to change. Then use the **Backspace** and the keyboard to change the value to what you desire.

    d. The idea here is to assign the same **Pen No.** to all of the **Colors** (layers) that you want to have the same pen width. Write down which layers are assigned to which pen numbers. You will need this information later for giving pen widths to pen numbers on the plotter.

    e. When you have changed the values that you want to change for one color, click on that line again in the box to the left to deselect that color. Then click on the next color for which you want to change values.

    f. When you have made all the changes that you want in the Pen Assignments box, click on **OK** to exit back to the **Plot Configuration** box.

3. Depending upon the plotter that you are using, there are a number of other things that can be done in the **Pen Assignments** box.

    a. You can also change the linetype that has been assigned to a layer here by altering the value of **Ltype** in the **Modify Values** section. This is not a procedure that I would recommend, however, as you can get thoroughly confused about which linetype is assigned to which layer. This does not modify the linetype in the actual layer itself, just in the plotter.

  b. For some plotters you can assign the specific line Width that you want the plotter to use here in the Pen Assignments box by changing that value in the Modify Values box. For others that assignment is made as a part of setting up the plotter for each particular plot. For older plotters it is done by physically changing pens in the plotter at prompts from AutoCAD. No matter which method your plotter uses you will need to know which layers, by color, are assigned to which pen numbers, so be sure to write that information down.

F. Plot Preview section:

  The last step in preparing the Plot Configuration box for plotting is previewing your drawing.

  1. Click on the Full circle in the Plot Preview section.
  2. Click on the Preview button.
  3. The drawing will appear on the screen inside a rectangle. This rectangle represents the size of the plot area that you have selected. Take a close look at your drawing inside this rectangle. If something is wrong try to figure out what you have done incorrectly in the Plot Configuration box and go back to that section and make a correction. The most common errors usually occur in the Scale, Rotation and Origin section and the Paper Size and Orientation section. Correct any errors and preview again.
  4. You can use the Pan and Zoom button in preview to move around in the drawing and to zoom down to a closer view.
  5. Exit the preview by clicking on the End Preview button or Esc on the keyboard.

G. Remember that if you exit the Plot Configuration box by clicking on the Cancel button, all of the changes that you have made will be lost. When you actually run a plot, all of those changes are saved for the next plotting session.

2. Running the plotter:

  A. Have AutoCAD running with the drawing you want to plot on the screen.
  B. Have your plotter turned on with the proper size paper loaded according to the manufacturer's instructions.
  C. Activate the plot command in AutoCAD.
  D. Establish all of the settings in the Plot Configuration box for your drawing following the instructions given above.

E. When completely ready to plot, click on the OK in the Plot Configuration box. If you need to escape before plotting, click on the Cancel button in the Plot Configuration box.

F. Prompt reads: Press Return to continue or s to Stop for hardware setup:.

    1. This is when you may need to know which pen numbers are assigned to which pen widths. Remember that you were supposed to write that down.

    2. If you need to do any further preparation to your plotter such as give it line width assignments for pen numbers, this is the time to do that.

    3. For older plotters that use actual pens, this is also a good time to check that you have all of the pens ready.

G. When your plotter is completely prepared, hit Enter on the keyboard.

H. For older plotters with actual pens the Message box opens prompting you to install a pen #.

    1. Install the appropriate pen in the plotter and click on OK in the message box.

    2. At each subsequent message box that gives you a pen prompt, install the appropriate pen and click on OK.

WORKING WITH A COMMERCIAL PLOTTER COMPANY

If you do not own a plotter you can make use of the plotters that are available at many commercial blueline/blueprint companies. In order to use a plotter at a remote site such as a commercial blueprint company you have to use the Plot To File command to plot your drawing to a 3.5-inch disk. It is easier to do this if your drawing is in the hard drive (c: drive) so that you can plot to the 3.5-inch drive (a: drive). You will also need to find out what kind of plotter the company is using so that you can add a plotter configuration that is compatible with it. When you have a compatible plotter configuration added follow this procedure to create a .plt file on a 3.5-inch disk. You will then take that disk to the commercial plotter. Remember also that the company will need to know the line width-assignments for the pen numbers that you have made in the Pen Assignments box.

1. To plot to file your drawing:

A. Have the drawing that you want to plot up and running on AutoCAD from your hard drive (c:).

B. Insert a fresh, formatted 3.5-inch disk in the disk drive (a:).

C. Activate the plot command.

D. Set up all areas of the Plot Configuration box as above. Remember that in the Device and Default Selection box you will have to select the plotter that conforms to the one being used by the company doing the work for you.

E. When all other areas of Plot Configuration box have been checked, click on the box next to Plot To File in the Additional Parameters section. An X should appear there.

F. Click on the File Name button.

G. The Create Plot File box will open.

H. Be sure that you have selected the a: drive and that the name that you want to give to the .plt file appears in the File Name area.

 I. Click on OK to exit the Create Plot File box.

 J. Click on the File Name button *again* and double-check the Create Plot File box. I have encountered some versions of AutoCAD in which the first setup of this box doesn't always take. Click on OK to exit the Create Plot File box.

K. Click on OK in the Plot Configuration box to plot to file on the a: drive disk you previously inserted. If you are not ready to plot to file or need to change something, click on Cancel to escape Plot Configuration box. Remember that when you exit the Plot Configuration box by clicking on Cancel all changes that you have made to the box will be lost.

L. When plot to file is completed, remove the disk from the a: drive and take it to your plotter company for plotting. Most companies will need you to supply some pieces of information about your plot. Many commercial plotters will need to know the following information.

  1. For all Pen Nos.:
     a. Pen Width in mm.
     b. Pattern to be used: Check with your blueline company about availability.

THE CREATE PLOT FILE BOX

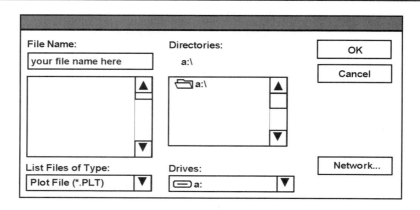

   c. **Pen Color** to be used: Check with your blueline company about availability.

   d. **Layer Color**: This identifies the layer color or colors to be assigned to a particular pen number.

2. Material to be plotted on: This will usually be **vellum**.
3. Name of file to be plotted: This is usually **your file name.plt**.
4. Information on where to get in touch with you if they have any questions.

Exercise No. 14: Plotting a Drawing

You will not be able to complete part A of this exercise unless you have a plotter. If you don't have a plotter, go to part B, which has instructions for configuring AutoCAD for creating a .plt file for a plotter to which you are not connected such as might be available at commercial blueline companies.

Part A: Setting up Your Own Plotter for Plotting a File

1. Open the file Projct14.dwg from the CD-ROM.
2. In the **Device and Default Selection** box select the name that you have given to your plotter. You will need to load a piece of vellum or other suitable material of at least 24 inches × 36 inches or as close to this that you can get for plotting the file.
3. In the **Paper Size and Orientation** box select the **Size** that is larger than, but closest to 24 inches × 36 inches.
4. In the **Scale, Rotation and Origin** box select a **Plot Rotation** of 0, an **Origin** of (X,Y) 0,0, and a **Scale** of 1/2" = 1'.
5. In the **Additional Parameters** box put a check by **Limits** and nothing else.
6. In the **Pen Parameters** box click on the **Pen Assignments** button and set up **Pens** by **Layer Colors** as follows.

   Color 1 (red): Pen 1, Pen Width: .35

   All Other Colors: Pen 2, Pen Width: .25

7. Activate the **Plot Preview** by clicking on **Full** and then on the **Preview** button. Check the preview very carefully to see that everthing is correct. If it doesn't look right, go back and check the parts of the **Plot Configuration** box that might affect it.
8. When you are ready to plot, click on the **OK** button.
9. You will also need to make whatever adjustments are necessary to set up your plotter to handle the pen assignments before continuing by hitting the **Enter** key at the prompt.

Part B: Configuring AutoCAD to Create a .plt File for an External Plotter

1. Review the information at the beginning of the book on configuring AutoCAD for your version (see page 15).

2. If you have information on how to set up for a commercial plotter near you, use that information now. If not, then this will talk you through setting up for a Hewlett Packard 7585, which is one of the most common commercial plotter configurations.

R12 and R13

A. Click on File/Configure. Prompt reads: Press Return to continue:. Hit Enter.

B. Type in number for Configure Plotter and hit Enter.

C. Type in number for Add a Plotter Configuration and hit Enter.

D. Under the Available Plotters menu that appears, find the driver for the commercial plotter near you or select the Hewlett-Packard (HP-GL) ADI 4.2. Type in that number and hit Enter.

E. Under the Supported Models menu that appears, find the model number for the commercial plotter near you or select the 7585. Type in that number and hit Enter.

F. Accept the defaults for Seconds to time out by hitting Enter.

G. Enter a period (.) to indicate None for port name.

H. Prompt will ask if you want to change anything. Hit Enter for <N>.

I. Prompt will ask you to enter a description for this plotter. Type in a name for your commercial plotter or 7585 and hit Enter.

J. Type in the number for Exit to Configuration Menu and hit Enter.

K. Type in the number for Exit to Drawing Editor and hit Enter.

L. Hit Enter again as a <Y> response to save configuration changes.

R14

A. Click on Tools/Preferences.

B. In the Preferences box, click on the Printer tab.

C. Click on the New button.

D. Click on the line with the driver for the commercial plotter near you or select the Hewlett- Packard (HP-GL) ADI 4.2. It will highlight the one you choose.

E. Click on OK. An AutoCAD text window will open with selections.

F. Type the number for the commercial plotter near you or the number for 7585. Hit Enter.

G. You will be asked to specify a port: **s** for serial or **N** for network. This is actually a configuration for a plotter that is not connected to your computer, but type in **s** for serial and hit **Enter**.

H. Accept the default of **<30>** for **Seconds to Time Out** by hitting **Enter**.

I. You are prompted to enter a name for the serial port or period (.) for none. Type . for none and hit **Enter**.

J. Prompt will ask if you want to change anything. Accept the **<N>** default by hitting **Enter**.

K. You will be returned to the **Printer** tab of the **Preferences** box. The commercial plotter or the 7585 will now appear in the list in the window under **Current Printer**.

L. Click on **OK** to close the Preferences box.

3. Open the file **Projct14.dwg** from the CD-ROM.

4. In the **Device and Default Selection** box select the name that you have given to the commercial plotter near you or 7585.

5. In the **Paper Size and Orientation** box select the size that is larger than, but closest to 24 inches × 36 inches. You will need to load a piece of vellum or other suitable material of at least 24 inches × 36 inches or as close to this that you can get for plotting the file.

6. In the **Scale, Rotation and Origin** box, select a **Plot Rotation** of 0, an Origin of (X,Y) **0,0**, and a **Scale** of 1/2" = 1'.

7. In the **Additional Parameters** box:

A. Put a check by **Limits**.

B. Put a check by **Plot to File**.

C. Click on the **File Name** button. The **Create Plot File** box opens:

   1. Enter a file name followed by .plt.
   2. Check that the File Type is **Plot File** (.plt).
   3. Select the a:\ (floppy drive) for the **Drive** or **Save In** section so that you will be plotting to a 3.5-inch disk. This will be necessary so that you can take the disk to your local plotting company.
   4. Click on **Save** or **OK**. You will be returned to the **Plot Configuration** box.

8. In the **Pen Parameters** box, click on the **Pen Assignments** button and set up **Pens** by **Layer Colors** as follows.

   Color 1 (red): **Pen 1, Pen Width: .35**

   All Other Colors: **Pen 2, Pen Width: .25**

9. Activate the **Plot Preview** by clicking on **Full** and then on the **Preview** button. Check the preview very carefully to see that everthing is correct.

If it doesn't look right, go back and check the parts of the Plot Configuration box that might affect it.

10. When you are finally ready to plot, be sure that you have a fresh, formatted 3.5-inch disk in your a: (floppy) drive and click on the OK button.

CREATING ISOMETRIC DRAWINGS

An isometric drawing is a two-dimensional representation of a three-dimensional object. These drawings will often be of great assistance to a shop or construction crew trying to visualize the finished product. They can provide information that is difficult to show on a strictly two-dimensional drawing.

AutoCAD has settings that will help you construct isometric drawings. If you type ddrmodes on the keyboard and hit Enter, the Drawing Aids box will appear. In R12 these are also found under the Settings/Drawing Aids pull down menu. In R13 they are located under Options/Drawing Aids. In R14 they are located under Format/Drawing Aids. The tools in the Drawing Aids box that will be of the most assistance in isometric drawings are the Isometric Snap/Grid, Grid, Snap, and Ortho.

In the Isometric Snap/Grid box you can turn on or off the isometric snap/grid and choose Left, Right, or Top isometric planes. These planes realign the X and Y crosshairs to isometric angles that can be used for drawing the appropriate sides of an isometric figure as shown in the figure labeled The Top, Left, and Right Isometric Planes.

When the isometric snap/grid is turned on, your draw commands will snap to the new alignment of your drawing crosshairs and with Ortho toggled on, you will be drawing lines parallel to the isometric snap/grid. For drawing in isometrics, it is also important to use the Grid and to Snap to it to get accurate measurements, as some of your construct commands such as offset will

THE TOP, LEFT, AND RIGHT ISOMETRIC PLANES

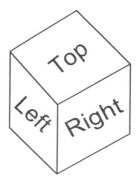

still be working on the old perpendicular coordinates and will give you incorrect distances in certain isometric planes.

In the Drawing Aids box you should set up the X and Y Grid spacing and the X and Y Snap spacing when drawing in isometrics. Use these tools to achieve the basic measurements of the figure that you are drawing. Then you may find it useful to turn ortho or snap off for some of the details of the figure and carefully establish certain parameters with construct commands such as offset. Remember that ortho and snap can also be toggled on and off on the toolbar.

Another tip to remember when drawing with the grid turned on is that the grid may not appear on the drawing screen if the size of the grid is very small and you are in a large view of the drawing. You will need to zoom down to a smaller view of the drawing to see a grid set in small increments.

Until you get used to it, isometric drawing in AutoCAD requires a little more thought in regard to the geometry of your drawing than regular 2-D drawing does. It also requires switching in and out of the isometric mode for some details of the drawing. Dimensions, for example, will not automatically align with the isometric planes in the horizontal and vertical modes. You will need to use Dimensions/Aligned to get your dimensions to align with both horizontal and vertical planes for the top isometric plane mode and with the horizontal plane for the left and right isometric plane modes.

If all of this sounds confusing, that's because it is. Isometric drawing in AutoCAD—and outside of AutoCAD—takes some practice before you get used to it. Remember that isometric drawings are not intended to take the place of accurate 2-D drawings, but rather to supplement them in providing an almost but not exactly 3-D view of a figure. Isometric drawings help provide information about a figure that may be difficult to visualize on a 2-D drawing.

Exercise No. 15: Creating an Isometric Drawing

1. Open Proto.dwg from either the CD-ROM or from the floppy disk that you saved it to earlier. Save it as Exer15.dwg on a floppy (3.5-inch) disk.
2. Work in drawing Exer15.dwg.
   A. Make an isometric drawing of a cube 1 foot on each side and dimension it.
   B. Make an isometric working drawing of a box that is to be constructed entirely from 3/4-inch plywood. The box should be 6 feet × 6 feet × 2 feet on its outside dimensions and have a bottom, but no top. Dimension it so that you could determine the exact cutting dimensions of each of the pieces from the drawing without having to do any calculations.

C. Erase the word Prototype at the top of the drawing and label it Exercise 15.

D. Using Script Simplex, put your name in the lower right-hand corner of the drawing.

3. Print Exer15.dwg on your printer in 1/2" = 1' scale using the plot command.

4. Open Projct15.dwg from the CD-ROM and print it in 1/2" = 1' scale.

5. Compare the two drawings. Pay special attention to the dimensions. This is where it is the easiest to go wrong when working in isometrics in AutoCAD. Note that there are several ways that the wood may be laid out to construct the box requested in the exercise. You may have chosen a different construction method from the one in Projct15.dwg.

THREE-DIMENSIONAL DRAWING— VIEWING THE DRAWING

Getting started in three-dimensional drawing in AutoCAD can at first be rather confusing. The first thing to understand is that you are now working not just in the familiar X and Y axes, but also the Z axis. Up until this point when working in AutoCAD that Z axis has been present, but you have not seen it because it was pointed straight toward you on the screen and it has had an assumed value of 0. As you start learning to add positive or negative values to the Z axis—the third dimension—you will need to learn how to reposition your viewpoint so that the Z axis becomes visible. Learning how to view the drawing and then how to establish a UCS—user coordinate system—so that you can draw from that viewpoint is half the battle in doing 3-D work in AutoCAD.

BACKGROUND ON WORLD COORDINATE SYSTEM AND USER COORDINATE SYSTEM

The principal difficulty of 3-D modeling is the 2-D nature of your work space. The screen you are looking at and the mouse you are working with are two-dimensional in nature. You can specify X and Y coordinates easily with them, but not Z coordinates. To solve this problem, AutoCAD lets you define your own user coordinate system or UCS. All entities in AutoCAD are actually defined in terms of the World Coordinate System or WCS. Up to now you have been working in just the X and Y coordinates of the WCS. There is only one WCS, but you can define as many UCSs as you need. The UCSs that you define will establish a drawing plane at any angle and from any location in the three-dimensional WCS.

The X,Y plane of a UCS is its construction plane. A construction plane is like a transparent sheet of plastic on which you can draw by using standard 2-D or 3-D AutoCAD commands. You can rotate and align that transparent sheet to any orientation in 3-D space by using the UCS command. Try to think of the WCS as a three-dimensional world with X, Y, and Z axes. A UCS is a two-dimensional slice taken across that world at any angle or location that you would like. You draw on it in X and Y axes much like you have already been doing. The Z value of points defaults to the construction plane, unless you explicitly specify a different elevation above or below the construction plane. You can give the construction plane a nonzero Z elevation, or you can relocate the UCS to control the Z coordinate. In both cases, the end result is the same, because entities are defined in terms of WCS coordinate values, regardless of how they are specified.

All 2-D drawing and editing commands work for drawing and editing in any construction plane set by the UCS anywhere in 3-D space. If you know how to locate and use your UCS, you have an immediate advantage because you can use everything you already know about 2-D drawing and editing to create work in 3-D. When you create a new UCS it is very much like creating a new viewpoint to your drawing, only now that viewpoint is in 3-D space and as a UCS also becomes a construction plane that you can draw upon. One way of creating a UCS is to actually work from a new 3-D viewpoint. In the next section I will cover setting a viewpoint. Once you have set up a viewpoint you can use it to establish a new UCS.

SETTING A VIEWPOINT (**vpoint**)

AutoCAD offers you a variety of ways to look at an entity using the **viewpoint** (**vpoint**) command. Later when you start establishing your own UCSs it will be important to remember which UCS you are currently in when using viewpoint and whether you are establishing a viewpoint relative to the current UCS or relative to the WCS. For now, though, all of the viewpoints that you will be establishing will be current to the WCS. To give you a reference for viewing entities with these viewpoints, you will be viewing the file **3D1.dwg**, which is a drawing of a three-dimensional cube. This file is on the CD-ROM accompanying this book. Open the file **3D1.dwg** and use it to work through the following discussion of vpoint. In 3D1.dwg the sides of the cube are drawn as follows: the **X axis** is drawn in black, the **Y axis** is drawn in green, and the **Z axis** is drawn in red. When you initially open 3D1.dwg in AutoCAD all that you will see are the X and Y axes unless you look very closely. If you look at the corners of the square you will see a small red dot at each corner. This is the endpoint of the Z axis. That the drawing is actually a cube rather than a square will only be evident when you look at it from a different viewpoint—one that you are not yet used to seeing in AutoCAD. The viewpoint that you are used to seeing is looking straight down the Z axis.

THE VIEWPOINT GLOBE AND AXES OR TRIPOD

The Viewpoint Globe and Axes or Tripod is a way of quickly setting a 3-D view of a drawing. It can be a little confusing when first viewed and does take a little practice to understand.

For R12, click on the pull down menu View/Set View/Viewpoint/Axes. For R13, click on the pull down menu View/Tripod. For R14, click on the pull down menu View/3D Viewpoint/Tripod. You will activate the Viewpoint Globe and Axes or Tripod. The screen shows two concentric circles with crosshairs and three axes labeled X, Y, and Z. As you move the cursor relative to the globe—the concentric circles and crosshairs—the axes will rotate.

The globe that you are looking at is a two-dimensional representation of the AutoCAD three-dimensional world. The center of the crosshairs represents the North Pole of the globe, the inner circle represents the Equator and the outer circle represents the South Pole. As you move the cursor—the small + mark—around the globe, you are moving around the outside of the globe looking at the drawing in the center of the globe. If the cursor is *inside* the inner circle you are looking down on your drawing. If the cursor is *outside* the inner circle you are looking up at your drawing from underneath. If the cursor is *on* the inner circle you are looking at the drawing on edge—the 2-D drawings that you have been making so far would be seen as a single line. The center of the crosshairs represents the 2-D view that you are used to seeing in AutoCAD— looking down the Z axis. Move the cursor around until you are in the position on the globe that you desire or have the axes aligned in the position that you desire and click the mouse button to see the viewpoint that you have chosen

THE VIEWPOINT GLOBE AND AXES

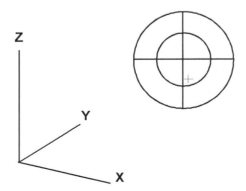

on the screen. View the file **3D1.dwg** from a variety of viewpoints using the globe and axes until you start getting a feel for the system.

USING VIEWPOINT PRESETS (**ddvpoint**)

You can also select viewpoints from the Viewpoint Presets dialogue box. This box is opened by typing ddvpoint and hitting Enter. In R12, you can click on the pull down menu View/Set View/Viewpoint/Presets. In R13, the pull down menu path is View/3D Viewpoint/Rotate. In R14, the pull down menu path is View/3D Viewpoint/Select. When this box opens you will see the following elements in the box:

1. **Absolute to WCS** Selection and **Relative to UCS** Selection: For now be sure that the **Absolute to WCS** selection is marked. Later, when you learn to establish your own user coordinate system, you will be able to establish viewpoints relative to it.

2. Horizontal Viewing Angle Selection Circle: This is a full circle with eight different horizontal viewpoints available for selection by clicking on the number of the chosen angle. You can also choose a more precise horizontal viewing angle than the selections available in the circle by entering a number in the From X Axis: box immediately beneath the circle. The horizontal

THE VIEWPOINT PRESETS BOX

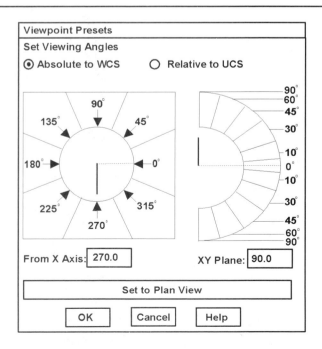

viewing angle represents the side of the drawing that you want to view from. Think back to your 2-D drawing. If you want to look at the drawing from the bottom of the screen, the selection to make is **270** degrees. From the top of the screen, the angle would be **90** degrees. From the right-hand side of the screen, the angle would be **0** degrees. From the left-hand side of the screen the angle would be **180** degrees.

3. Vertical Viewing Angle Selection Semicircle: The semicircle to the right of the horizontal viewing angle circle is used for selecting the vertical viewing angle. The 90 degrees point at the top of the semicircle represents looking straight down on the drawing from the North Pole of the viewing globe—just like the regular 2-D screen. The 0 degrees point represents the Equator of the viewing globe. The 90 degrees point at the bottom of the semicircle represents looking straight up at the drawing from the South Pole of the viewing globe. You can also enter a more precise angle than the ones available on the semicircle by entering the number in the **XY Plane:** box underneath the semicircle.

4. Once you have selected your horizontal viewing angle and vertical viewing angles, click on **OK** to see the viewpoint that you have chosen.

5. Clicking on **Set to Plan View** will return you to the standard 2-D view of the drawing.

Using Polar Angles to Select a Viewpoint (**vpoint** and **rotate**)

A faster way to select the horizontal and vertical viewing angles defined in the Viewpoint Presets box described above is to enter them directly by using the keyboard. Once you completely understand the Viewpoint Presets box the method given below will let you move your viewpoint around very quickly.

1. Type **vpoint** and hit **Enter**.
2. Prompt reads: Rotate/<View point><0'-0",0'-0",0'-1">:.
3. Type **r** and hit **Enter**.
4. Prompt reads: Enter angle in XY plane from X axis:.
5. Type the horizontal viewing angle that you desire and hit **Enter**. Note that 270 represents a front view, 90 a back view, 180 a view from the left, and 0 a view from the right side of the drawing.
6. Prompt reads: Enter angle from XY plane:.
7. Type the vertical viewing angle that you desire and hit **Enter**. Note that when typing vertical viewing angles, a positive angle gives you a view from above the global equator, to get a view from below the global equator, preface the angle with a minus sign (–).

USING A POINT ON THE X, Y, AND Z AXES TO SELECT VIEWPOINT (vpoint AND X,Y,Z)

Another method of selecting a viewpoint is entering distances on the X, Y, and Z axes from which the drawing is viewed. To understand this option remember that the origin point of the drawing on the X,Y,Z scale is 0,0,0. When you select a viewpoint using the X, Y, and Z axes you are determining a point in space from which you are looking back at the origin point. The view of the regular 2-D drawing, for example, is from 0,0,1". From there you are looking down the Z axis back at the X and Y axes. This method can be difficult to master for those who are geometrically challenged. Below I give some of the typical viewpoints that you might find useful with this method.

1. Type vpoint and hit Enter.
2. Prompt reads: Rotate/<View point><0'-0", 0'-0", 0'-1">:.
3. Type in the distances on the X, Y, and Z axes (X,Y,Z) from where you want to view the drawing and hit Enter. For example, typing 1,1,1 would give you a view from a 45 degree angle in the X,Y plane and a 45 degree angle above the X,Y plane.
4. Many people find this method of establishing a viewpoint confusing, but this is how the information on a viewpoint is actually stored in AutoCAD. It may help if you remember these basic views that can be entered by using the X,Y,Z axes command:
   A. 0,0,1: top view, looking back at the Z axis to origin (basic 2-D view)
   B. 0,0,-1: bottom view, looking down the Z axis to origin
   C. 0,1,0: back view, looking back at the Y axis to origin
   D. 0,-1,0: front view, looking down the Y axis to origin
   E. 1,0,0: right side view, looking back at the X axis to origin
   F. -1,0,0: left side view, looking down the X axis to origin

PRESET VIEWPOINTS: R13 AND R14

AutoCAD R13 and R14 also offer you a quick method of accessing preset viewpoints by clicking on toolbar icons. These icons show you graphically which view of the drawing you will be choosing by representing it as a cube with one side darkened. The darkened side is the side from which you will be viewing the drawing if you click on that icon. The icons are illustrated in the figure labeled: The Preset Viewpoints Toolbar: R13 and R14. They can be accessed by clicking on the top icon in the column on page 175 on the Standard toolbar or by opening the View toolbar. They can also be accessed in either version under the View pull down menu. If you have R13 or R14 try out several of the viewpoints available on the Preset Viewpoints toolbar.

**THE PRESET
VIEWPOINTS
TOOLBAR:
R13 AND R14**

Viewing the Drawing from a Distance

Another thing to remember about the viewpoint commands is that you always enter a viewpoint from the extents of the drawing. If you would like to back off and take a look at the drawing from a distance, you are going to have to use the zoom vmax command to do that.

1. Type z for zoom and hit Enter.
2. Type v for vmax and hit Enter.
3. Use the zoom windows command to frame the view of the drawing you would like to see.

Returning to a Plan View

After moving around the drawing using all of the different methods of 3-D viewing it can sometimes be difficult to remember exactly how to get back to a basic plan view in the WCS—"home base," as it were. There are a number of different ways that you can do this.

1. Using the vpoint command:
   A. Type vpoint and hit Enter.
   B. Type 0,0,1 and hit Enter.
2. Using the pull down menu:
   A. R12: Click on View/Set View/Plan View/World.
   B. R13: Click on View/3D Viewpoint Presets/Plan View/World.
   C. R14: Click on View/3D Viewpoint/Plan View/World UCS.
3. Using the Viewpoint Presets box:
   A. Type ddvpoint and hit Enter.
   B. Make sure there is a dot next to Absolute to WCS.
   C. Click on Set to Plan View bar.
   D. Click on OK.

SAVING A VIEW OF THE DRAWING (**ddview** AND **view**)

No matter what method that you use to establish a view of the drawing, you can still save that view for later use. While still in the viewpoint that you want to save, follow this procedure:

1. Type ddview and hit Enter or:
   A. R12: Click on View/Set View/Named View.
   B. R13 or R14: Click on View/Named Views.
2. This opens the View Control box.
3. Click on New.
4. This opens the Define New View box.
5. Type in a name for this view in the New Name: box and click on Save View.
6. You are returned to the View Control box.
7. To return to the same view that you were in click on OK.
8. To switch to another saved view while already in the View Control box click on the name of the view, then click on Restore, and then click on OK.
9. To go from the drawing screen to a view that has already been saved:
   A. Click on View, then on Set View (R12), and then on Named View.
   B. This opens the View Control box.
   C. Click on the name of the view that you want to go to, then click on Restore, and then click on OK.
10. You can also use the view command to do the same thing without opening the View Control box by using the view (view) keyboard command:

A. Type view and hit Enter.

B. Prompt reads: ?/Delete/Restore/Save/Window:.

C. Type first letter or symbol of desired option below and hit Enter.

   1. ?:

      a. Hit Enter again and it will list the already named views for this drawing in an AutoCAD text box.

      b. Type in the name of a view and hit Enter and it will give you specifications on the view.

   2. Delete: Type in the name of the view you want to delete.

   3. Restore: Type in the name of the view you want to open.

   4. Save: Type in a name for the current view you are in.

   5. Window: Use this to name a window that you specify by typing in drawing coordinates for the two corners.

11. Note that anything that you save or delete using the view keyboard command will be saved to or deleted from the View Control box. Similarly, any view that you have saved using the View Control box can also be restored or deleted using the view keyboard command.

MULTIPLE VIEWS OF A DRAWING (mview AND vports)

If you haven't used the mview and vports commands in a while, now is the time to go back and review them. Both of these commands can be a big help in getting around in 3-D drawings. Remember that mview will let you put multiple viewports of a drawing on a single screen, but that it only works while you are in paper space.

Vports, on the other hand, lets you save a number of different viewport configurations. This command lets you create tiled viewports that you can switch between or return to a single viewport. With mview you can only switch between the single viewport and one set of viewports.

In R14, you also have the floating model space option that lets you setup multiple working spaces.

Review these commands (see pages 58–64). It is much easier to work in 3-D if you have several different views set up on the screen simultaneously. Mview and vports lets you set up as many different views at the same time as you would like.

Exercise No. 16: Viewing a Drawing

Let's try looking at a couple of 3-D drawings using the different methods covered in this section.

1. Open the file 3d1.dwg from the CD-ROM. You are looking at the X and Y axes and straight down the Z axis—the traditional "ground plan" view

of a stage. This is a drawing of a cube. Some arrows with angles by them have been added to help you in understanding many of the Viewpoint commands.

2. Activate the **Viewpoint Globe and Axes** or **Tripod** command. Click on the globe where its "Equator" crosses the lower portion of the crosshairs. This should give you something pretty close to a front view of the cube. Notice the arrows to the right that give you an indication of vertical degrees above and below zero.

3. Continue to play around with the **Viewpoint Globe and Axes** command, trying different views. Take the time to try to understand how the point that you clicked on the globe and axes got you to the view that you are looking at.

4. Get back to the original WCS plan view by typing **vpoint**, hitting **Enter**, and then typing **0,0,1** and hitting **Enter**.

5. Now let's try using the **Viewpoint Presets** dialogue box. Type **ddvpoint** and hit **Enter**. You will note that the arrows and degrees on the drawing correspond to the arrows and degrees in the **Viewpoint Presets** dialogue box. This should help you more easily understand how this box works.

6. Select an **X Axis** angle and a **XY Plane** angle by clicking inside the red enclosed sections of the diagram and then click on **OK**. Notice that you can either click on the diagrams to select an angle or enter a specific angle in the boxes using the mouse to click in the box and then the keyboard to enter an angle. After you have viewed the result of your choice, to repeat the command and return to the **Viewpoint Presets** box simply click with the right mouse button or hit **Enter**.

7. When finished looking at a number of different viewpoints using this box, return to the WCS plan view.

8. Next let's use polar angles to select a viewpoint (**vpoint** and **rotate**). Remember how the from X Axis and from XY Plane sections of the Viewpoint Presets box worked? This works exactly the same way. Type **vpoint** and hit **Enter**. Then type **r** and hit **Enter**. Your prompt is **Enter angle in XY plane from X axis**. Enter an angle like you would have on the left portion of the Viewpoint Presents box—270 = front view, 90 = back view, 180 = left view, 0 = right view. Hit **Enter**, and you will be prompted to **Enter angle from XY plane**. Type the vertical angle you want—just type an angle to get that angle from above, put a minus (–) in front of the angle to get the view from below—and hit **Enter**. Try out several different combinations until you get the feel for this. If you get confused, go back to the Viewpoint Presets box and study it for a little while. Remember that after you are in the view, hitting **Enter** or the right mouse button will repeat the command for you to set up a different viewpoint.

9. Finally, let's use a point on the X,Y,Z Axes to select a viewpoint. Type vpoint and hit Enter. Now type in one of the three-number combinations given in the section covering this command such as 0,-1,0—front view, looking down the Y axis to origin—and hit Enter. Try all of the combinations listed until you get a feeling for this command. Once you remember the combinations, this can be the quickest of the Viewpoint commands.

10. You can also use the zoom and pan commands to move about in the viewpoint that you have established. Get into a 3-D view of the drawing and pan and zoom around in it. Try the zoom vmax command to move back and take a long-distance view.

11. Review the view command. Use it to establish several named views of the drawing and then to restore them.

12. Review the mview command. Use it to establish multiple viewports and then set up a different viewpoint in each viewport.

13. Review the vports command. Use it to establish tiled viewports.

14. All of these viewing commands are essential to being able to draw in 3-D in AutoCAD. To draw 3-D images efficiently you must first be able to establish different viewpoints to the drawing, use those viewpoints to establish UCSs, and then be able to return to those viewpoints later when you need them.

THREE-DIMENSIONAL DRAWING— WORKING WITH UCSs

Up to now you have been working in AutoCAD's WCS, or world coordinate system. This is the master coordinate system for AutoCAD in terms of which all entities are defined. Establishing a number of UCSs, or user coordinate systems, however, will allow you to work more easily in 3-D space. The WCS has the familiar X,Y plane in which you are used to working and a Z plane that is perpendicular to the X,Y plane. When you set up a UCS you are establishing a new X,Y plane at any angle that you desire to the WCS X,Y plane. You can then draw and edit objects on this new X,Y plane and your commands will automatically be translated into the WCS by AutoCAD. Drawing on the UCS that you have established will allow you to more easily create 2-D and 3-D objects at an angle to the X,Y and Z planes of the WCS.

ESTABLISHING A UCS

You can establish a UCS by a number of different methods. You can:

1. Specify a new origin, a new X,Y plane, or a new Z axis.
2. Copy the orientation of an existing entity.

3. Align the new UCS to your current view.

4. Rotate the current UCS around any one or all of the X, Y, and Z axes.

You can make as many UCSs as you would like, giving each a different name; however, only one UCS can be used at a time. If you are using multiple viewports, for example, they all share the same UCS even though they may be different views.

You can establish or call up a UCS by typing ucs and hitting Enter. In R12, you can also use the pull down menu by clicking on Settings/UCS and then a variety of other options. In R13, the path is View/Named UCS, View/Preset UCS, or View/Set UCS. In R14, the path is Tools/UCS.

Keyboard Method

When you type ucs and hit Enter, the following prompt appears: Origin/ZAxis/ 3point/Entity/View/X/Y/Z/Prev/Restore/Save/Del/?/<World>:. This offers you the following options:

1. Origin: This specifies a new UCS origin point, without changing the orientation.

2. ZAxis: This specifies a new UCS origin point and defines a new UCS by specifying a positive point on the Z axis.

3. 3point: This specifies a new UCS by selecting three points: an origin, a positive point on the X axis, and a positive point on the Y axis.

4. Entity: This aligns the current UCS with the coordinate system of a selected entity.

5. View: This aligns the UCS with your current viewpoint.

6. X: This rotates the UCS around the X axis.

7. Y: This rotates the UCS around the Y axis.

8. Z: This rotates the UCS around the Z axis.

9. Prev: This restores the previous UCS. Note that you can repeat this command to back up a maximum of ten coordinate systems.

10. Restore: This restores a previously named and saved UCS. Note that ? will give you a list of named UCSs.

11. Save: This saves the current UCS. You can specify a name of up to thirty-one characters.

12. Del: This deletes a saved UCS by name.

13. ?: This lists all named UCSs. A current unnamed ucs is listed as *NO NAME*, unless it is the WCS, which is listed as *WORLD*.

14. World: This restores the world coordinate system.

THE UCS CONTROL DIALOGUE BOX

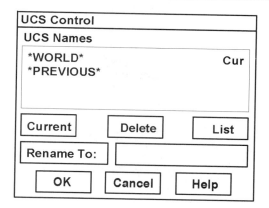

Pull Down Menu Method

In R12, go to Settings/UCS/. In R13, go to View/Named UCS, View/Preset UCS, or View/Set UCS/. In R14, go to Tools/UCS/. When you click on the pull down menu path for your version, the following options are available to you:

1. **Named UCS . . . :** This option displays the UCS Control dialogue box, which is also available by typing **dducs** and hitting **Enter**. Here you can establish the plane of the current viewpoint as a UCS by giving it a name,

THE UCS ORIENTATION BOX

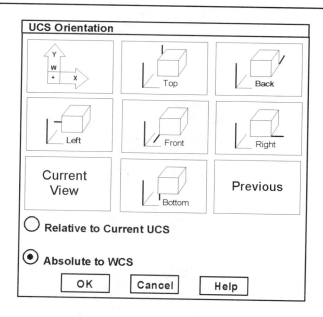

delete a UCS, rename a UCS, or click on the name of an already named UCS to make it the current UCS.

2. Presets . . . : This option displays the UCS Orientation dialogue box. This box offers you a choice of predefined UCSs as well as letting you define a UCS in the plane of the current view and switch to the previous UCS. All of these can be established Relative to the Current UCS or Absolute to the WCS. You can also get into this box by typing dducsp and hitting Enter.

3. Origin: This lets you change the origin of the current UCS.

4. Axis
   A. X: Use this to rotate the current UCS around the X axis.
   B. Y: Use this to rotate the current UCS around the Y axis.
   C. Z: Use this to rotate the current UCS around the Z axis.

HELP! I'M LOST: GETTING BACK TO WHERE YOU WERE

In all of the exercises so far, the different viewpoints that have been explored have been based on the WCS. When you establish your own UCSs you will be able to establish viewpoints from a number of different UCSs. When you start moving around in different viewpoints in different UCSs it becomes very easy to get lost. So here's how to get back to the WCS and a plan view quickly and easily.

1. Reestablishing yourself in the WCS:
   A. Type ucs and hit Enter.
   B. Type w and hit Enter.

Or:

   A. Open the UCS Control box:
      1. R12: Click on Settings/UCS/Named UCS.
      2. R13: Click on View/Named UCS.
      3. R14: Click on Tools/UCS/Named UCS.
   B. Under UCS Names, click on *World*, then on the Current button, and then on OK.

2. Reestablishing yourself in the WCS plan view:
   A. Type plan and hit Enter.
   B. Type w and hit Enter.

Or:

   A. R12: Click on View/Set View/Plan View/World.
   B. R13: Click on View/Set UCS/World.
   C. R14: Click on Tools/UCS/World.

UCS Icon (**ucsicon**) Options

The UCS icon has several different settings that can help you keep track of your UCS as you change views of a drawing. These settings can be changed by typing **ucsicon** and hitting **Enter**. The prompt reads: **ON/OFF/All/Noorigin/ ORigin<ON>:**. This offers the following options:

1. **ON:** This turns on the UCS icon so it appears in the drawing area.
2. **OFF:** This turns off the UCS icon so it no longer appears in the drawing area.
3. **All:** This displays the UCS icon in each viewport when you use multiple viewports.
4. **Noorigin:** This always displays the UCS icon at the lower left corner of each viewport.
5. **ORigin:** This displays the UCS icon at the 0,0 point of the current UCS, unless the origin is outside the drawing area; then it is visible in the lower left corner of the viewport. When the UCS icon is displayed, it appears at an angle to the current viewport, reflecting the orientation of the UCS to that viewport. You are used to seeing the UCS icon showing the X and Y axes with a box in the corner and a W on the Y axis, but there are a number of other views. Take a look at the diagrams in the figure labeled USC Icon Displays for some samples of other views that may occur as you start creating UCSs and viewpoints. Understanding the icon can help you orient yourself as to where you are in a viewpoint relative to a UCS.

The model space icon (in top left corner of figure) uses X and Y arrows to point along the axes of the drawing. The + on the icon means that it is located at the origin of the current UCS. The W on the Y axis means that the current coordinate system is the WCS. A box at the icon's base means you are viewing the

UCS ICON DISPLAYS

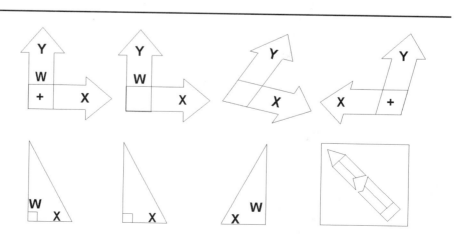

UCS from above—in a positive Z direction. No box means that you are look-ing at the UCS from below—in a negative Z direction. The triangle instead of two arrows means that you are in paper space rather than model space and cannot draw. The broken pencil means that your view is within one degree of parallel (edge on) to the current UCS, making point picking unreliable.

Some of the uscicon options are also available under pull down menus:

R12: Settings/UCS/Icon
R13: Options/UCS
R14: View/Display/UCS Icon

Exercise No. 17: Working with UCSs

1. Open the drawing Projct17.dwg from the CD-ROM. Save it to a floppy disk as Exer17.dwg.

2. You will notice a line near the top of the screen labeled A. This line actually has a Z-axis thickness of 2 feet to it, though you can't see that from the WCS, which is what you are currently in. As we work our way through the UCS command, this line will become important to establish-ing some of the UCSs.

3. First let's work with the keyboard command ucs. There are several com-mands available here that are not available with the UCS Control dialogue box. Type ucs and hit Enter. Prompt reads: Origin/ZAxis/3point/Entity/View/X/Y/Z/Prev/Restore/Save/Del/?/<World>.

   A. Origin: This specifies a new origin point other than the lower left-hand corner of the drawing screen. This command is occasionally useful, but dangerous if you forget that a new origin has been spe-cified. The origin must be restored to the lower left corner before printing, or the origin must be entered in the Print/Plot dialogue box. Skip this one for now.

   B. ZAxis: If you would like to draw something oriented the same as the WCS, but above or below the WCS drawing plane on the Z axis, this command will establish a new UCS from which you can do that. Let's try it:
      1. Type za and hit Enter.
      2. Prompt reads: Origin point <0,0,0>:.
      3. Enter a value for the height on the Z axis that you want the new drawing plane to be. For example, type 0,0,2' and hit Enter. This will establish a new drawing plane 2 feet above the WCS.
      4. Prompt reads: Point on positive portion of Z axis < 0'-0", 0'-0", 2'-1">:. Hit Enter.

5. You are now in a new UCS 2 feet above the WCS—notice that the W has disappeared from the UCS icon in the lower left-hand corner of the screen. You are now out of the WCS.

6. Now you have to get into the viewpoint for that UCS that you just created. Click on View/Set View/Plan View/Current UCS.

7. Draw a small rectangle just below the line labeled A on the screen.

8. Using the globe and axes, establish a viewpoint that is slightly above the "Equator" and slightly to the left. Notice that the rectangle that you just drew is actually on a level with the top of line A.

C. 3point: This is one of the most useful UCS commands. It lets you establish a drawing plane by clicking on 3 points. To do this you are going to need to be very precise about the 3 points you use so use object snaps. From the viewpoint that you are currently in, you should be able to see that line A looks like a rectangle that is vertical relative to the WCS. Let's say that you want to establish a UCS drawing plane using that rectangles so that you can draw some more entities on the same plane as the rectangle—think of these as flats relative to a ground plan, with the WCS being the ground plan. The 3point command is a good way to do this.

1. Type ucs and hit Enter.

2. Type 3 and hit Enter.

3. Prompt reads: Origin Point <0,0,0>: In the toolbox click on the object snap Intersection and then click on the lower left-hand corner of the A rectangle.

4. Prompt reads: Point on the positive portion of the X axis <2'-10 5/8",15'-9 1/4",-2'0">:. Click on the nearest object snap and then click on a point on the lower line of the A rectangle somewhere to the right of the lower left-hand corner that you clicked on in the previous step).

5. Prompt reads: Point on the positive-Y portion of the UCS XY plane <2'-9 5/8",15'-10 1/4",-2'0">:. Click on the nearest object snap and then click on a point on the vertical line emanating from the origin point that you selected earlier.

6. Notice that the icon has shifted. You have just established a new UCS on line with the A rectangle.

7. Get into the plan view for the current UCS that you have established.

8. Draw a rectangle to the right of the rectangle currently on the screen. Think of this as drawing a flat next to the flat that is rectangle A in this UCS or line A in the WCS.

9. Now let's save this UCS so that you can come back to it later. Type ucs, hit Enter, then hit s.

10. Prompt reads: ?/Desired UCS name:. Type in flats and hit **Enter**. You have just saved this UCS under the name flats.
11. **Restore** the WCS and the WCS plan view.
12. Notice that the rectangle that you drew now appears to be a line right next to the A line.
13. Now restore the UCS flats by using the keyboard and the **UCS/Restore** command and then go into the plan view for the current UCS. **Restore** the WCS and the WCS plan view.

D. Entity: Type ucs, hit **Enter**, type e, hit **Enter**.
1. Prompt reads: **Select object to align UCS:**.
2. Click on the small rectangle that you drew below line A earlier, but did not save a UCS for.
3. Notice that you are no longer in the WCS. You are now in a UCS that is parallel to the WCS, but 2 feet above it where you earlier drew that rectangle. Draw another small rectangle next to this one. Save this UCS as smrect. **Restore** the WCS and WCS plan view. Get into a viewpoint that lets you see the height above the WCS of both of the small rectangles.
4. Activate the **UCS/Entity** command again. This time click on the rectangle that you drew next to the A rectangle. This will restore you to the UCS called flats that you used to draw this rectangle. Go into the plan view for the current UCS.
5. **Restore** the WCS and plan view for the WCS.

E. Now you should have a basic idea about UCS and how to use the UCS command. Try establishing UCSs using the view, and X, Y, Z options of the UCS command. Draw a small figure in each of them and then get into views that show you best how these UCSs are working. You can save these new UCSs if you would like.

4. Next let's work with the **UCS Control** dialogue box. Type dducs and hit **Enter** or click on the appropriate pull down menu path. The **UCS Control** box opens. Notice that in addition to *World* the UCSs that you saved earlier, *flats* and *smrect*, are also present in the box. If you would like to go to one of these UCSs click on the name of the UCS in the box, click on **Current**, and then click on **OK**. You can then go into the plan view for that UCS. Go to these UCSs and watch the icon carefully in each case. You can also use this box to name a UCS that you are in but haven't named, rename a UCS, delete a UCS, and restore the WCS.

5. Finally let's work with the **UCS Orientation** dialogue box. If you are not in the WCS and plan view, restore them. Then either type dducsp and hit **Enter** or use the appropriate pull down menu path. This opens the **UCS Orientation** box. This box has a number of preset UCSs that you can get

into by clicking on the pictures in the upper portion of the box and then clicking on **OK**. By clicking on the appropriate circle in the lower portion of the box, these UCSs can also be established relative to either the WCS or the current UCS. Options available are:

A. **WCS**: The icon in the upper left box restores you to the WCS.

B. **TOP**: This is absolute to WCS and is the same as WCS. Relative to the current UCS, this would be looking down from the Z axis of the UCS, that is, the same as the current UCS. In other words, this is a pretty useless command.

C. **BACK and FRONT**: These are parallel to the Z axis of the WCS or current UCS and looking at it from opposite sides.

D. **LEFT and RIGHT**: These are parallel to the Z axis of the WCS or current UCS and turned 90 degrees to the left or right.

E. **BOTTOM**: This is the same as the WCS or current UCS, except that you are looking at it from underneath.

Establish several UCSs using the UCS Orientation box. Draw a simple figure in each of them and then look at the figures from several viewpoints so that you understand how these presets work.

6. Probably the most difficult part of AutoCAD to understand is the concept of the UCS and how to use it. Work through this exercise very carefully, being sure that you understand each step of the process. Understanding and using UCSs is essential to working easily in 3-D in AutoCAD.

THREE-DIMENSIONAL DRAWING— USING DRAWING COMMANDS

DRAWING WITH 2-D ENTITIES IN 3-D SPACE

One of the simplest ways to create a 3-D shape in AutoCAD is to use the 2-D entities with which you are already familiar and add a Z-coordinate value, or elevation above or below the X,Y plane, and/or a thickness. Both of these are added relative to the current UCS in which you are working or to the WCS if you are working in the WCS. Here are some tips for creating 3-D objects from 2-D shapes:

A. Circles create closed cylinders. Donuts create open-ended cylinders.

B. Ellipses create open-ended cylinders.

C. Solids such as squares, rectangles, polygons, etc., create closed objects. For example, use the rectangle or polygon command to make a solid cube.

D. Lines and open polylines are used to create open objects. For example, draw your cube using lines to create a cube you can see through.

E. Closed polylines can also be used to create solid, irregular objects and shapes.

F. Lines can approximate any object in wireframe, but cannot hide anything unless they are extruded, meaning a thickness is added.

ADDING Z-COORDINATE VALUES TO POINTS IN DRAWING FIGURES

When you have been drawing a 2-D figure so far in AutoCAD you have been drawing on the X,Y plane of the WCS. If you add a Z-coordinate value to each point as the figure is drawn, that will position each point of the figure above or below the X,Y plane. For example, if you are drawing a line from a point at 8',6' to a point at 7',6' you have drawn a horizontal line 1 foot long on the X,Y plane. If you draw a line from a point at 8',6',1' to a point at 7',6',1' you have drawn a line 1 foot long that is 1 foot above the X,Y plane. Z values can also be negative, so a line drawn from a point at 8',6',-1' to a point at 7',6',-1' would be a line 1 foot long, but also 1 foot below the X,Y plane. Adding a Z-coordinate value in this manner requires that you specify each point of the figure that you are drawing with three coordinates—X,Y,Z. The figure that you have drawn using this method is still a 2-D figure, but it is displaced from the X,Y plane by the amount of the Z coordinate that you have specified.

THICKNESS (**thickness**) AND ELEVATION (**elev**) COMMANDS

If you want to create a 3-D figure using 2-D entities you will need to add a thickness to the entity. Thickness will give the figure a dimension along the Z axis of the drawing. The value for thickness is set by using the thickness command.

Similarly, elevation (elev) sets the height above or below the current drawing plane—WCS or UCS—on which you are drawing. To set the value for thickness and elevation:

1. Type thickness and hit Enter. In R14, you can also click on Format/ Thickness.
2. Prompt reads: New value for THICKNESS <0'-0">:.
3. Type in the desired thickness and hit Enter.
4. Set a value for Elevation by typing elev and hitting Enter.

Keep in mind that thickness and elevation can be positive or negative values. A positive value will create a thickness above the X,Y plane in which you are drawing the figure, as determined by the Z-coordinate value. A negative value will create that thickness below the X,Y plane, as determined by the Z-coordinate value. The Z-coordinate value for each of the points used in drawing the figure determines where the thickness will begin. Once you have set thickness, that value will be used by AutoCAD in drawing *all figures* until you reset the value for thickness. The default value for thickness is 0, which creates a 2-D figure.

A positive value for elevation creates a figure with its base at that distance above the current drawing plane. A negative value for elevation creates a figure with its base at that distance below the current drawing plane. Again, once you have set a value for elevation, that value will remain until it is reset.

ENTITY CREATION MODES (**ddemodes**) IN **R12** AND **R13**

The Entity Creation Modes box allows you to simultaneously set a value for both elevation—Z-coordinate value above or below the X,Y plane—and thickness. You open the Entity Creation Modes box by typing **ddemodes** and then hitting **Enter**. In R12, you can use the pull down menu path **Settings/Entity Modes**. In R13, you can use the pull down menu path **Data/Object Creation**. In R13, there is also an **Object Creation** icon on the **Object Properties** toolbar that will open the box. This command is not available in R14.

Entering a value in the **Elevation** area of the box sets a Z- coordinate value for all entities that you draw above or below the current X,Y plane in which you are working. Entering a value in the **Thickness** area of the box sets a thickness above or below the elevation that you have set. This is a fast way to set or change both elevation and thickness simultaneously.

CHANGE PROPERTIES (**ddchprop** IN **R12**), (**ai_propchk** IN **R13** AND **R14**)

This command opens the **Change Properties** box, which allows you to simultaneously change a number of different properties of an entity such as color, layer, linetype, thickness, location of end points, etc. The exact properties that can be changed will vary with the entity selected. Activate the command by typing **ddchprop** in R12 or **ai_propchk** in R13 and R14 and hitting **Enter**. In R12 it can also be entered by clicking on **Modify/Change/Properties**. In R13 and R14 this command is the same as the **ddmodify** command. See the **ddmodify** command in the next section for more information.

1. Prompt reads: **Select Objects:**.
2. Click on entity to be changed.
3. Prompt reads: **Select Objects:1 found Select Objects:**.
4. Select more entities and the same prompt will appear again. When you have selected all the entities that you want to change you can activate the command by hitting **Enter** or clicking on the right mouse button.
5. Remember that while it is possible to select more than one entity using the **change properties** command, the changes that you make will be made to *all* entities selected.

6. Once you have selected all the entities on which you want to change properties, a dialogue box will open in which you can make the changes.

MODIFY ENTITY OR PROPERTIES (**ddmodify**)

The Modify Entity or Modify Properties (ddmodify) command is an editing command that opens a box with information about the selected entity. It also allows you to make a wide variety of changes in the selected entity.

1. Activate the modify entity command.
2. Once you have entered ddmodify, you will be prompted to select the entity that you would like to modify by clicking on it.
3. Clicking on the entity to be modified will open a Modify dialogue box. The particular dialogue box opened will depend upon the entity that you have selected and its attributes. If you have a number of changes to make to an entity, the ddmodify command can be a quick way to make them all at once. This is a command that becomes more useful the more complex that the drawing becomes. You may not need to use all of its capabilities right away, but as you get better at AutoCAD you will.
4. For example, if the entity selected is a circle you could change the layer, color, linetype, center coordinates, radius, diameter, circumference, or area. If the entity selected is text, you could change the layer, color, text itself, origin, justification, style, height, rotation, width, or obliquing.

R12: AME MODELER AUTHORIZATION CODE

The first time that you try to use any of the AME modeling commands in R12 you may find that you receive a message from AutoCAD requesting an authorization code. If you cannot locate the AME authorization code in your paperwork, call AutoDesk. Have the serial number of your version of AutoCAD ready, and a representative will be able to give you an authorization code.

The AME modeling commands are those commands that are part of the Automatic Modeling Extension in AutoCAD R12. These are most of the

THE MODIFY ENTITY/ PROPERTIES COMMAND

AutoCAD Command	Function
Modify Entity/Properties	**Changes characteristics of an entity.**

Keyboard Command	Pull Down Menu Path	Icon (R12)	Icon (R13 & R14)
DDMODIFY	**R12: Modify/Entity** **R14: Modify/Properties**		**Object Prop.**

commands that are used to create 3-D objects. In R12, this AME is actually loaded separately from the main program during installation. When you try to use an AME command in R12, the AME will be activated if it has been installed and if after installation the AME authorization code has been entered. Usually, you are prompted for the AME code the first time that you try to use an AME command. After the AME code has been entered once it will not need to be entered again. In R13 and R14, all of the 3-D commands are incorporated into the main program and there is no AME or associated codes.

DRAWING 3-D OBJECTS

There are also a number of commands in AutoCAD that let you draw solid objects or 3-D objects directly rather than creating them by modifying two-dimensional ones. The solid command draws solid objects that can be made three-dimensional by adding thickness. The various commands for 3-D objects create basic three-dimensional shapes that can then be combined to create more complex shapes.

THE SOLID (**solid**) COMMAND

The solid command can be used to create 3-D entities. It creates solid, filled regions as either triangles or quadrilaterals.

1. Prompt reads: First point:. Enter a point.
2. Prompt reads: Second point:. Enter a point.
3. Prompt reads: Third point:. enter a point.
4. Prompt reads: Fourth point:. Either enter a point for a quadrilateral or hit Enter for a triangle.
5. Prompt reads: Third point:. Enter a point or hit Enter to end solid.
6. The solid command will keep prompting you for the third and fourth point until you hit Enter, letting you continue to draw solid, filled regions. The subsequent prompts for a third or fourth point let you enter new points so that you can create a figure using five, six, or more points.

THE SOLID COMMAND

AutoCAD Command	Function	
Solid	**Draws 2D solid geometric shapes.**	

Keyboard Command	Pull Down Menu Path	Icon (R13 & R14)
SOLID	**R14: Draw/Surfaces/2D Solid**	 **Draw Surfaces**

THE SOLID COMMAND SEQUENCE

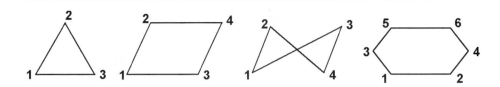

Predicting the precise shape of figures using more than five or six points, however, can get very complex. Note that the order in which you select points will determine the shape of the figure that you draw. It is natural, for example, in drawing a quadrilateral to start at one point and then go sequentially around the figure with points. This will give you a "bow tie" when using the **solid** command. Study the diagrams shown in the figure labeled The Solid Command Sequence to understand the sequential selection of points when using the **solid** command. Also note that when using the **solid** command it can be very useful to have the **Blips** feature selected under **Settings/Drawing Aids**, as the figure will not appear until you have finished.

3-D OBJECTS—SURFACES

AutoCAD also has available for your use a number of 3-D objects that are formed from surfaces for which you can specify dimensions in your drawing. This is often a way to rapidly get a solid object drawn in 3-D. With a little imagination you can also combine these objects to create a wide variety of other shapes and objects as well. In R12, the **3D Objects** box will open when you click on **Draw/3D Surfaces/3D Objects**. Click on the object that you would like on the left side of the box and then click on **OK**. You will then be prompted for the specifications necessary for each individual object. In R13 and R14, open the **Surfaces** toolbar and click on the object that you would like.

The following are the keyboard commands for each individual object that is available in all versions:

1. 3D Box (ai_box): Use this command to draw any 3-D box-shaped object by defining two corners and a height. You can use it, for example, to draw a flat, platforms, step units, etc. in 3-D.

2. Wedge (ai_wedge): Use this to form any wedge-shaped object such as a ramp, a buttress, etc.

SURFACE ICONS: R13 AND R14

3. Pyramid (ai_pyramid): Use this option to draw any generally pyramidal-shaped object by defining four corners and a top point. The sides do not have to be even.

4. Cone (ai_cone): This can be used to form a cone of specified base radius, top radius, and height. Note that this cone does not have to come to a point. The base radius and the top radius can be the same, in which case you have drawn a column.

5. Sphere (ai_sphere): Use this to form a sphere of specified center point and radius.

6. Dome (ai_dome): This can be used to form a dome—top 1/2 of a sphere—of specified center point and radius.

7. Dish (ai_dish): This can be used to form a dish—bottom 1/2 of a sphere—by picking a center point and radius.

8. Torus (ai_torus): This option forms a torus—a 3-D donut—with a specified center point, an outside radius, and a radius for the tube of the donut or torus.

9. Mesh (ai_mesh): This option forms a mesh—flat surface—with four specified corners. Note that sides do not have to be even. You can also later use the pedit command to move the vertices of the corners to twist this flat surface through three dimensions.

3-D Objects—Solids, or Primitives

Also available in AutoCAD are a number of true solids, or primitives. In R12 you access these commands by the pull down menu Model/Primitives. In R13 and R14, they are available on the Solids Toolbar.

The following are the keyboard commands for each individual object that is available in all versions:

1. Box (box): Use this to form a 3-D cube by defining a corner, a second corner, and a height.

2. Sphere (sphere): Use this to form a 3-D sphere by defining the center and diameter or radius.

3. Cylinder (cylinder): Use this to form a 3-D cylinder by defining a center, a diameter or radius, and a height. This also has an option for forming an elliptical cylinder.

SOLIDS TOOLBAR ICONS: R13 AND R14

4. **Cone (cone):** Use this to form a 3-D cone by defining a center, a diameter or radius, and a height. It also has an option for forming an elliptical cone.

5. **Wedge (wedge):** Use this to form a 3-D wedge by defining a corner, a second corner, and a height.

6. **Torus (torus):** Use this to form a 3-D donut by defining a center, a diameter or radius of the center, and a diameter or radius of the tube.

Note: You can use a number of the 3-D editing commands that will be covered in the next section to modify these basic shapes by cutting them, rotating them, etc.

Exercise No. 18: Working with Drawing Commands

1. Open the drawing Proto.dwg from either the CD-ROM or the disk that you saved it to earlier.
2. Save the drawing as Exer18.dwg on a 3.5-inch disk.
3. Erase the word Prototype.
4. First, let's cover some of the ways that you can use the already familiar 2-D drawing commands to draw 3-D figures.
   A. Adding Z-coordinate values in drawing figures:
      1. Draw a circle using the following coordinates: center—3',18',2'; radius—1'.
      2. View the circle you have drawn from a perspective (vpoint) that shows that it is now raised 2 feet above the drawing plane. Restore to plan view. Remember, if the Z-coordinate value entered had been -2' the circle would have been below the drawing plane.
   B. Using the thickness command:
      1. Erase the circle.
      2. Make the value for thickness in the drawing 2'.
      3. Draw the same circle that you did in A.
      4. View the circle from the same—or similar—perspective that you did above. Notice that you now have a cylinder raised 2 feet above the drawing plane and 2 feet in height.
      5. Return to plan view and draw a short line right next to the circle; do *not* add Z-coordinate values. Return to the same perspective view that you were in before. Notice that what you have drawn is a vertical rectangle 2 feet in height, the bottom of which is on the drawing plane—WCS. As long as thickness is set to 2 feet, any figure drawn will have this thickness.
      6. Return to plan view and reset the thickness to 0.

C. Setting elevation and thickness using the Entity Creation Modes box (ddemodes):

Note: This command is not available in R14. You will have to draw the figure and then use ai_propchk to modify it in R14.

1. Open the Entity Creation Modes box by typing **ddemodes** and hitting Enter or clicking on Settings/Entity Modes.
2. Set elevation at 1'0" and thickness at 3'0" and click on OK.
3. Draw another circle and another line just using your mouse.
4. View these from a perspective similar to the one used earlier. Remember that until you reset elevation and thickness, all figures drawn will have this elevation and thickness. Reset the values for elevation and thickness to 0'0".

5. You can also create 3-D figures by modifying already existing 2-D figures. Let's draw some 2-D figures and then change their elevation and thickness using editing commands to turn them into 3-D figures.

A. Erase the figures that you have already drawn and return to plan view.

B. Draw a circle, a line, a rectangle, and a hexagon all in a row.

C. Activate the change properties (chprop) command or open the Change Properties box (ddchprop in R12 or ai_propchk in R13 and R14).
   1. You will be prompted to select objects:. Click on all of the entities that you have drawn and then hit Enter or click the right mouse button.
   2. Change the thickness to 2'.
   3. View the figures that you have drawn using a perspective similar to the one you used earlier.
   4. If you used chprop above to change the thickness of the figures, then use ddchprop or ai_propchk to change the thickness back to 0'0", or vice versa.
   5. Stay in a view where you can see a perspective view of the figures.

D. Activate the modify entity command by typing ddmodify and hitting Enter.
   1. You will be prompted to select object:. Click on the circle. Notice that you can select only one object at a time using this command.
   2. The Modify Circle box will open.
   3. Change the thickness to 2' and the Z value of the center to 1'. Click on OK.
   4. Activate Modify Entity again and click on the line.
   5. Change the thickness to 1'. Change the From Point: Z value to 1' and the To Point: Z value to 2'. Click on OK. You now have a vertical rectangle that is 1 foot high, but at different elevations at each end.

6. Activate **Modify Entity** again and click on the rectangle.

7. The **Modify Polyline** box opens.

8. Change the thickness to 2'. Notice that you cannot change the Z value. This is because a rectangle is actually a 2-D polyline. You can see the values of each of the points that form the corners of the rectangle by clicking on **Next** under **Vertex Listing**. Click on **OK**. In order to change the values for these points you would have to use the **pedit** command using the **edit vertex** and **move** options. If you had written down the X, Y, and Z value of each of the vertices, you could enter a new keyboard value for Z under **pedit/edit vertex/move**, or you could click with the mouse on a vertical point from a perspective or side view of the rectangle. If you want to try this, review the **pedit** command in the section on modify commands (see page 106).

9. Again activate the **modify entity** command.

10. Click on the hexagon.

11. Change the thickness to 3'. Notice that again you are dealing with a 2-D polyline. You cannot change the Z value of the vertices in this box. Once again, you would have to use the **pedit** command to do this.

12. When you are done, return to plan view and erase all the figures that you have drawn.

6. Now let's draw some figures using the **solid** command. Refer back to the section on this command (see page 191) and review how the order in which you select points determines the shape of the figure.

A. Activate the **blips** command. This will help you keep track of where you have clicked in drawing the figures.

B. Set a thickness of 2'.

C. Draw a figure using the **solid** command. View the figure from a suitable perspective.

D. Return to the plan view.

E. Activate the **solid fill** command.

F. Draw another figure using the **solid** command. View the figure from the same perspective.

G. Return to the plan view and draw several more figures using the **solid** command until you have a feel for how the command works. When done, return to plan view, reset thickness to 0, and erase all of the figures.

7. Next, let's try drawing some of the 3-D surface objects that AutoCAD has available for you.

A. In R12, click on **Draw/3D Surfaces/3D Objects**. In R13 or R14, open the **Surfaces** toolbar.

B. Type ai_box and hit Enter or select a 3-D box from the 3D Objects box in R12 or the Surfaces toolbar in R13 or R14.

C. Prompt reads: Corner of box:. Click on a point or enter one with coordinates.

D. Prompt reads: Length:. Click on a point or enter one with coordinates.

E. Prompt reads: Cube/<Width>:. Click on a point or enter one with coordinates. Note that if you select the Cube option, by typing c and hitting Enter, the length, width, and height will be the same and you will skip ahead to the Rotation about Z axis prompt (step G).

F. Prompt reads: Height:. Type a value by keyboard and hit Enter.

G. Prompt reads: Rotation about Z axis:. Type a figure in degrees counterclockwise and hit Enter, or click with the mouse to enter a rotation.

H. View the box that you have just drawn from a suitable perspective.

I. Return to the plan view and draw each of the other 3-D surface objects that are available. Note the options that are available at each step of the drawing process and try each of them out like the Cube option above. Remember also that you can activate the command for the particular 3-D object by keyboard as well as using the 3-D Objects box. You can also save the work that you have done at any step in the process and return to it later.

8. Finally, let's try drawing some of the 3-D primitives or solids that AutoCAD has available.

A. In R12, click on Model/Primitives. In R13 or R14, open the Solids toolbar.

B. Type box and hit Enter or select the AME Primitives box in R12 or the Box from the Solids toolbar in R13 and R14.

C. Prompt reads: Center/<Corner of box> <0,0,0>:. Click on a point or enter one with coordinates.

D. Prompt reads: Cube/Length/<other corner>:. Click on a point or enter one with coordinates.

E. Prompt reads: Height:. Enter a height such as 2'.

F. View the box that you have just drawn from a suitable perspective.

G. Return to the plan view and draw each of the other 3-D solid objects that are available. Note the options that are available at each step of the drawing process and try each of them out like the Cube option above. Remember also that you can activate the command for the particular 3-D object by keyboard as well. You can also save the work that you have done at any step in the process and return to it later.

THREE-DIMENSIONAL DRAWING—
USING EDITING COMMANDS

USING 2-D EDITING COMMANDS AS 3-D TOOLS

Certain of the familiar 2-D editing commands will also work in 3-D. **Copy,**
move, and **rotate** all have uses when working in 3-D. **Copy** and **move** will
accept 3-D points and displacements. You can use one of the object snaps, for
example, to **move** an object to a 3-D intersection. The **rotate** command, however, will only rotate an object that is parallel to the current UCS. By setting different UCSs, though, you can rotate objects to any orientation in space.

Other editing commands that may work a little differently in 3-D are
stretch, break, trim, extend, fillet, chamfer, and **offset.**

Stretch works in 3-D, but the results may depend upon the entity and the
current UCS. Three-dimensional entities such a lines and meshes can be
stretched to and from any point in 3-D. For 2-D entities and extruded 2-D
entities (thickness added), however, unless you are stretching along the
construction plane, the results can be difficult to predict.

Break projects the entity to be broken and the break points into the current
UCS.

Trim projects the trim edge and entities to the current UCS.

Extend projects the extend edge and entities to the current UCS.

Fillet and **chamfer** will work with objects that lie parallel to the current UCS.

- Note that there is also a **Fillet Solids** and a **Chamfer Solids** command
  under **Model/Modify** in R12.

Offset works relative to the current UCS.

You may find it easiest to work with these commands in plan view while
observing the results in multiple 3-D viewports.

3-D EDITING COMMANDS

There are certain other AutoCAD commands that are useful for or specific to
editing in 3-D. Among the most useful of these are align, rotate 3D, mirror 3D,
array 3D, solcut, solunion, extrude, revolve, subtract, intersect, solidify, chamfer solids, and fillet solids.

ALIGN (**align**)

This command works like a combination of **move** and **rotate.** To use this command you select three **Source Points**—points on the object to be aligned—and
three corresponding **Destination Points**—points on the object to which the

THE ALIGN COMMAND

AutoCAD Command	Function	
Align	**Aligns 3 points on one object w/another.**	

Keyboard Command	Pull Down Menu Path	Icon (R13)
ALIGN	**R12: Modify/Align** **R14: Modify/3D Operation/Align**	 Modify

source object is to be aligned. This is one of the most useful of the 3-D editing commands. You can construct two pieces separately and then put them together using align. For example, you could construct a flat using the 3-D box command, then build some molding by drawing a section of the molding and then giving it a thickness, and finally put the molding on top of the flat using the align command. Align also works as a transparent command so you could escape from the middle of the command to zoom down to a closer view in order to select a source or destination point.

ROTATE 3D (rotate3d)

This command lets you rotate in the X, Y, or Z direction. You select the object to be rotated; what it is to be rotated around, if an axis the point on the axis it is to be rotated around; and the angle of rotation. This will work either in the WCS or any UCS.

MIRROR 3D (mirror3d)

This command lets you mirror a set of objects around a 3-D plane. The plane can be defined by an existing entity, the last used plane, a viewpoint, or by you defining the plane. You select the object(s) to be mirrored, define the rotation plane, define a point on the plane if it is an axis, and then decide whether to delete the old object.

THE ROTATE 3D COMMAND

AutoCAD Command	Function	
Rotate 3D	**Rotates an object around X, Y, or Z axis.**	

Keyboard Command	Pull Down Menu Path	Icon (R13)
ROTATE3D	**R12: Modify/Rotate 3D** **R14: Modify/3D Operation/Rotate 3D**	 Modify

AutoCAD Command	Function
Mirror 3D	Mirrors an object around X, Y, or Z axis.

Keyboard Command	Pull Down Menu Path	Icon (R13)
MIRROR3D	R12: Construct/Mirror 3D R14: Modify/3D Operation/Mirror 3D	Modify

ARRAY 3D (array3d)

This command lets you create rectangular or polar arrays that can be nonparallel to the current UCS. It does not let you create an array in three directions.

THE ARRAY 3D
COMMAND

AutoCAD Command	Function
Array 3D	Creates Arrays not parallel to current UCS

Keyboard Command	Pull Down Menu Path	Icon (R13)
ARRAY3D	R12: Construct/Array 3D R14: Modify/3D Operation/Array 3D	Modify

SOLCUT (solcut) IN R12 OR SLICE (slice) IN R13 AND R14

The solcut or slice command cuts solids with a plane. The cutting plane must intersect the solid to be cut and the object to be cut must be a solid, not a thickness. First establish a plane to define the cutting line or see if there is already something in the drawing that will work as a cutting line. Then activate the solcut command. Select the solid(s) to be cut. Define the cutting plane. Then

THE SOLCUT
OR SLICE
COMMAND

AutoCAD Command	Function
R12: Solcut R13 &14: Slice	Cuts a solid.

Keyboard Command	Pull Down Menu Path	Icon (R13 & R14)
R12: SOLCUT R13 &14: SLICE	R12: Model/Modify/Cut Solids R14: Draw/Solids/Slice	Solids

THE SOLUNION OR UNION COMMAND

AutoCAD Command		Function
R12: Solunion R13 &14: Union		**Joins two solids into one.**

Keyboard Command	Pull Down Menu Path	Icon (R13 & R14)
R12: SOLUNION	**R12: Model/Union**	
R13 &14: UNION	**R14: Modify/Boolean/Union**	**Modify Modify II**

indicate which part of the cut solid is to be kept—or you may specify that you want both sides kept. This is another very useful command. In the example above of fitting a molding to the top of a flat, if you wanted to make a 45-degree cut at one end for a mitre joint, this would be the command to use.

SOLUNION (solunion) IN R12 OR UNION (union) IN R13 AND R14

The solunion or union command joins two or more separate solids—not thicknesses—into one. At the Select objects: prompt, simply specify which solids you want to join. If you have to construct something out of several separate parts, you can then join all the parts together using solunion.

   If you need to separate these parts at some later time you can do that in R12 by using the separate (solsep) command. There is no solsep command in R13 and R14. In R13 and R14, however, there are subtract and intersect commands that will subtract the area occupied by one solid from another or extract only the area where two solids intersect with one another. The explode command will work somewhat like separate, except it breaks two solids that have been unioned into their own component parts as well as apart from one another.

EXTRUDE (extrude)

The extrude command will let you add a uniform thickness to a polyline or figure that is a 2-D polyline such as a rectangle or polygon. Select the object and

THE EXTRUDE COMMAND

AutoCAD Command		Function
Extrude		**Adds a uniform thickness to a figure.**

Keyboard Command	Pull Down Menu Path	Icon (R13 & R14)
EXTRUDE	**R12: Model/Extrude**	
	R14: Draw/Solids/Extrude	**Solids**

AutoCAD Command	Function	Revolves a 2D object around
Revolve		a set of points. Acts like a lathe.

Keyboard Command	Pull Down Menu Path	Icon (R13 & R14)
REVOLVE	**R12: Model/Revolve** **R14: Draw/Solids/Revolve**	**Solids**

then indicate the thickness desired. This is another way of adding thickness to an object that you have already drawn. The important difference between extruding a shape and just adding thickness to a shape is that extruding truly turns the shape into a solid, whereas merely adding thickness does not. In R12, for example, after adding thickness, you have to solidify before you can mesh and export the shape to 3D Studio MAX. If you extrude, you do not have to solidify in R12, you just have to mesh.

REVOLVE (revolve)

Revolve takes a 2-D figure such as a rectangle, polygon, etc., rotates it around an axis line by the number of degrees specified, and then turns that entire revolution into a solid figure. In many ways this is almost the equivalent of turning something on a lathe. You could, for example, draw a vertical section of a lathe-turned banister post and then revolve that section to get the entire post. In one of the later exercises you will be doing exactly that.

HIDE (hide)

When working in 3-D, much of your drawing will be made using wireframes in addition to solid objects. Wireframe drawings can be made more realistic-looking by using the hide command. The hide command will remove from the

AutoCAD Command	Function	Masks the parts of 3D figures not
Hide		in direct sightlines.

Keyboard Command	Pull Down Menu Path	Icon (R13 & R14)
HIDE	**R12: Render/Hide** **R14: View/Hide**	**Render**

THE SUBTRACT
COMMAND

AutoCAD Command	Function	Subtracts an overlapping part of
Subtract		**one solid from another solid.**

Keyboard Command	Pull Down Menu Path	Icon (R13 & R14)
SUBTRACT	**R12: Model/Subtract**	
	R14: Modify/Boolean/Subtract	**Modify Modify II**

screen lines that should be hidden by other objects in that viewpoint. It does not actually remove these lines and it only works in the current view. If you move to another view, these lines will reappear and have to be hidden again if you desire.

SUBTRACT (subtract)

The subtract command lets you remove part of one solid by overlapping the part to be removed with another solid. It and the intersect command both work with overlapping solids. The subtract command first asks you to select the solid from which a part is to be removed. Then it asks you to select the second solid that defines what part is to be removed from the first solid. The parts of the second and the first solids that overlap then disappear. This command can be much easier to use than the sometimes difficult slice or solcut command. If you are having trouble getting slice or solcut to work properly, try using subtract.

INTERSECT (intersect)

The intersect command is similar to the subtract command in that they both work with overlapping solids. Intersect, however, saves the part of two solids that overlap and discards the rest of the two solids. The order in which the solids are selected does not matter with intersect.

THE INTERSECT
COMMAND

AutoCAD Command	Function	Leaves you with only the
Intersect		**overlapping part of two solids.**

Keyboard Command	Pull Down Menu Path	Icon (R13 & R14)
INTERSECT	**R12: Model/Intersect**	
	R14: Modify/Boolean/Intersect	**Modify Modify II**

R12 Solid Commands

The following are commands used with solids that are only available in AutoCAD R12. These commands were either outdated by changes in R13 and R14 or were deemed unnecessary. For those of you who are still running R12, however, they can be extremely useful when working with solids.

Solidify (solidify)

Solidify turns an object into a solid. Just select the object(s) to be solidified at the prompt. This command only works on polylines, a polygon, a circle, an ellipse, or a donut. If the object was not drawn with polylines you can use the pedit command to turn them into plines before applying the solidfy command to them. If you have an object that has a thickness, this command will turn it into a solid before you can use solcut, solunion, etc. on it. The pull down menu is Model/Solidify.

Chamfer Solids (solcham)

This command bevels the edge of a solid. First you pick a base surface on the solid, then pick the edge to be beveled, and then enter the dimensions of the chamfer. The pull down menu is Model/Modify/Chamfer Solids.

Fillet Solids (solfill)

This command rounds the edges of a solid. You select the edges to be filleted, and then define the size of the fillet by diameter or radius. The pull down menu is Model/Modify/Fillet Solids.

Mesh (mesh)

The mesh command covers an object with a network of lines to act as a surface. This creates a much better 3-D illusion when you are working with solids. Just type mesh, hit Enter, and click on the object to be meshed. There are also commands for varying the mesh density and 3-D mesh commands, but for theatrical purposes just the simple mesh command will usually do the job. The pull down menu is Model/Display/Mesh.

Exercise No. 19: Working with Editing Commands

1. Open file Projct19.dwg from the CD-ROM and save it as Exer19.dwg on a 3.5-inch disk.
2. First, let's work with some of the familiar 2-D editing commands:
    A. Draw a small rectangle with a thickness of 6".
    B. Establish a UCS 2 feet above the WCS. Name this UCS1.

C. Draw a short line a small distance away from the rectangle with one end pointing toward the rectangle and one end pointing away from it.

D. Get into a perspective view (vpoint) from which you can see both of these objects in 3-D.

E. Copy the rectangle so that its lower right-hand corner is at the end point of the line. Use the intersection object snap to select the lower right-hand corner of the box as its base point, and then the endpoint object snap to select the end point of the line as the second point of displacement.

F. Move the first box so that its lower right-hand corner is lined up with the lower left-hand corner of the copy. Use the intersection object snap.

G. Undo the move.

H. Use the rotate command on the box on the lower level (the WCS). Select it for rotation. Select the end point of the line as the base point. Be sure that ortho is toggled off and use your mouse to rotate the box. Notice how the object rotates relative to a point in a different UCS from its own.

I. Undo the rotation.

3. Now let's try some of the 3-D editing commands.

A. Align:

   1. Activate the align command.

   2. Prompt reads: Select Objects:. Click on the object to be moved. In this case click on the box down on the WCS—the original box that you drew.

   3. Prompt reads: Select Objects:. Click with the right mouse button or hit Enter to indicate that this is the only object to be selected.

   4. Prompt reads: 1st Source Point:. Using the intersection object snap, click on the lower right-hand corner of the box selected.

   5. Prompt reads: 1st Destination Point:. Using the intersection object snap, click on the lower left-hand corner of the other box up on UCS1.

   6. Prompt reads: 1st source point _int of 1st destination point _int of 2nd source point:. Hit Enter.

   7. The box moves up in alignment. Note that this was a simple alignment. Only one source point and one destination point were necessary. In more complex alignments you may have to specify up to three source and destination points. Think through the source and destination points carefully before you pick them, or AutoCAD will tell you that it cannot be done.

   8. Undo the alignment.

B. Rotate 3D:
1. You still should be in UCS1. Return to the plan view for the current UCS.
2. Draw a short line to the right side of and parallel to the right side of the original rectangle.
3. Get into a perspective view (vpoint) that will let you see both the box and the new line clearly in 3-D.
4. Activate the rotate3d command.
5. Prompt reads: Select Objects:. Click on the original box.
6. Prompt reads: Select Objects:. Hit Enter or click the right mouse button.
7. Prompt reads: Axis by Entity/Last/View/Xaxis/Yaxis/Zaxis/ <2 points>:. Type e for entity and hit Enter.
8. Prompt reads: Pick a line, circle, arc, or 2-D polyline segment:. Click on the line that you just drew.
9. Prompt reads: <Rotation angle>/Reference:. Type 45 for degrees counterclockwise and hit Enter.
10. Watch carefully how the box has rotated relative to the line that you chose. If you had drawn a line in the WCS instead of UCS1, think about how it would have rotated relative to it.
11. Try out some of the other options in rotate3d to see how they work.
12. When you are done, undo back to the original box down on the WCS level and the second line that you drew up on the UCS1 level, but still in the perspective view that lets you see both of them clearly (step B3 above).

C. Mirror 3D: Remember that the entity option of mirror3d only works when the object is a circle, arc, or 2-D polyline segment.
1. Turn the second line that you drew into a pline using pedit.
2. Activate the mirror3d command.
3. Prompt reads: Select Objects:. Click on the original box.
4. Prompt reads: Select Objects:. Hit Enter or click the right mouse button.
5. Prompt reads: Plane by Entity/Last/Zaxis/View/XY/YZ/ZX/<3 points>:. Type e for Entity and hit Enter.
6. Prompt reads: Pick a circle, arc or 2-D polyline segment:. Click on the pline.
7. Prompt reads: Delete old objects? <N>:. Hit Enter.
8. Notice that the box has been mirrored around the plane established by the pline in UCS1.
9. Now try some of the other options available with mirror3d.
10. When you are done, undo back to step C1 above.

D. Array 3D:
1. Activate the array3d command.
2. Prompt reads: Select Objects:. Click on the original box.
3. Prompt reads: Select Objects:. Hit Enter or click the right mouse button.
4. Prompt reads: Rectangular or Polar array (R/P):. Type p and hit Enter.
5. Prompt reads: Number of items:. Type 5 and hit Enter.
6. Prompt reads: Angle to fill <360>:. Hit Enter.
7. Prompt reads: Rotate objects as they are copied? <Y>:. Hit Enter.
8. Prompt reads: Center point of array:. Click on one end point of the pline.
9. Prompt reads: Second point on axis of rotation:. Click on the other end point of the pline.
10. Notice how the choices that you made above affect the look of the array. Try the command again using some of the other options.
11. Return to the WCS and the WCS plan view and erase all that you have done so far.

E. Solcut or slice:
1. Set your elevation to 0 and your thickness to 2' using the Entity Modes Creation box (ddemodes). **Note:** If you are working in R13 or R14, ignore this step.
2. Draw a rectangle.
3. Solidify (solidify) the rectangle if you are working in R12. If you are working in R13 or R14, extrude the rectangle to a height of 2 feet.
4. Draw a line that cuts across the rectangle at an angle; be sure that the line completely crosses the rectangle with some overlap on each side. If you are working in R13 or R14, extrude the line to a height of 2 feet.
5. Get into a viewpoint that gives you a good 3-D view of both the rectangle and the line.
6. Activate the solcut or slice command.
7. Prompt reads: Select Objects:. Click on the solid to be cut—the rectangle.
8. Prompt reads: Select Objects:. Hit Enter or click the right mouse button.
9. Prompt reads: Cutting plane by Entity/Last/Zaxis/View/XY/YZ/ZX/<3 points>:. Hit Enter to select 3 points.
10. Prompt reads: 1st point on plane:. Use the intersection object snap to click on one corner of the Line (Plane).
11. Prompt reads: 1st point on plane: _int of 2nd point on plane: Use the Intersection Object Snap to click on another corner of the line.

12. Prompt reads: 1st point on plane: _int of 2nd point on plane: _int of 3rd point on plane:. Use the intersection object snap to click on another corner of the line.

13. Prompt reads: Both sides/<Point on desired side of plane>:. Click on the side of the line that you would like to retain. AutoCAD will take a little while to work out the math of the whole thing, but shortly it will cut the solid along the line you have established and discard the side that you chose not to retain. If you would like to keep both sides of the cut, at the last prompt, type b and hit Enter. Then you can move, align, etc. both sides as you would like. Note: In some versions of AutoCAD you may have trouble getting the b option to operate.

14. Try out some of the other options available with solcut or slice.

15. When you are done, return to the WCS plan view and erase all of your work.

F. Solunion or union:

1. If you have R12, leave your elevation set at 0 and your thickness set at 2'.

2. Draw a rectangle.

3. Solidify the rectangle if you have R12. If you have R13 or R14, extrude it to a height of 2'.

4. Get into a good 3-D view of the rectangle—from the front and a little bit to the side and above.

5. Copy the rectangle so that the copy is sitting directly on top of the original rectangle. Choose your object snaps (intersection) carefully so that this happens.

6. Now we're going to turn those two solids into one by using solunion or union. Activate the solunion or union command.

7. Prompt reads: Select Objects:. Click on both boxes and hit Enter or click on the right mouse button.

8. After a short math break, AutoCAD will combine the two boxes into one.

G. Solsep: If you have R12, let's take them apart again.

1. Activate the solsep command.

2. Click on the box that you have created above with solunion.

3. AutoCAD will separate the box into two objects.

H. Revolve (revolve): You may have noticed a strange-looking object down at the bottom of the drawing space and wondered what it was. Get back into WCS plan view and then zoom down to this object for a closer look. Think of this object as a section view of half of a banister post, sort of a template for turning the post on a lathe. We're now going to use the revolve command to turn it into a whole 3-D banister post.

1. Activate the revolve command.
2. Prompt reads: Select Objects:. Click on the object.
3. Prompt reads: Select Objects:. Hit Enter or click on the right mouse button.
4. Prompt reads: Axis of revolution - Entity/X/Y/<Start point of axis>:. Using the Intersection object snap, click on the intersection at the top of the object where the two straight lines meet.
5. Prompt reads: Axis of revolution - Entity/X/Y/<Start point of axis>: _int End point of axis:. Using the intersection object snap, click on the intersection at the bottom of the object where the two straight lines meet.
6. Prompt reads: Angle of revolution - <full circle>:. Hit Enter or click with the right mouse button.
7. Voila! You now have a banister post. Before you start playing around with creating things on your own with revolve, however, I'd like to use this post to demonstrate a couple of other commands in AutoCAD.
8. Get into a 3-D view of the post that shows it in a better perspective—a front view slightly to the side and above. Zoom down for a closer look.
9. If you have R12, type mesh and hit Enter. If not, skip to step 13.
10. Prompt reads: Select Objects:. Click on the banister post.
11. Prompt reads: Select Objects:. Hit Enter or click the right mouse button.
12. You now have a very different look to the post. You have just meshed it, which creates a network of lines on the 3-D surface. This will be a very important command when you start exporting objects out of AutoCAD R12 into 3D Studio MAX.
13. Now type hide and hit Enter.
14. This is again a very different look. The hide command makes the lines that would be hidden from view in a solid object disappear. This will only work as long as you stay in this view, however. If you go into a different view or zoom or pan, you will have to hide again. You will also find that many objects will need to be meshed before they can be hidden in R12.
15. Try creating an object and revolving it around itself or a line somewhere else in the drawing. Before you do this, however, check to be sure that the thickness command is set to 0. Use your drawing commands like line, arc, etc. to draw a section of half of an object. When you are finished drawing it you need to turn the whole thing into a polyline. Use the pedit command to do this. Then revolve it around either part of itself like you just did with

the banister post or draw another line to revolve it around. I had you revolve it around itself to create a solid post. If you revolve it around another line you will get a hollow object. You could also revolve it around part of itself to create a dish-shaped object. Use your imagination, but keep the geometry of the object and what you are doing in mind.

I. Subtract
1. Return to the WCS plan view if you are not there.
2. Use the polygon command to draw a hexagon about 2 feet wide.
3. Extrude it to a height of 1 foot.
4. Choose the Cylinder option under Solids to create a cylinder in the middle of the hexagon. It should have a radius of 3 inches and a height of 2 feet.
5. Get into a perspective view that will let you see both of the figures that you have drawn in 3-D. Slightly above and to the side would work well.
6. Activate the subtract command.
    a. Prompt reads: Select solids and regions to subtract from . . . Select objects:. Click on the hexagon.
    b. Prompt reads: Select solids and regions to subtract from . . . Select objects: 1 found . . . Select objects:. Hit Enter or click on the right mouse button.
    c. Prompt reads: Select solids and regions to subtract . . . Select objects:. Click on the cylinder.
    d. Prompt reads: Select objects:. Hit Enter or click on the right mouse button.
    e. You have just subtracted the cylinder from the hexagon, creating a hexagon with a hole in the middle.

J. Intersect
1. Undo the subtract command.
2. Activate the intersect command.
    a. Prompt reads: Select objects:. Click on the hexagon.
    b. Prompt reads: Select objects:. Click on the cylinder.
    c. Prompt reads: Select objects:. Hit Enter or click the right mouse button.
    d. The only thing left is the area where both the cylinder and the hexagon intersected.

The next two commands are for R12 only:

K. Chamfer Solids (solcham): Erase enough of what you have done so that you have got some working space at the top of the drawing.

Go back into the WCS plan view. Draw a rectangle. Give the rectangle a thickness of 2 feet. Solidify the rectangle. Go into a good 3-D view of the rectangle from the front and slightly to the side and above. Zoom in for a closer look at the box.

1. Activate the **solcham** command.
2. Prompt reads: **Pick base surface:**. Click on the surface—face of the solid—where the chamfer(s) will be. This can sometimes get a little tricky, as you have to click on a line between two surfaces and you are not always sure which of the two surfaces AutoCAD will decide that you want. However, you do get a chance to tell it if it picked the wrong one later in the command.
3. Prompt reads: **Next <OK>:**. This is AutoCAD's way of asking you if it's got the right surface—the selected surface will be indicated on the screen in dotted lines. If this is the surface that you want just hit **Enter** or click the right mouse button. If it isn't the one that you want, type **N** and hit **Enter**.
4. Prompt reads: **Pick edges of this face to be Chamfered (press Enter when done):**. Click on the edges on which you would like to create a chamfer and then hit **Enter** or click the right mouse button.
5. Prompt reads: **Enter distance along base surface: <0>:**. Type **6"** and hit **Enter**.
6. Prompt reads: **Enter distance along adjacent surface: <0>:**. Type **4"** and hit **Enter**. I'm giving you different figures here so that you can see the difference between the base surface and the adjacent surface distances in the end chamfer.
7. Give it a second or two, and AutoCAD will create your chamfer.
8. Now I'll show you why you usually need to mesh before you hide. Type **hide** and hit **Enter**.
9. As you can see, nothing happened. Now **mesh** the box you just chamfered and then type **hide** again.
10. **Undo** the chamfer you just did. You will have to go several steps back past the hide and mesh commands until you are back at just the box, but still in the 3-D view.

L. Fillet Solids (solfill):
1. Activate the **solfill** command.
2. Prompt reads: **Pick edges of solids to be filleted (press Enter when done):**. Click on the edges where you would like a fillet to occur and then hit **Enter** or click the right mouse button. Because a fillet takes the same amount from both sides of an edge, you don't have to specify a base surface and an adjacent one like you do with chamfer.

3. Prompt reads: Diameter/<Radius> of fillet<0.00>:. Type **6"** and hit **Enter**. This determines the radius of the fillet. You can also pick a diameter instead by hitting **d**, **Enter**, and a figure for the diameter.
4. Wait for the AutoCAD math to catch up and it will display your fillet. Try meshing and hiding the box.

Exercise No. 20: Putting It All Together

By now it should be easy to see how all of these AutoCAD commands can be put together to create a drafting for a technical drawing or a lighting plot; however, it may still be somewhat puzzling how a set designer can fully assemble a 3-D drawing of a set and how that might be more useful than just doing it the old-fashioned way.

The critical thing to remember in that regard is that first, a set is built out of pieces exactly the way that items in AutoCAD are drawn. So the "flat" in an AutoCAD 3-D "model" can quickly be pulled out and used as the basis for the drawings that will need to be done for the shop either by the set designer or the technical director. If the set designer has been precise in creating the pieces and fitting them together, then most of the measurements and calculations will already be done. Secondly, the 3-D perspective views of AutoCAD can be printed out from a variety of different viewpoints to go over details with the director, and any changes that come out of the early design meetings can be made much faster in AutoCAD than by hand. These views can become your "thumbnail sketches" and can quickly have changes incorporated into them. From the same basic "3-D model," you can also derive the ground plan and import it into a drawing of the theatre that already exists. The lighting designer will have not just a ground plan and section to work from, but also a model with all of the heights for calculating lighting angles, etc. As well as serving as the basis for the technical drawings, the "3-D model" in AutoCAD can also be exported to 3D Studio MAX and/or Painter and serve as the beginning of as stylized or photo-realistic a rendering as you would like. Once the process is mastered by all of the participants, everyone's work speeds up and the inevitable changes involved in the theatrical production process become easier. The details of how the work is done and used in any theatrical situation will vary from theatre to theatre and will have to be worked out to the needs of any particular production team. I won't attempt to kid you that you will be doing this overnight. AutoCAD is a demanding program and it takes time to learn to use it well, but in the long run it can be time well invested.

For this final AutoCAD exercise, I'll attempt to guide you through the construction of a simple 3-D model of a box set. It will be greatly simplified but should help you to begin honing some of the skills that you have already acquired and serve as a guide to more sophisticated work hopefully yet to come. You'll start with detailed instructions and then taper off to more general instructions after I think that you should have picked up the concept. Throughout, I'll be trying to give you tips about trouble spots and how to do things easier. You will find as you progress in AutoCAD that there are usually about two to three different ways to do almost anything—the trick to using the program well is to find the ones that work best for you. You do not have to attempt this exercise all in one sitting. At any time in the middle of the exercise you can save what you have done up to that point as the file **Exer20.dwg** and then open it again and continue later. Depending upon the skill level that you have managed to develop with AutoCAD, this project could take you from four to eight hours to complete.

1. Start in the AutoCAD opening screen this time and create a drawing space with limits of (X,Y) 50',30'.
   A. Create a layer called Centerline, make its linetype Center, color Blue.
   B. Create a layer called Hidden, make its linetype Hidden2, and its color Green.
   C. Create a layer called Set, with a linetype Continuous, and a color of White, which is really black in some versions if you've changed the color of the background and crosshairs to a lighter background with darker crosshairs.
   D. Create a layer called Theatre with a linetype of Continuous and a color of Grey.
   E. Create a layer called Plaster for the plaster line with a linetype of Hidden2 and a color of Red.

   That should be enough to get you started. When you are working in 3-D you should, however, get into the habit of creating lots of layers and of labeling all of them clearly so that you can identify what is in that layer. When you start importing elements of the set into 3D Studio MAX each element that has a different texture or color will have to be imported separately.

2. Set ltscale to 12 if you are going to want to print out in 1/2 inch = 1 foot scale or 24 if you'll be printing in 1/4 inch = 1 foot scale. Go ahead and set your dimscale to the same figure.

3. Draw and label a center line down the middle of the space using the Centerline layer.

4. Down near the bottom of the screen—3 to 4 feet up from the bottom of the limits—draw a plaster line using the Plaster layer. *Hint:* Both of these lines will be easier to draw if ortho is toggled on. Just like you use the center line and the plaster line in a theatre to keep track of where

something is located and to take measurements, these two lines can help you in your drawing. You can offset from them to easily find locations and use the inquiry commands to determine measurements.

5. Next let's set up multiple viewports so that the 3-D work that you're about to do will be easier.

   A. Set Tilemode to 1.

   B. Use vports to set up four viewports that fit the space.

   C. Then use vports to save this view as View4.
      1. Leave the view in the top left viewport as a top view.
      2. Change the view in the top right viewport to a front view. *Hint:* Click in that viewport to activate it. Type vpoint and then enter a value of 0,-1,0.
      3. Change the view in the bottom left viewport to a left view.
      4. Change the view in the bottom right viewport to a right view.

   D. To work in each of the viewports you will have to activate that viewport and then use the UCS/View command to set your UCS to the view in that viewport.

   E. Now you can also use the vports command to move between a single viewport and View4, which you have saved. The single viewport can be very useful when you are working on detail and need a larger view than you can get in one of the smaller viewports. Unfortunately, every time that you go to the single viewport, you will have to reset the views and UCSs of View4.

6. Work in the top left viewport (the WCS viewport). If you are not in the WCS and plan view get into it now. There should be the regular X,Y double arrow icon in the lower left corner of this viewport. The other three viewports all have the broken pencil icon in them. Let's get set up to make a proscenium arch with an opening of 40 feet.

   A. Make the Theatre layer active.

   B. Offset the center line 20 feet S.L. and 20 feet S.R.

   C. Offset each of these 6 feet more offstage.

   D. Offset the plaster line 1 foot D.S. You now have a rectangle on each side of the proscenium arch that you can use to make the upright sections of the arch.

   E. Use the box (Solid) command to make two boxes that are the size of each of these rectangles and 20 feet high. *Hint:* Use the intersection object snap to snap to each corner of the rectangle and then give it a height of 20 feet.

   F. Next make the top of the proscenium arch. Again use the box command to make one box that has the D.S.R. corner of the S.R. upright as one corner and the U.S.L. corner of the S.L. upright as the other corner. Give it a height of 4 feet.

G. You have just created the top of the proscenium, but it is down at ground level, not up on top of the uprights. Go to the Front viewport and activate it.

H. Use UCS/View to make its UCS current.

I. Move the top of the proscenium arch into position.

J. Union the three parts of the proscenium into one piece.

K. Go back to the top viewport, activate it, and make its UCS current.

L. Erase the offsets that you used to construct the proscenium arch.

7. Save the drawing that you have already begun as Exer20.dwg and open up the drawing Projct20.dwg from the CD-ROM. This is the set that you will be drawing. It should open in a perspective view, but it is a full drawing and you can move around in viewing it as you could any other drawing. It already has some views set up that you might want to check out. It would be helpful to go ahead and print out a plan view and a perspective view just so that you have an idea of how the pieces all fit together.

8. Next you'll draw in some basic flats for the walls of the room. Work in the upper left viewport and the WCS.

A. Turn the Theatre layer off.

B. Get ready to draw in the Hidden layer.

C. To start the S.R. wall, draw a line from 20 feet 6 inches S.R. of center line, 18 inches U.S. of plaster line to a point 10 feet S.R., 15 feet U.S.

D. Draw another line from 10 feet S.R., 15 feet U.S. to 16 feet S.L., 10 feet U.S.

E. Draw another line from 16 feet S.L., 10 feet U.S. to 20 feet 6 inches S.L., 18 inches U.S.

F. Offset each of these lines 1 inch offstage or upstage. You can now use the end points of each of these sets of double lines to define the corners of three "flats."

G. Get into the Set layer.

H. This time instead of using the box command you'll use the pline command and extrude a closed pline into a solid.

1. Start the pline at one end point of a double line.

2. Then snap to the end point of the line 1 inch away.

3. Then snap to the end point of the other end of that line.

4. Then snap to the end point of the line 1 inch away.

5. Then close the pline. It is very important that the pline be closed. Otherwise, it cannot be extruded.

I. Repeat this with the other two sets of double lines.

J. Turn off the Set layer.

K. Erase the hidden lines that you used to define the location of the plines that you just drew.

L. Turn the Set layer back on.

M. Use the extrude command to give each of the closed plines that you just drew a height of 12 feet. You now have the three basic flats for the set.

9. Next you're going to cut three doors, an arch, and a window into the flats. First you'll define the shape that is to be cut out and then use either the subtract or solcut command to make the cutout.

A. Use the box command to make a solid box that is 3 feet × 3 feet × 7.5 feet (length × width × height).

B. Make two copies of it. These will be used to form the three doors.

C. Make another box that will form the window: 4 feet × 4 feet × 5.5 feet.

D. Make another box for the lower part of the arch: 6 feet × 6 feet × 6 feet. You'll form the upper part of the arch later.

10. Next you need to move the boxes into position and rotate them so that they are parallel to the wall from which they are going to be subtracted. Their final position will be sticking through the wall so that the subtract command can work.

A. First use the dimension angular command for each wall so that you will know how many degrees to rotate the boxes.

B. There will be two doors in the S.R. wall. The arch and the window will be in the U.S. wall. There will be one door in the S.L. wall.

C. Rotate all of the boxes so that they are parallel to their respective walls.

D. Then move them into position.

1. On the S.R. wall, one door starts at a point 3.5 feet U.S. of the D.S. end of the flat. The second door starts at a point 10.5 feet U.S. of the D.S. end of the flat.

2. On the U.S. wall, the arch starts 2 feet S.L. of the S.R. end of the flat. The window starts at a point 16 feet S.L. of the S.R. end of the flat.

3. On the S.L. wall, the door starts 2 feet D.S. of the U.S. end of the flat.

E. After the boxes for the doors and the arch have all been moved into position, go ahead and use the subtract command to remove the part of the flats for all of the doorways. Before you can remove the part of the flat that forms the window, however, you need to move it into a position 2 feet above the floor. This may need to wait until you have a UCS established for the U.S. flat. Try moving the window box up using the front viewport. If that works, go ahead and subtract its space from the U.S. flat. If it doesn't work, then wait.

F. After you have subtracted the spaces for the doors, etc. from the three flats you will need to mesh them if you are using AutoCAD R12. If you are using R13 or R14 you do not need to do this. Remember that in R12 any solid, extrusion, etc. must be meshed before the hide command will work. It also must be meshed before it can be exported to 3D Studio MAX.

11. Before you can start adding the baseboards, door frames, crown molding, etc., you will need to establish viewpoints and UCSs that are perpendicular to the face of the three flats. You will also need the ones for the U.S. flat to finish the arch. To make this easier, turn off the Theatre layer.

A. First let's make three new layers:
  1. a layer named SRFLAT, linetype Continuous, color Black
  2. a layer named SLFLAT, linetype Continuous, color Black
  3. a layer named USFLAT, linetype Continuous, color Black

B. Use the ddmodify command to change the layer of each of the flats that you have drawn.

C. Next get into a viewpoint that lets you see the S.R. flat from a view as close to perpendicular to its front face as possible. The Viewpoint/ Globe and Axes or Tripod method is a good way to do this.
  1. Once you are in a view close to perpendicular to the face of the S.R. flat you can then establish a UCS that is parallel to the face of the S.R. flat by using the UCS/3point command.
  2. Save this UCS as SRFLAT.
  3. Then get into a plan view for that UCS. Save the view as SRFLAT.

D. Repeat the operation with the U.S. flat and the S.L. flat so that you have UCSs named USFLAT and SLFLAT and views named USFLAT and SLFLAT. *Hint:* If you are having trouble establishing a UCS for the U.S. flat, try turning off the layers for the other two flats so that you are dealing with it all by itself. It is very important that you establish these UCSs and their corresponding views accurately or you will have a great deal of trouble drawing the door frames, molding, etc.

12. If you weren't able to move the window box up 2 feet earlier, do that now:

A. Get into the USFLAT UCS and view.

B. Move the window box up 2 feet.

C. Subtract the window box from the U.S. flat.

13. Next you are going to finish off the arch in the U.S. flat.

  A. Go into the **USFLAT** UCS and view. If you are not in the **Set** layer, get into it now.

  B. Zoom in on the top of the doorway that you cut earlier with the 6-foot box. You need to be able to see both ends of the top line of the doorway. You are going to construct an elliptical cylinder to subtract from the top of the arch.

  C. Activate the **Cylinder** command.

   1. Type **e** for **Elliptical** and hit **Enter**.
   2. Use the **endpoint** object snap to establish one end of the top line of the doorway as one **Axis Endpoint**.
   3. Use the **endpoint** object snap to establish the other end of the top line of the doorway as the other **Axis Endpoint**.
   4. At the **Other axis distance:** prompt, type 1.5' and hit **Enter**.
   5. Give it a height of -2'.

  D. Examine the cylinder that you have created carefully from several different viewpoints. Make sure that it is properly lined up to subtract out the part of the flat that you want. It is very easy when working in 3-D to accidentally snap to the wrong end point and get the cylinder on the wrong side of the flat. When you are sure that you have the cylinder lined up properly, use the **subtract** command to remove the part of the flat that creates the arch over the doorway.

14. Now you are ready to start applying the thickeners and molding around the doorways and windows.

  A. Start with the S.R. flat. Go into the **SRFLAT** UCS and view. You will first make thickeners for inside the doorway.

  B. Set your elevation to -6" and thickness to 6".

  C. Create a new layer named **SRTHICK**, linetype **Continuous** color **Black**, and go into it.

  D. Activate the **pline** command. This time you are going to do a closed pline with thickness applied. Then you will **solidify** and **mesh** the closed pline.

   1. Start the pline at the lower left-hand corner of one of the door openings. **Note:** If you **snap** to an intersection here, it will override the **elev** command.
   2. At the next prompt, Arc/Close/Halfwidth/Length/Undo/Width/ <Endpoint of line>:, type in the polar coordinates @.75"<0 and hit **Enter**.
   3. Then go to a point @7.5'<90.
   4. Then go to a point @.75"<180.

5. Then enter a **c** for close. That completes a thickener along the left-hand side of that doorway.

E. Go ahead and put in thickeners all the way around the inside of the opening of both of the doors on the S.R wall. Remember the format for giving polar coordinates: 0 is to the right, 90 is up, 180 is to the left, and 270 is down. Make sure that the last command always closes the pline.

F. *Hint:* After you have finished the thickeners for one doorway you can **copy** them over to the other and save time. You could also **copy** it again and then **move** it over to the S.L. flat and **rotate** it into position there.

G. After you have finished the thickeners for the S.R. doorways go to the **USFLAT** UCS and view. Create a new layer called **USTHICK**, linetype **Continuous** color **Black**. With the same elevation and thickness settings, make thickeners all the way around the window opening. Then create thickeners for the edges of the arch from the floor up to 6 feet high where the actual arch starts.

H. And finally, still with the same elevation and thickness settings, make the thickeners for the S.L. doorway if you didn't copy and rotate for it. Create a new layer called **SLTHICK**, linetype **Continuous**, color **Black**. Use this layer for the S.L. thickener. If you are working in R12, go back and **solidify** all of the thickeners and **mesh** them.

I. Check all of your thickeners from a WCS plan view.

15. Next comes the trickiest thickener: the top of the arch. There are a variety of ways that this curved thickener could be done. This section will talk you through one method that may be suggestive of other uses for itself as well.

A. Open **USFLAT** view, UCS, and layer.

B. Reset elevation and thickness to 0.

C. Remember the **cylinder** command that you used to cut the arch in the flat originally? From this view and UCS, redo that **cylinder** command with the same **Elliptical** option and values as before, except make the height -6".

D. Next make another cylinder that fits precisely inside the cylinder that you just made, but is .75 inches smaller all around.

E. Use the smaller cylinder to **subtract** from the larger cylinder. This gives you an elliptical-shaped oval, the top half of which fits the arch perfectly.

F. Draw a solid line that divides the cylinder in half, or draw a box that covers the bottom of the cylinder. Either of these must be of the same or greater thickness as the cylinder.

G. Use the solid line to solcut/slice, or the box to subtract the bottom half of the cylinder.

H. There is your arch thickener. If you are working in R12, be sure to solidify and mesh it.

Note: This is your last warning about solidify and mesh in R12. Remember that anything that you create in R12 that is 3-D must be meshed, or the hide command will not work and you will not be able to export it properly to 3D Studio MAX. If it was created using thickness rather than being extruded it must be solidified before it can be meshed.

16. It's time now to do the door-frame and window-frame molding. This is going to be plain and simple molding. Later, when you do the crown molding you'll see how to do more elaborate work.
    A. Create three new layers:
       1. USMOLD: linetype Continuous, color Black.
       2. SRMOLD: linetype Continuous, color Black.
       3. SLMOLD: linetype Continuous, color Black.
    B. Stay in the USFLAT view and UCS and get to a close-up view of the window. You'll do the molding for it first.
    C. Go into layer USMOLD.
    D. Activate the pline command. Build the window molding by drawing rectangles with pline and then extruding them to a height of .75", except for the windowsill, which you will extrude to a height of 4".
    E. Give all of your door-frame and window molding a width of 5".
    F. Use the MOLD layers for the molding.
    G. Make the molding around all the doorways in the same manner. Do not do molding around the arch. If you have any questions, refer to the drawing Projct20.dwg on the CD-ROM.

17. Next do your baseboards.
    A. Creat three new layers for them:
       1. USBASE: linetype Continuous, color Black.
       2. SRBASE: linetype Continuous, color Black.
       3. SLBASE: linetype Continuous, color Black.
    B. Make them 5 feet wide like the window and door-frame molding.
    C. Work from the SRFLAT, SLFLAT, and USFLAT UCSs and views.
    D. Use the pline command with polar coordinates and then extrude them to a height of .75 inches.
    E. *Hint:* This would also be a very good place to practice transparent commands.

18. Build the window itself. Make the bottom half using closed plines, and then copy it to the top half.
    A. Then get into the USFLAT UCS and view.
    B. Create a new layer—USWINDOW—and get into it.
    C. Set an elevation that will recess it back 3 inches into the thickener.
    D. When you have the whole window completed, union it into one piece.
    E. Be sure to reset the elevation when you are done.

19. Next let's make some doors.
    A. Create two new layers for them:
       1. SRDOOR: linetype Continuous, color Black
       2. SLDOOR: linetype Continuous, color Black
    B. Start in the SRFLAT UCS and view.
    C. Open the SRDOOR layer.
    D. Set your elevation to recess the door about 3 inches.
    E. Then draw a full-size, plain door that is just a little bit smaller than the opening, using a closed pline.
    F. Extrude it to 1 inch thick.
    G. Reset your elevation to 1 inch less recessed than before and then draw and extrude the panels on top of the plain door.
    H. When you are done with the door, you might want to union it and then rotate it open slightly. Repeat the operation on all of the other doors or copy the first one and move it into the other locations.
    I. Be sure that each door is in the proper layer.
    J. Reset your elevation and thickness to 0 when done.

20. Next, we are going to make the crown molding for the top of the flats. You'll make the first piece and extrude it in place, then make copies of that molding and move it into place with the align command.
    A. Create three new layers for it:
       1. USCROWN: linetype Continuous, color Black
       2. SRCROWN: linetype Continuous, color Black
       3. SLCROWN: linetype Continuous, color Black
    B. Set up a UCS that is perpendicular to the D.S. end of the S.R. flat.
       1. Name the UCS SRMOLD.
       2. Then get into a plan view for that UCS.
       3. Name that view SRMOLD.
    C. You want to get into a view and UCS that is aligned with the end of the flat and then use a closed pline to draw a section of some crown molding right at the D.S. end of the flat and extrude it -30'.

1. Draw a section of crown molding that will work with the set. I did one that was about 6 inches high and 3 inches wide in section. You can use the **arc** as well as the **line** methods of the **pline** command to do this. Play around with pline and create an interesting crown molding.

2. **Extrude** a length that is long enough for not just this flat, but also for the U.S. flat as well (-30').

D. After you have extruded it, make two **copies** of it, one for the U.S. flat and one for the S.L. flat.

E. Then you can **solcut**, **slice**, or **subtract** to create a mitre joint at the corner where the S.R. and U.S. flats meet. *Hint:* Make a copy of the positioned object that you are using to make the mitre cut before making the cut on the S.R. crown molding. This copy will then already have the angle of the mitre cut and can be used to make the mitre cut on the U.S. crown molding. **Rotate** and **move** one of the copies that you made of the crown molding into a position close to where you want it on the U.S. flat. Then use **align** to get it into the final position. Make your mitre cuts at both ends of the U.S. crown molding and then position and cut the S.L. crown molding.

21. Next you should build the greenhouse outside of the arch. If you look at it closely you will see that it is constructed mostly of identical 12-foot-high by 3-foot-wide sections. The exception is the door module, which is still 12 feet high by 3 feet wide but is not identical to the other greenhouse units. Here is how I would recommend going about building the greenhouse:

A. Create a new layer named **Green**, linetype **Continuous**, color **Black**.

B. Check to make sure that your elevation and thickness are set to **0**.

C. Get into the **USFLAT** UCS and view.

D. Turn off the layers **USFLAT, USMOLD, USBASE, USCROWN, Theatre** and any others that might obstruct your view.

E. Do layout for the greenhouse modules in the **Hidden** layer. Then draw over the top of the layout in the **Green** layer.

F. Draw one of the wall units for the greenhouse using **pline** and **extrude**.

G. After you have the entire unit drawn:
   1. Turn off the **Green** layer.
   2. Erase the layout lines in the **Hidden** layer.
   3. Turn on the **Green** layer.

4. Then union the unit into one piece and copy it twice to complete all of the wall units for the U.S. greenhouse wall.

H. Build the one door unit that you need, using pline and extrude. Union it together as two pieces. The door should be one piece and the rest of the unit another.

I. Get into the WCS and plan view. Copy one of the U.S. wall units and rotate it 90 degrees.

J. Copy it three more times. Two of these will form the S.R. wall of the greenhouse and two will form the S.L. wall of the greenhouse.

K. Turn on the layers that you have turned off.

L. Move the pieces of the greenhouse into position.

22. Next, you are going to draw the borders over the top of the set.

A. Create a new layer named Border, linetype Continuous, color Black.

B. Work in the plan view, WCS, and the Border layer.

C. Set your elevation to 13' and thickness to 10'.

D. Offset the plaster line 6 feet and 12 feet U.S. These are the positions for the borders.

E. Turn off any layers that will interfere.

F. It would be a good idea to go into the Plaster layer and create some marks to guide you for creating the arcs of the borders.

   1. Draw a line perpendicular to the offset plaster line at its end and then offset it all the way across the stage in 2-foot increments.

   2. Offset the border line upstage and downstage by a set amount— 6 inches.

G. Go into the layer Border.

H. Now you can use the arc command to create the borders. *Hint:* Use the lines that you just set up as visual guides, but do not snap to them. If you do, that snap will override the elevation and your borders will end up on the stage floor instead of 13 feet up in the air.

I. When done, erase all the guide lines that you created.

J. You might also want to use pedit to turn all of the arc segments into one big long pline or if you have R13 or R14 you could combine all of them into a group.

23. Use the View/Set View/Viewpoint/Axes or View/Tripod command to get back into a good perspective view of the set and do a hide to see how it all looks. If you are working in R12, you may find that you have forgotten to do some of your solidify and mesh commands.

Exporting the Drawing—Working with Files and Views from AutoCAD in Other Programs

One of the big advantages of working with computers is that many of the files from one program can be used directly in other programs as well. Even if the files may not be directly compatible they still may be usable in another form. As you have already seen you can use AutoCAD to construct perspective views of scenery that you have drawn. These perspective views can form the basis for a rendering in Painter. They can easily serve as the "sketch" underneath the rendering, thus saving you layout time. In 3D Studio MAX you can—and should—directly import files from AutoCAD and use them as the foundation underneath the 3-D rendering work that can be done in that program.

Sometimes it can be difficult to use files from one program in another if they're not directly compatible. Files created in one program may not be directly usable in another, but you may be able to go through a transition program that converts the first file type to a different file type that is usable in the second program. All of the different file types that exist can in themselves get quite confusing. In this section I will cover the different ways that AutoCAD files can be used in 3D Studio MAX and Painter, the two "rendering" programs covered in the companion volume to this book.

Exporting for Use in 3D Studio MAX

3D Studio MAX was designed by AutoDesk to directly use AutoCAD for the construction of objects. The quickest way to work in 3D Studio MAX is to first construct all of the parts of the set in AutoCAD. Because of the way that 3D Studio MAX adds textures to objects, it is necessary to construct each of the imported objects separately. Any part of the set that is going to have a different texture must be a separate file. In the case of a typical box set, for example, the walls to which wallpaper or paint would be applied would be one file, the woodwork—baseboards, molding, etc.—would each be a separate file, the cyc would be another file, and so on. Anything that is going to have a different texture, color, etc. on it has to be a separate file.

This is really not as hard as it may at first sound, because once you have gotten the entire set constructed in one file in AutoCAD, it is easy to pick out any element of it that you would like and wBlock it into a different file. Once the block is created, if you are careful to *not* save the changes to the original file, then nothing will be lost from it. So it is a simple matter to take the single AutoCAD file and create as many smaller files from it as you need. These smaller files are then brought into 3D Studio MAX one at a time and texture, color, etc. is added to them as you desire to create the look that you want.

It will be easier to understand precisely how this is done when you read the 3D Studio MAX section of the second volume. The procedure for saving and exporting the files from AutoCAD is as follows:

1. When you have finished your 3-D drawing in AutoCAD think about how you are going to be applying texture and color to each of the pieces. Say, for example, that you have a bench that will have brass legs and wooden slats for a seat. They need to be imported into 3D Studio MAX separately and have a brass texture and color applied to the legs while a wooden texture and color is applied to the slats that form the seat.

2. You will need to use the **wblock** command for each item that you pick out of the AutoCAD drawing so that it will be saved as a file separate from the main file for the drawing. If you use the **block** command instead it is only saved to the original drawing and won't be available for export. There are four things to keep in mind when using the **wblock** command:

    -   First, give the file a name that tells you what is in it, for example, bnchseat.dwg and bnchlegs.dwg.

    -   Second, be sure that you remember where you saved the file—did you save it in a directory in the hard drive or did you put it on a floppy disk? I strongly recommend saving the files to a directory in your hard drive that has the name of the show on it so that it can be easily found *and* backing them up on a 3.5-inch disk.

    -   Third, after you have created the new file by using **wblock**, as you exit the main drawing that you were working from, AutoCAD will ask you whether you want to save the changes to the file or discard them. Ordinarily you want to save any changes that you make to a file so that they will not be lost. This is the major exception to that rule. The changes to this file consist of creating the block. That means that something was taken out of the file to create another one. *Do not save this change!* If you save this change, everything that you used to create the block will be gone from the main file.

    -   Fourth, when you create the block and are prompted for the insertion point, use the origin (0,0,0). This way, as each part of the overall set is imported into 3D Studio MAX, it will already be in the correct location, elevation, and orientation. You won't have to spend as much time moving things around.

3. When you have created all of your blocks by using the **wblock** command, you will have a number of new files with names like bnchseat.dwg, bnchlegs.dwg, etc. These files have to undergo one further change to be readily usable in 3D Studio MAX. All of these files will have to be **exported** from AutoCAD as **.dxf** files if you are using R12 or R13. Sometimes you can

use a .dwg file directly in 3D Studio MAX, but sometimes you cannot. It is safer to export all the files that you will be using as .dxf files. If you are working in R14, you will be able to export the file as either a .dxf or a .3ds file.

EXPORTING A FILE FROM AUTOCAD R12

The export a file from R12:

1. Open the file to be exported in AutoCAD.
2. If you have not already meshed all objects that you are going to be exporting, do so now.
3. Click on File, then on Import/Export, then on DXF Out.
4. The Create DXF File box will open. This looks almost identical to the Save and Save As boxes with which you are already familiar. Check these points in the Create DXF File box:
   A. Is the name of the file under File Name: correct and does it have a .dxf extension on the end of it?
   B. Under List Files of Type:, is *.DXF selected?
   C. Under Drives:, is the proper drive selected—c: for the hard drive, a: for the floppy drive?
   D. Under Directories: is the proper directory or folder selected?
   When all of this is correct, click on OK.
5. Prompt reads: Enter decimal places of accuracy (0 to 16)/Entities/Binary <6>:. Hit Enter. If you were doing an engineering drawing in which it were necessary to be accurate to hundredths of a milimeter, this would be something to be concerned about. For theatrical drawings the default selection <6> works just fine.
6. That's it. You now have a .dxf file of the name you selected in the drive and directory or folder that you selected or on a 3.5-inch disk if that is what you chose. This file is ready to be brought directly into 3D Studio MAX.

EXPORTING A FILE FROM AUTOCAD R13 OR R14

To export a file from R13 or R14:

1. Open the file to be exported in AutoCAD.
2. Click on File, then on Export.
3. The Export Data box will open.
   A. Give the file a name in the File Name window.
   B. In the List Files of Type or Save as Type window, select .dxf in R13 or .3ds in R14.

C. In the **Save In** or **Drives and Directories** window, select the drive and folder where you want to save the file.

D. Click on **Save** or **OK**.

4. If you have saved as a .dxf file, prompt reads: **Enter decimal places of accuracy (0 to 16)/Entities/Binary <6>:**. Hit **Enter**. If you were doing an engineering drawing in which it were necessary to be accurate to hundredths of a milimeter, this would be something to be concerned about. For theatrical drawings the default selection <6> works just fine.

5. That's it. You now have a .dxf or .3ds file of the name you selected in the drive and directory or folder that you selected or on a 3.5-inch disk if that is what you chose. This file is ready to be brought directly into 3D Studio MAX.

Exporting for Use in Painter

You can bring saved views of AutoCAD files directly into Painter in much the same way that you can bring them into 3D Studio MAX. In 3D Studio MAX you are importing a 3-D image that you are working with in the program to create a 3-D representation of a set that can be viewed from any angle. In Painter you are working, in effect, on a canvas. What most designers would usually like to bring in from AutoCAD is a perspective view of the set that can be used as the "sketch" underneath the rendering. This is easy to do. You could also bring into Painter any part of the set to do a painter's elevation, prop rendering, etc. By the time the rendering is finished the "sketch" from AutoCAD may have been completely covered, but it will have helped with the layout, proportions, perspective, etc. One of the nice features of Painter, which is covered in the Painter section of the second volume, is that you can bring in a "sketch," lay a piece of "tracing paper" over the top of it, work on the "tracing paper," and when you are done, even the lines from the "sketch" are no longer a part of the rendering. This lets you get as stylized as you want with the rendering without having to worry about all those geometrically straight lines showing through.

Set designers can make use of AutoCAD in combination with Painter in yet another manner, namely the construction of scenic models. If you or your director likes to work in models, AutoCAD and Painter together can greatly speed the process of layout and construction of these models. "Elevations" of the flats, platforms, and model pieces can be created to perfect scale using AutoCAD. These can be printed out and used as templates for the model construction. They can also be exported to Painter and used as the basis for "painter's elevations" that are done in that program. When these are printed out, they can then be attached to the model pieces to create highly detailed "painting" on the model. There are a several methods that you can use to get your work from AutoCAD into Painter.

1. Get into the perspective view of the set or part of it that you want using AutoCAD.

2. Use the Print/Plot command to print out that view. Use the scale portion of this command to control the size of the print. It can be printed directly in a particular scale that you may want to use in the rendering, or by selecting the Scaled to Fit option you can have it fill the size of paper that you have selected under Paper Size.

3. Take the printout from AutoCAD to a scanner and scan it into a file. From the scanner you will be able to save it to a disk or to your hard drive. It is important here to be sure that it is saved as a file type that Painter can use. After it has been scanned in, almost all scanners will let you save the image as a variety of file types. Read the instructions for your particular scanner carefully to find out how to do this. Different file types will give you different image qualities and different file sizes. Here is some information on what to expect from the different file types. The number in parentheses after the name of the file type gives the size in kilobytes of a typical 8.5-inch × 11-inch file at 72 pixels/inch for that format. For Painter you will need to save your scan as one of the following file types:

    1. RIFF File (*.rif) 52K: It is very unlikely that this will be an option with your scanner, since this format is almost exclusive to Painter. If it is available, however, it is your best choice.

    2. TIFF File (*.tif) 477K: This is a very detailed format, but it is also rather large. A good-size rendering in this format may not fit on a 3.5-inch disk.

    3. Photoshop File (*.psd) 72K: This is Adobe Photoshop's own format. This format gives good quality in a medium-size file.

    4. JPEG File (*.jpg) 9K: This is probably the best of the extremely compact formats even though it was originally designed for monitors rather than printing.

    5. GIF File (*.gif) 5K: This format was developed by CompuServe. It is the most common graphic format used on the World Wide Web. It was designed for monitor screens rather than printing. It has an extremely compact file size.

    6. PC Paintbrush File (*.pcx) 54K: This type is designed for use in many simple drawing programs. It has a compact format but not as good detail as RIFF, TIFF, or Photoshop files.

7. MAC PICT File (*.pct) 49K: This type was designed by Mac programmers for its simple drawing programs. It has a compact format but not as good detail as RIFF, TIFF, or Photoshop files.

8. Bitmap File (*.bmp) 1421K: This was designed for high-quality image reproduction on a computer monitor rather than in printing. These files are extremely large.

9. Targa File (*.tga) 1421K: This format is often used in commercial printing. It is detailed, but extremely large.

10. Postscript File (*.eps) 2274K: This format was designed for extremely detailed commercial printing. It has a huge file size.

11. Pyramid Image File (*.pyr) 3390K: This is another commercial printing format with an incredibly large file size.

4. Once you have scanned the image into a file on your hard drive or a disk then you can open it in Painter from there.

USING THE COPY IMAGE COMMAND: R12

Use the copy image command in AutoCAD to save the image as a file.

1. Get into the perspective view of the set or part of it that you want in AutoCAD. Move or get rid of the toolbox on the screen so it won't be in the middle of the image. This command will capture anything on the screen including the toolbox, pull down menus, icons, etc.

2. Under Edit, click on Copy Image.

3. Click on the first corner of the screen area that you want to capture.

4. Move the mouse diagonally to the opposite corner of the screen area that you want to capture.

5. Click on this corner. The image will go directly to your clipboard as a bitmap image.

6. Minimize or close AutoCAD.

7. Open a program that will accept bitmap files pasted from the clipboard. There are many programs that are designed to do this. Even if you haven't purchased one separately, almost all computers come with a simple drawing program such as: Paint, Draw, or Paintbrush.

8. Locate the paste command in this program and click on paste.

9. The image will appear in the drawing area of the program.

10. Save the file as a name that you want and format (file type) that you can import into Painter. Be sure to remember the directory and folder and subdirectories that it has been saved into on your hard drive or a floppy disk. The formats available on these simple drawing programs

are usually very limited, but Painter will accept a fairly wide variety of formats. See the list above.

11. Once you have saved the image into a file on your hard drive or a disk, you can open it in Painter.

Using the Save Image Command

Use the **save image** command in AutoCAD to save the image as a file.

1. Get into the view of the file in AutoCAD that you would like to save. Do not worry about toolboxes, etc. that might be in the way. This process will ignore them.

2. In R12, click on **Render/Files/Save Image**. The **Save Image** box will open. In R13, click on **Tools/Image/Save**. The **Save Image** box will open. In R14, click on **Tools/Display Image/Save**. The **Save Image** box will open.

    A. Select the format that you would like by clicking either **BMP**, **TGA**, or **TIF**. For an export to Painter, I would recommand using the **TIF** format.

    B. Under **Size**, the **X** and **Y** boxes represent the size of the image in pixels. You can change the size of the image in the windows next to the **X** and **Y** if you would like.

3. Click on the **OK** button.

4. The **Image File** box opens.

    A. Give the image a name in the **File Name** window.

    B. Choose the location where the file will be saved in the **Drives and Directories** windows or in the **Save In** window.

    C. Click on **OK** or **Save**.

Creating and Using a Lighting Instrument Library

The two commands in AutoCAD that make it possible for the lighting designer to do light plots are the **wblock** and **insert** functions. The **wblock** command lets you draw a variety of lighting instrument symbols and attach attributes to them that can include all the information around the instrument that one uses such as the color, instrument number, etc. Then, when you use the **insert** command you are prompted for these attributes as you insert the instrument symbol and you can specify the particular information that you want for each individual instrument. Without the **wblock** command you would have to draw the instrument symbol every time that you wanted to use it. Without attributes, the information around the individual instruments would similarly have to be inserted each time by hand. Therefore, when the lighting designer is going to use AutoCAD to do a light plot, the first thing he or she has to do is build an instrument library of blocks (files) to allow him or her to quickly and easily insert the instrument symbols on the plot.

I have already talked you through doing one of these in the section on working with blocks. Using the information there and some measurements on your lighting instruments you can create a library of files. It can then be customized by defining both the appearance of the symbols and the information included in the attributes. However, I have also included on the CD-ROM accompanying this book an instrument library that should more than get you off to a good start. This library of files is drawn to the latest USITT Recommended Practice for Lighting Design Graphics. It includes all of the symbols from the Recommended Practice. The attributes that are already a part of the files follow it as well. The Recommended Practice acknowledges a fact with which all of us in theatre are familiar, namely that not every lighting designer in every situation will want to or should use all of the information around the symbols. Some of the attributes may not be needed or wanted for your particular situation. You will probably want to eliminate some of them, possibly move some of them around, and maybe even create some new ones for your particular situation. Similarly, you may need to create some variations on the basic symbols or even invent your own symbols. All of this can be easily done in AutoCAD.

The next step in making AutoCAD work to save you time is creating your own theatre drawing library. If you work in one or several theatres, you should keep basic drawings of the theatres in your hard drive as well. You can set these up with a typical key and title block and all of the other elements that would be on any light plot and have them ready to go when you start working on a show. With the theatre structure already in place a good part of your work is already done. Freelancers can have the basics of their plot all ready on a file before they start and this will save them time. If you spend a little time working on things that you know you would have to repeat on every drawing and save them in a file, they will always be ready to go, needing only minor editing.

CHANGING AND CREATING SYMBOLS

To create your own symbols, follow the instructions outlined in the section on drawing and using blocks (see page 143). Draw the symbol that you want, add the attributes that you want, and then use the wblock command to turn it into a file. It is better to use the wblock command rather than just saving it as a file because that way you can more easily control the insertion point on the symbol.

If you want to change one of the files (blocks) that already exists in the library on the CD-ROM, that is also a simple procedure. First you will have to take the file off of the CD-ROM and save it to your hard drive or disk since you will not be able to save a file to the CD-ROM. Once you have the file on a hard drive or disk, open it in AutoCAD and make any changes that you would like. Erase attributes that you don't want, add new ones that you would like, make a modification to the symbol, etc., and then save the changes that you have made. When you insert the block into your light plot, whatever changes that you have made will appear.

The symbols on the CD-ROM also represent an instrument that would typically be inserted straight-forward on the light plot. You may want to add variations on this basic symbol as well. When inserted these symbols will be facing in one direction with the attributes readable in the direction in which they are initially inserted. You could, of course, rotate them to any angle that you would like as a part of the insert command. When you do this, however, the attributes might not be as easy to read. If you turned the instrument 180 degrees to indicate a back light, the wording of the attributes would be upside down. What I have found to be really useful is creating four files for each instrument symbol. One for front lights, one for lights coming from S.R., one for lights coming from S.L., and one for back lights. In each of these files, I rotate the attributes so that they face in the appropriate direction and move the circle and hexagon to a different side of the symbol that is appropriate for that direction. The key to making this easy to work is to give each file a name for the basic symbol with just a slight variation for the direction of orientation. The file for the 6-inch Fresnel symbol in the library, for example, is named Fres6.dwg. In my own library I have a Fres6f.dwg, Fres6l.dwg, Fres6r.dwg, and a Fres6b.dwg to indicate one coming from the front, left, right, and back, respectively. Then I just insert the file that I want.

WORKING WITH THE INSTRUMENT LIBRARY

One key to making the library work for you is making a handy reference. One of the files in the instrument library is not an instrument block at all. This is the file titled Blockinv.dwg. This file is something that I always have printed out and have next to me when I am working on a light plot. It contains all the symbols in the library with their file names right next to them. So if I don't remember the correct file name, a quick glance will tell me the name of the file that I have to type in at the insert command. This can save a lot of frustrating searching around through your hard drive to locate a file name.

Another important element in making the library work is having all of the files located in the main AutoCAD directory or folder of your hard drive. Yes, you should keep them on a disk as a backup, but if you try to insert them off of a 3.5-inch disk you will have to type a:\filename at the insert command. If you wanted to work from the CD-ROM you would have to type e:\instlibr\ filename—or whatever letter represents the CD-ROM drive on your computer. With the files in the main AutoCAD directory of your hard drive all you have to type at the insert command is the file name. You don't have to type a:\ or include the extension .dwg. This makes everything go much more quickly. If you don't know what your main AutoCAD directory is or understand how to copy the files into it, have someone who does explain the process to you. The name given to the directory is different between versions and in installing the program it is possible to change the name of the directory. If someone else installed the program he or she may have done exactly that either during the installation or at a later date. Copy everything in the instrument library from the CD-ROM to the main AutoCAD directory in your hard drive.

Take the time to customize the library to your particular needs and thoroughly familiarize yourself with how blocks are created and changed. It will pay off in a better-looking light plot and one that will work more efficiently for you. Learn how to insert the blocks efficiently and start developing work habits in AutoCAD that speed up the process. For example, it will speed things up if you insert as many of the same block following one another as possible. When you have just inserted a block, all you have to do to insert the same block again is hit Enter or click the right mouse button. You don't have to hit the Insert button and type in the name of the block again. Figure out which AutoCAD commands you will be using the most and then customize your toolbar or toolbox with buttons for those commands. A lighting designer would definitely want an insert button readily available on the toolbar or toolbox. You may want to create buttons for several aspects of one command such as one button for zoom all and another button for zoom window. Creating your own customized toolbar and toolbox will make all of your work in AutoCAD go more smoothly.

Have ready on your computer's hard drive files that will be the basis of a ground plan and/or section lighting plot for each of the theatres in which you work on a regular basis. These can include not just the basic theatre structure that you always include on your lighting plot, but also a title block, the beginning of a key, etc. When it comes time to start a new plot for that theatre, you can simply call up the file for that theatre, save it to a new name, and be ready to start drawing without having to repeat the work each time. AutoCAD can be a highly efficient way to create well-drawn light plots, but like any tool it is only as good as the person who uses it. If you are presently drawing sloppy light plots, AutoCAD will not seriously help the situation.

CREATING AND USING
A SET OR CONSTRUCTION LIBRARY

The set designer and the technical director should also consider how they might be able to create a permanent set of files that could save them time in doing their working drawings. Obviously, having a ground plan and section of a theatre already created and saved could greatly speed up the beginning of the design/drafting process. The next time that you began a scenic ground plan for that theatre you would not have to draw in the theatre structure and could instead begin working directly on the set itself.

There are numerous other instances of drawings that could form the basis of a library, however. These would be drawings that you could use to begin another drawing or that you could quickly modify to meet the needs of a particular production. Files of stock platforms, parallels, or flats, for example, could quickly be inserted into new drawings and thus would not have to be recreated from scratch each time that they were needed. Any stock or standard item that your particular theatre uses on a regular basis could be part of a library that could save you time when they were called for in drawings.

Stock pieces of scenery aren't the only things you can put in a library to save you time. Any part of a drawing can also be saved as a file and then inserted as you need it. If you use a fairly standard title block, for example, it could be all ready to go except for the details for the particular show on which you are currently working. The details such as show title, date, drawing title, etc. could all be set up as attributes in the file. You would just have to insert it in the drawing and you would automatically be prompted for the details. The layout, font size, etc. would already be there. If you have a standard paper size for your drawings or always work in a particular scale, you could also have files already created with the limits, ltscale, dimscale, etc. preset and ready to go.

In short, AutoCAD can speed up your drawing/drafting process immediately by relieving you of having to draw the same item or almost the same item over and over again each time that you begin a new drawing or a new show. If you think about all of the things that go into any theatrical drawing or drafting you will quickly realize how many of them are repetitive or similar. These items should be the basis of your AutoCAD set or construction drawing library.

AutoCAD .bak FILES

Most AutoCAD files contain a lot of information and relative to other programs such as word-processing programs are fairly large in size. Most AutoCAD files also represent hours of work. Like all computer files it is easy for these files to be lost, destroyed, or corrupted through a variety of accidents, computer glitches, or just plain mistakes on your part. Given the amount of time that it will take you to create AutoCAD files it just makes sense to always back them up on one or more floppy disks.

The AutoCAD program itself, however, automatically creates a further backup file every time that you **save** in the program. If you look at the directory for the disk that you have been working on you will find that for each file name there are actually two files. There is the file name that you have been working in—a .dwg file—and there is another file with the same name, but a different extension—a .bak file. This .bak file is a file that AutoCAD creates to back up your regular file. If your regular file becomes corrupted or lost you can usually retrieve most of your work by using the .bak file. Remember that the .bak file is updated every time that you **save**. So if you are working on something that is a very complicated process, it is a good idea to **save** often in the working process to keep your .bak file updated.

This .bak file, however, cannot be read by AutoCAD as a regular file. If you try to **open** a .bak file as you would an ordinary file, you will get an error message from AutoCAD telling you that it cannot read this file. In order to read the .bak file in AutoCAD you will have to change the extension on it from .bak to .dwg. In Windows 3.1 you can use **File Manager** to do this. If you are working in Windows95/98 or WindowsNT you can use **Windows Explorer** to change the extension. If you are working in other programs you will need to use the **MS-DOS** prompt to change the extension from .bak to .dwg.

The following sections explain the procedures you will have to follow to change a .bak file to a .dwg file using Windows Explorer, File Manager, and the MS-DOS prompt.

CHANGING FILE EXTENSIONS USING WINDOWS EXPLORER

1. Open Windows Explorer:
   A. You can usually find Windows Explorer on the Desktop or under **Start** and then **Programs**.
2. Select the **drive** that contains the .bak file and locate the file:
   A. Click once on either the **a:** icon or the **c:** icon depending upon where your file is located. If your file is on a floppy disk it is in the **a:** drive. If it is on the hard disk it is in the **c:** drive. If it is in the **c:** drive you will also have to work your way down through the **folders** and/or **directories** to locate the file.
3. Make sure that Windows Explorer is configured to show file extensions. When you look at the name of your file using Windows Explorer if it doesn't show the **extension**—if there isn't a .bak or a .dwg after the filename, then:

A. On the pull down menu bar at the top, click on View and then on Options.

B. In the Options box that opens, under the View tab make sure that there is no check in the Hide MS-DOS File Extensions box.

4. Find the .bak file for which you want to change the extension.

5. Click once with the left mouse button on the name of the file that you want to change.

6. Click on File on the pull down menu bar.

7. Click on Rename.

8. The file name that you earlier selected will be surrounded by a box with a blinking cursor.

9. Type in the complete name of the new file name including a .dwg extension.

10. Hit Enter.

11. You may get a warning that changing the file name could have dire consequences. Ignore it.

12. Exit Windows Explorer, return to AutoCAD, and open the renamed file.

CHANGING FILE EXTENSIONS USING FILE MANAGER

1. Open File Manager:
   A. In Windows 3.1 you will usually find the File Manager program under the Main program group, but depending upon how the computer was initially set up it could be somewhere else. You may need to search through several program groups to find the File Manager program.

   B. In Windows95 File Manager is usually located under Accessories. You would activate the program by clicking on Start, then on Programs, then on Accessories, then on File Manager.

2. Select the drive that contains the .bak file and locate the file: There are icons that represent drives just above the large window that shows the files. Click once on either the a: icon or the c: icon depending upon where your file is located. If your file is on a floppy disk it is in the a: drive. If it is on the hard disk it is in the c: drive. If it is in the c: drive you will also have to work your way down through the folders and/or directories to locate the file. Once you have located the .bak file with the name that you want, click on it once to highlight it.

3. Rename the file:
   A. In the upper left-hand corner of the screen, click on File:.

B. In the pull down menu that opens, click on **Rename**.

C. The **Rename** box opens with the file name that you have selected under From: and a blinking cursor under To:.

D. In the To: box, type in the file name, but with the extension .dwg rather than .bak. For example, if the file name project1.bak appears in the From: box, type project1.dwg in the To: box.

E. Click on **OK** in the Rename box.

F. Close File Manager, reenter AutoCAD, and open the file just as you usually would.

G. This will open a copy of the file that you were working on as of the last time that you **saved**.

CHANGING FILE EXTENSIONS USING THE MS-DOS PROMPT

1. Open the MS-DOS prompt: In MS-DOS-based computers, this will be the opening prompt when the computer has finished booting up. In Windows 3.1-based computers, this will also usually be the opening prompt unless the computer has been configured to automatically start Windows. If your computer is configured to automatically start Windows then you will either have to exit Windows to access the MS-DOS prompt or there will be an **MS_DOS** prompt icon located in one of your program groups. In most versions of Windows95 or WindowsNT this is under the **Programs** directory. Click on **Start**, then on **Programs**, then on **MS-DOS** prompt.

2. When the MS-DOS prompt opens, the screen will read:

   C:\WINDOWS> on Windows-equipped computers, or

   C:\> on MS-DOS computers.

3. Type in the command **rename**, followed by a space, followed by the complete path to the file that is to be renamed, followed by a space, followed by the new name of the file and then hit **Enter**. Note that the new name of the file does *not* include the complete path to the file, just the new name of the file itself. Let's say that you had lost the file project1.dwg, but that you had its backup file project1.bak on the disk that you had placed in the a: drive. To rename the file project1.bak to project1.dwg you would type the following at the MS-DOS prompt:

   rename a:\project1.bak project1.dwg

   Then you would hit the **Enter** key.

4. For a file that is in the hard drive—usually the c: drive—you will need to know the complete path to the file that you want to rename. Let's say that

the file project1.bak was in the hard drive (c:) under the directory or folder acad. At the MS-DOS prompt you would type:

    rename c:\acad\project1.bak project1.dwg

Then you would hit the Enter key.

5. Also note that the drive and any folders, directories, or files within the drive are separated by a backslash (\).

6. To exit the MS-DOS prompt, type exit when the prompt comes up on the screen again and hit the Enter key.

APPENDIX A

INTEGRATION: SHARING, MOVING, IMPORTING, AND EXPORTING PROGRAM FILES

This is one of the most important sections of these two volumes. All of the information contained in this section is also found in a variety of locations in the two volumes of this work, but in this Appendix, I have gathered all of the instructions for sharing, moving, importing, and exporting files together in one location for easier reference. Here is the basic information that you will need to integrate the four programs: what the different file types are and how they work, how to export the different file types from the programs involved, and how to import them into the other programs. This is where you will start learning how to go about sharing the files between programs and thus also with your fellow designers and technicians. Most of this information is also included in the text on the specific programs, but it is summarized in this section for easier access.

As I stated at the beginning of this volume, programmers have yet to devote the time and effort that it would take to arrive at the one program that will do everything that we in the theatre would desire on a completely integrated basis. Until that time arrives we will have to make the best use possible of the already available programs. These two volumes in general and this section in particular were written toward that end: to show you how to integrate these four programs as completely as you can.

File Types

The first step in the integration process is understanding the different file types that are involved in the four programs. Before you can move a file from one program to another, you need to know whether it is compatible and what are some of its more important characteristics. This is a listing of all of the file types that can be created by the programs, detailing which are compatible with which other programs and describing some of their major characteristics.

AUTOCAD FILE TYPES AND EXTENSIONS

AutoCAD Internal Files

These file types are used by AutoCAD in creating its drawings. Some of them are usable in other programs as well.

DWG File (*.dwg): This is the basic AutoCAD drawing format. The same extension is used for all three releases, but R14 files cannot be read by R12 or R13. R13 files can be read by R14, but not by R12. R12 files can be read by both R13 and R14. R14, however, can save files in either an R12 or R13 format. 3D Studio MAX claims to be able to read a DWG file, but unless you are using R14, I don't recommend trying to use one in 3-D Studio MAX. DXF files work much better.

Drawing Template File (*.dwt): This file type is only used in R14. It is used internally to save a template that can be used to set up later drawings.

AutoCAD Export and Import Files

These file types can be used as 3-D files in other programs.

DXF File (*.dxf): This is a drawing export file. This type is used by AutoCAD and other programs as a general export format. These files can be exported from all releases. They can be opened in R14 or imported into R12 and R13. They can be imported into 3D Studio MAX. They can also be imported into Poser as props.

3D Studio Mesh File (*.3ds): This file type can be exported only from AutoCAD R14. These files can be imported into 3D Studio MAX or Poser. They can also be imported into AutoCAD R13. They can be inserted into AutoCAD R14.

AutoCAD Rendering Files

These file types are 2-D file types that you can get from AutoCAD. They can be used in Painter and many other drawing programs. Some of them can also be used as texture or bitmap files in 3D Studio MAX and Poser.

TIFF Image File (*.tif): This is a popular graphics file format with commercial printers. These files have a large file size, but excellent detail. They can be created in all releases of AutoCAD. They can be read in Painter and Adobe Photoshop. They can be used as texture files in 3D Studio MAX and Poser. They can also be used as background files in Poser.

GIF File (*.gif): This is the most common graphic file type used on the World Wide Web. These files are compact in size. They can be created in all releases of AutoCAD. They cannot be opened in Photoshop, but they can be created there. GIF files can be opened in Painter, and other file types can be saved as GIF files.

Targa Image File (*.tga): Originally developed for video, this is a widely used commercial graphics file type. These are relatively large files, but they have good detail. They can be created in all releases of AutoCAD. They can be created in Painter, but not in Adobe Photoshop. Other file types can be converted to this type in Painter.

BMP Image File (*.bmp): This is often referred to as a "bitmap" file. A BMP file is a type of graphic file used for display on computer monitors. Most of the icons that you see on your computer screen are BMP files. BMP files are large in size. They can be created in all releases of AutoCAD. They can be used as background files in Poser.

Encapsulated Postscript File (*.eps, *.ps): This file type is used by many commercial printers. This type cannot be opened in Painter, but it can be opened in Adobe Photoshop. It cannot be read in Poser or 3D Studio MAX. It can be exported from all releases of AutoCAD.

3D STUDIO MAX FILE TYPES AND EXTENSIONS

3D Studio MAX Internal Files

This file type is what is created when you save or save as in the program.

MAX File (*.max): 3D Studio MAX uses this file type to create its 3-D scenes. However, this type cannot be used in any other of the four programs in this book and its companion volume.

3D Studio MAX Export Files

These are the file types that you can use to export 3-D objects or scenes to AutoCAD for making technical drawings or to Poser to be used as props.

3D Studio Mesh File (*.3ds): This file type can be exported from 3D Studio MAX. These files can be inserted into AutoCAD R14 or imported into AutoCAD R13. They cannot be used in AutoCAD R12. They can be imported into Poser as a prop.

DWG File (*.dwg): This is the standard AutoCAD drawing format. These files can be exported from 3D Studio MAX and used in AutoCAD R12, R13, and R14.

DXF File (*.dxf): This is an export format that is used by many programs besides AutoCAD and 3D Studio MAX. These files can be opened in AutoCAD R14. They can be imported into AutoCAD R12 and R13. They can be imported into Poser as props.

3D Studio MAX Texture and Bitmap Files

These are the file types that can be used by 3D Studio MAX as materials, textures, and bitmaps after being brought in through the Material/Map Browser.

TIFF Image File (*.tif): This is a popular graphics file format with commercial printers. These files have a large file size, but excellent detail. They can be created in Painter and Adobe Photoshop. They can be created in AutoCAD. They can be created with many scanners. Other file types can be converted to this type in Painter.

Targa Image File (*.tga): Originally developed for video, this is a widely used commercial graphics file type. These are relatively large files, but they have good detail. They can be created in Painter, but not in Adobe Photoshop. They can be created in AutoCAD. Other file types can be converted to this type in Painter.

JPEG File (*.jpg): This is a widely used compact graphic format. These files can be created in Painter, Adobe Photoshop, and many other graphic programs. This is the most popular format used in digital cameras. Other file types can be converted to this type in Painter.

GIF File (*.gif): This is the most common graphic file type used on the World Wide Web. These files are compact in size. They cannot be opened in Photoshop, but they can be created there. They can be created in AutoCAD. GIF files can be opened in Painter, and other file types can be saved as GIF files.

RLA File (*.rla): This format lets you include separate channels for different elements of the graphics. The files cannot be opened in Painter or Adobe Photoshop.

AutoDesk Flic Image File (*.flc, *.fli, *.cel): This file type is used by AutoDesk for several of its animator programs. Unless you have one of these programs you will probably not want to use this file type.

Image File List File (*.ifl): IFL files are actually text files that are a list of image files. They can be used in animation to switch or change the texture, bitmap, etc. on an object during the course of the animation. This can create such effects as changing the color of the surface of an object.

3D Studio MAX Rendering Files

These are file types that can be created in 3D Studio MAX to save the renderings of scenes. Do not confuse these file types with the object file types that are used in 3D Studio MAX to save objects or whole 3-D scenes such as .max, .dxf, .dwg, or .3ds.

JPEG File (*.jpg): This is a widely used compact graphic format. These files can be opened in Painter, Adobe Photoshop, and many other graphic programs.

This is a good choice for exporting a file to Painter or another graphics program. These files cannot be used in Poser.

TIFF Image File (*.tif): This is a popular graphics file format with commercial printers. The files have a large file size, but excellent detail. They can be opened in Painter and Adobe Photoshop. They can be used as background files in Poser.

BMP Image File (*.bmp): This file type is often referred to as a "bitmap" file. Do not confuse this use of the term with the way that 3D Studio MAX uses the term *bitmap* to refer to any file type that can be applied to an object as a texture. A BMP file is a type of graphic file used for display on computer monitors. Most of the icons that you see on your computer screen are BMP files. BMP files are large in size. They can be opened in Painter, but not in Adobe Photoshop. They can be used as background files in Poser.

Targa Image File (*.tga): Originally developed for video, this is a widely used commercial graphics file type. These are relatively large files, but they have good detail. They can be opened in Painter, but not in Adobe Photoshop. They cannot be used in Poser.

AVI File (*. avi): This is one of the most common file types used in animation viewers. If you are creating an animation, this is the file type you will most likely use. Single AVI files can also be opened in Painter, but not in Adobe Photoshop.

AutoDesk Flic Image File (*.flc, *.fli, *.cel): AutoDesk uses this file type for several of its animator programs. Unless you have one of these programs you will probably not want to use this file type.

Encapsulated Postscript File (*.eps, *.ps): This file type is used by many commercial printers. This type cannot be opened in Painter, but it can be opened in Adobe Photoshop.

PNG Image File (*png): This is a compact graphics file type that is intended to supplant the GIF file type. So far it has not found widespread use in spite of its advantages. These files cannot be opened in Painter, Adobe Photoshop, or many other graphics programs.

RLA Image File (*.rla): This format lets you include separate channels for different elements of the graphics. These files cannot be opened in Painter or Adobe Photoshop.

PAINTER FILE TYPES AND EXTENSIONS

These are file types that can be created in Painter or brought into Painter from other sources.

RIFF File (*.rif): RIFF files are exclusive to Painter. If you save a file as a RIFF file, you will not be able to use it in any of the other programs in this book and its companion. If, however, you are going to use it just in Painter or you are going to store it on a floppy disk, there are a number of advantages to using a RIFF file. It is a highly detailed file type, but still compact. If you need to save space it might be a good idea to save the file as a RIFF file and then convert it to another file type in Painter before you use it in another program. There are a number of special techniques used in Painter such as floaters that will only be saved if the file is saved as a RIFF file.

TIFF File (*.tif): TIFF files are large, detailed files that can be imported into a wide variety of other programs. TIFF files can be imported into Poser for use as backgrounds, bump maps, and texture maps. They can also be used in 3D Studio MAX as textures and bitmaps. TIFF files can be created from renderings in 3D Studio MAX. TIFF files can also be created in AutoCAD. They can be opened in Adobe Photoshop as well. This format is not used in most digital cameras. It is a format that is often used in scanners. Scanned files may first appear in this format and then be converted to other formats in Painter. TIFF files can be opened in Painter and other files can be saved as TIFF files.

JPEG File (*.jpg): This graphic file type is often used on the World Wide Web. The files are compact in size. They can be used as textures or bitmaps in 3D Studio MAX. They can be created as rendering files from 3D Studio MAX. They cannot be used in Poser. They can be opened in Photoshop. They can be created with some scanners. This is the most common format used in digital cameras. JPEG files can be opened in Painter, and other files can be saved as JPEG files.

Targa File (*.tga): This is another relatively large file type that is used in many graphics programs. These files can be used as textures or bitmaps in 3D Studio MAX. They can be created as rendering files in 3D Studio MAX. They can be created in AutoCAD. They cannot be used in Poser. They can be opened in Photoshop. They can be created with some scanners. This format is not used in digital cameras. Targa files can be opened in Painter, and other files can be saved as Targa files.

Bitmap File (*.bmp): This is a large file type often used for computer screen graphics. These files can be used as backgrounds, bump maps, and texture maps in Poser, but they cannot be used in 3D Studio MAX. They can be created as rendering files from 3D Studio MAX. They can be exported from AutoCAD R13 or R14 and can be created by using the Tools/Save Image pull down menu in AutoCAD R14. They cannot be opened in Photoshop. They can be created with some scanners. This format is not used in digital cameras. Bitmap files can be opened in Painter and other files can be saved as bitmap files.

Video for Windows File (*.avi): This is one of the most common file types used in animation viewers. If you are creating an animation, this is the file type you will most likely use. These files can be created as rendering files in

3D Studio MAX. Single AVI files can also be opened in Painter, but not in Adobe Photoshop. Other file types cannot be saved as AVI files by Painter.

PICT File (*.pct): This file type is common to Macs. These files can be opened in Adobe Photoshop but cannot be used in Poser or 3D Studio MAX. PICT files can be opened in Painter, and other files can be saved as PICT files.

Photoshop File (*.psd): This is an Adobe Photoshop file type. These files cannot be opened in Poser or 3D Studio MAX. Photoshop files can be opened in Painter and other files can be saved as Photoshop files.

PC Paintbrush File (*.pcx): This file type is common in PC graphics programs. These files cannot be used in Poser, 3D Studio MAX, or Photoshop. PC Paintbrush files can be opened in Painter, and other file types can be saved as PC Paintbrush files.

GIF File (*.gif): This is the most common graphic file type used on the World Wide Web. The files are compact in size. They can be used as textures or bitmaps in 3D Studio MAX. They can be created in AutoCAD. They cannot be used in Poser. They cannot be opened in Photoshop, but they can be created there. GIF files can be opened in Painter, and other file types can be saved as GIF files.

Pyramid Image File (*.pyr): Pyramid images are very large, highly detailed files sometimes used in commercial printing. They cannot be used in any of the other programs in these volumes. They can be opened in Painter, and other file types can be saved as Pyramid Images.

Frame Stack File (*.frm): Frame Stack files are also commonly used in animation. They cannot be used in any of the other programs in these volumes. Frame Stack files can be opened in Painter, but other file types cannot be saved as Frame Stack files.

Postscript File (*.eps): This file type is often used in commercial graphics. These files cannot be used in Poser or 3D Studio MAX. They can be opened in Photoshop. Postscript files cannot be opened in Painter, but other file types can be saved as Postscript files.

Adobe Illustrator File (*.ai): This file type was developed for the Adobe Illustrator program. The files cannot be used in any of the four programs covered in these volumes. They can be opened in Photoshop. They can be exported from Painter.

POSER FILE TYPES AND EXTENSIONS

Poser Internal File Types

These file types are used to save the work that you have done so that it can be worked on again in Poser. They cannot be used directly in any of the other programs in these volumes.

POZ (*.poz): This is the Poser 1 file type. It can also be opened in Poser 2 or Poser 3.

PZR (*.pzr): This is the Poser 2 file type. It can be opened in Poser 3, but not Poser 1.

PZ3 (*.pz3): This is the Poser 3 file type. It cannot be opened in Poser 1 or Poser 2.

Poser 3-D Image Export File Types

These are file types that can be exported from Poser so that they can be used in other programs as 3-D images of figures.

3D Studio Mesh File (*.3ds): This is the easiest format to use with either AutoCAD or 3D Studio MAX. It can be imported into AutoCAD R12 and R13 or 3D Studio MAX and can be inserted in AutoCAD R14.

DXF File (*.dxf): This is a drawing export file. These files can be imported into AutoCAD R12, R13, and 3D Studio MAX. They can be opened in AutoCAD R14. They cannot be used in Painter or most other drawing programs.

Poser 2-D Image Export File Types

These are file types that can be exported from Poser and then used in other programs as 2-D representations of figures. Both of these file types can be used in Painter to create renderings.

TIFF File (*.tif): When exported from Poser, this file type can be opened in Painter. This image can then be manipulated in any way you would like in Painter. These files are usually smaller in size than BMP files. See "Painter File Types" for more description.

Bitmap File (*.bmp): When exported from Poser, this file type can be opened in Painter. This image can then be manipulated in any way you would like in Painter. See "Painter File Types" for more description.

Poser Import File Types

These file types can be imported into Poser for use as backgrounds, props, and bump and texture maps.

Background Files

These file types can be used by Poser to create backgrounds behind the figures.

TIFF File (*.tif): This file type can be created in Painter or saved from a rendering in 3D Studio MAX. These files can be brought in from scanned images. They can be created in AutoCAD. They can also be created by taking digital photos and then converting the images from JPEG to TIFF files in Painter.

Bitmap File (*.bmp): This file type can be created in Painter or saved from a rendering in 3D Studio MAX. The files can also be exported from AutoCAD R13 and R14. They can also be brought in from scanned images or created by taking digital photos and then converting the images from JPEG to BMP files in Painter.

Bump or Texture Map Files

These file types can be used by Poser to create bump or texture maps for the figures.

TIFF File (*.tif): This file type can be created in Painter or brought in from a scanned image. Another file type can be converted to a TIFF file in Painter.

Bitmap File (*.bmp): This file type can be created in Painter or brought in from a scanned image. Another file type can be converted to a BMP file in Painter.

Prop Files

These file types can be brought into Poser and used as props along with the figures.

3D Studio Mesh File (*.3ds): Three-dimensional objects created in 3D Studio MAX can be exported from that program as 3D Studio Mesh files and then imported into Poser as props. This format can also be exported from AutoCAD R13 and R14.

DXF File (*.dxf): Three-dimensional objects created in AutoCAD can be exported from that program in DXF format and then imported into Poser as props. **Note:** DXF files do not work as well as 3D Studio Mesh files in Poser. If you have an option, go for a 3D Studio Mesh file instead of a DXF file. See the section on importing into Poser (see page 251).

Importing and Exporting Files from the Programs

This section will provide you with a quick summary of how to import and export the various file types out of each of the programs covered in these volumes. If you need more details on dealing with a specific program, that information is available in the text on the program.

AutoCAD

Exporting 3-D Image Files

These files can be used as 3-D objects or figures in other programs.

DXF Files (*.dxf): These files can be brought into 3D Studio MAX as objects or into Poser as props. They are created in all releases of AutoCAD by clicking on **File/Export** on the pull down menu.

3D Studio Mesh Files (*.3ds): These files can be used in 3D Studio MAX as objects or in Poser as props. They can only be created in AutoCAD R14. Click on File/Export on the pull down menu.

Exporting 2-D Image Files

These files can be used as 2-D backgrounds, images, or the bases of renderings.

TIFF Image Files (*.tif), GIF Image Files (*.gif), and Targa Image Files (*.tga): All of these file types can be opened in Painter. TIFF files can be used as backgrounds and texture maps in Poser and as textures in 3D Studio MAX. In R12, click on Render/Files/Save Image on the pull down menu. In R13, click on Tools/Image/Save. In R14, click on Tools/Display Image/Save.

BMP Image Files (*.bmp): These files can be opened in Painter. They can be used as backgrounds and texture maps in Poser and as textures in 3D Studio MAX. In AutoCAD R12, click on File/Save As. In R13 and R14, click on File/Export.

Encapsulated Postscript Files (*.eps, *.ps): These files cannot be used in any of the other programs in these volumes. In all releases, click on File/Export.

Importing Files

These are files that can be brought into AutoCAD to create drawings.

DXF Files (*.dxf): After being created in another program such as 3D Studio MAX, these files can be brought into AutoCAD. For R12 and R13, click on File/Import. For R14, click on File/Open.

3D Studio Mesh Files (*.3ds): These files cannot be brought into R12. For R13, click on File/Import. For R14, click on Insert/3D Studio.

3D Studio MAX

Exporting 3-D Image Files

These are file types that can be used in other programs as objects or to create accurate technical drawings.

3D Studio Mesh Files (*.3ds): These can be used in AutoCAD R13 and R14, but not R12. They can be used in Poser as props. To create, click on File/Export.

DWG Files (*.dwg): These can be used in all versions of AutoCAD. To create, click on File/Export.

DXF Files (*.dxf): These can be imported into all versions of AutoCAD. The can also be imported into Poser as props. To create, click on File/Export.

Exporting Rendering Files

These are files that are created from 3D Studio MAX renderings and can be saved for use in rendering programs such as Painter or as backgrounds in Poser.

JPEG (*.jpg), TIFF (*.tif), BMP (*.bmp), Targa (*.tga), AVI (*.avi), FLIC (*.flc), EPS (*.eps), PNG (*.png), and RLA (*.rla) Files:

1. To save to one of these formats after the rendering has already been created, click on the icon above the rendering window that looks like a 3.5-inch disk.
2. To save to one of these formats before the rendering is created:
   A. Click on the Render Scene button.
   B. In the Render Scene box:
      1. Click on Single under Time Output.
      2. Select the output size desired.
      3. Click on the File button under Render Output.
         a. Select the drive and folder where you want to save the file.
         b. Select the file type that you desire.
         c. Enter a file name and extension.
         d. Click on OK. You are returned to the Render Scene box.
      4. Be sure there is a check next to Save File under Render Output.
      5. Click on the Render button.

Importing 3-D Image Files

These are the files that can be brought into 3D Studio MAX as objects or entire scenes.

3D Studio Mesh Files (*.3ds): These files can be created in Poser and AutoCAD R14. To bring one into 3D Studio MAX, click on File/Import on the pull down menu.

DWG Files (*.dwg): These files can be created in all releases of AutoCAD. To bring one into 3D Studio MAX, click on File/Import on the pull down menu. You may experience some difficulties importing this file type into 3D Studio MAX. If so, use a DXF file instead.

DXF Files (*.dxf): These files can be created in Poser and all releases of AutoCAD. To bring one into 3D Studio MAX, click on File/Import on the pull down menu.

Importing Texture and Bitmap Files

These file types can be used by 3D Studio MAX as materials, textures, and bit-maps to be applied to objects. They can be created in a variety of sources such as Painter and by using scanners and digital cameras.

TIFF (*.tif), Targa (*.tga), JPEG (*.jpg), GIF (*.gif), RLA (*.rla), AutoDesk
Image (*.flc), and Image File List (*.ifl) Files:

1. Open the Material Editor and select a Sample Slot.
2. Under the Maps bar, click on the None bar to the right of the diffuse spinner.
3. The Material/Map Browser opens.
   A. In the Browse From section, click on New.
   B. Click on Bitmap in the large window.
   C. Click on OK.
4. You are returned to the Material Editor.
5. Click on the blank bar next to Bitmap in the Bitmap Parameters section.
6. The Select Bitmap Image file box opens.
   A. Choose the drive and folder where the file is located.
   B. Click on the file name that you want to use.
   C. Click on OK.
7. The file will appear in the sample slot that you have selected in step 1.
8. You can now assign that material to a selected object in the program.

Importing Files to Use with Lighting Instruments

These file types can be used by 3D Studio MAX with target spots and directional spots in their projector option. They will then act like patterns, templates,
gobos, or projected images. They can be created in a variety of sources such as
Painter and by using scanners and digital cameras.

TIFF (*.tif), Targa (*.tga), JPEG (*.jpg), GIF (*.gif), RLA (*.rla), AutoDesk
Image (*.flc), and Image File List (*.ifl) Files:

1. In the Spotlight Parameters area of the lighting instrument's Modify
   Parameters section, click on the box next to Projector.
2. Click on the Assign button.
3. The Material/Map Browser opens. Click on New in the Browse from: section. Click on Bitmap in the large box on the right-hand side. Click on OK.
4. Back in the Spotlight Parameters area, click on the button next to Map:.
   The Put to Material Editor box opens. Select a slot # and click on OK.
5. Open the Material Editor. The slot number that you selected in the last
   step is black. Click on this slot to select it. In the Bitmap Parameters section of the Material Editor, click on the large blank button next to Bitmap.
6. The Select Bitmap Image File box opens.
   A. Find the file that you desire in whichever drive it is located.
   B. Be sure that the name of the file appears in the File name: window.
   C. Click on OK.

7. You are returned to the Material Editor. The file that you selected appears in the slot previously selected.

8. Close the Material Editor and do a quick render to see the result.

PAINTER

The following file types can all be opened (File/Open) in Painter. Once they have been opened they can be saved as (File/Save As) any of the other file types. For more information on the various file types, see the part of this section dealing with file types. To bring a file into Painter, it must be in one of these formats:

RIFF files (*.rif)	TIFF files (*.tif)
JPEG files (*.jpg)	Targa files (*.tga)
Bitmap files (*.bmp)	GIF files (*.gif)
PICT files (*.pct)	Photoshop files (*.psd)
PC Paintbrush files (*.pcx)	Video for Windows files (*.avi)
Pyramid Image files (*.pyr)	Frame Stack files (*.frm)
Postscript files (*.eps)	

There is one file type that cannot be opened in Painter, but can be exported from Painter. That is an Adobe Illustrator file (*.ai). To save another file type as an Adobe Illustrator file, click on File/Export.

POSER

Exporting Files

To export a file from Poser you, click on File/Export/Name of the Filetype on the pull down menu. 3D Studio Mesh files (*.3ds) and DXF files (*.dxf) export as 3-D figures and can be used in AutoCAD and 3D Studio MAX. TIFF (*.tif) and bitmap (*.bmp) files export as 2-D views of figures and can be opened in Painter as the beginning of a rendering.

Importing Files

Background Files

TIFF (*.tif) and bitmap (*.bmp) files can be brought into Poser to use as backgrounds behind the figures. To import one of these file types to use as a background, click on File/Import/Background Picture on the pull down menu. After you have imported the background you must still tell the program to use it in the rendering. Click on Render/Render Options. This opens the Render Options box. In the Render Over section, select Background Picture and click on OK.

Bump and Texture Map Files

TIFF (*.tif) and bitmap (*.bmp) files can be brought into Poser to use as bump and texture maps for the figures. These files are loaded in the following manner after a figure type and pose has been selected:

1. Click on **Render/Surface Material** on the pull down menu.
2. Click on **Load** in either the **Bump Map** or **Texture Map** area, depending upon which kind you want to load into the program.
3. The **Open** box appears.
   A. Locate the file that you want and click on it so that its name appears in the **File Name** window.
   B. Click on **Open**.
4. If you are loading a bump map you will be prompted to convert it to a .bum file. Convert it into a .bum file.
5. Click on the arrow button under **Bump** or **Texture Map**, depending upon which kind you are loading, and select the file that you just loaded.
6. Click on the **OK** button to exit the Surface Materials box.

Prop Files

3D Studio Mesh (*.3ds) or DXF (*.dxf) files can be brought into Poser and used as props along with the figures. A prop can also be substituted for a part of a figure.

   To import one of these files as a prop:

1. Click on **File/Import/Name of the filetype** for either 3D Studio or DXF.
2. Locate the file that you want to import and click on it so that its name appears in the **File Name** window.
3. Click on **Open**.
4. The **Prop Import Options** box opens. Here you will make choices about the prop's size relative to the figure and location. Click on **OK**.
5. The prop will appear in the scene. It is already selected when it appears and has been given a name such as OBJ_IMPORT_1. You can move it around as you desire.
6. You can color the prop using the **Render/Surface Material**.

APPENDIX B

BIBLIOGRAPHY

Bertol, D. 1994. *Visualizing with Cad: An AutoCAD Exploration of Geometric and Architectural Forms.* Santa Clara, CA: TELOS.

Bertoline, G. R. 1994. *The Essestial AutoCAD.* New York: Maxwell Macmillian International.

Billing, K. W., et al. 1993. *AutoCAD—The Professional Reference.* Carmel, IN: New Riders Publishers.

Busch, D. D. 1999. *Painting Amazing Web Images with Fractal Design Painter 5.* Orlando, FL: Academic Press Inc.

Dix, M. 1989. *Discovering AutoCAD.* Englewood Cliffs, NJ: Prentice Hall.

Hood, J. D. 1988. *Easy AutoCAD.* New York: McGraw-Hill.

Juracek, J. A. 1996. *Surfaces: Visual Research for Artists, Architects, and Designers.* New York: W. W. Norton.

Karaiskos, P. 1995. *AutoCAD for Mechanical Engineers and Designers.* New York: Wiley.

Kirsher, L. 1997. *Painter 5: Users Guide.* Santa Clara, CA: Citation Press.

London, S. 1997. *Fractal Design Painter.* Research Triangle Park, NC: Ventana Communications Group Inc.

Love, L. 1997. *Painter 5: Tutorial.* Santa Clara, CA: Citation Press.

Martier, S. 1998. *MetaCreations Poser 3 Handbook.* Rockland, MD: Charles River Media.

Matossian, M. 1998. *Teach Yourself 3D Studio Max in 14 Days.* Indianapolis: Sams.

———. 1999. *3D Studio MAX: Visual Quick Start Guide.* Berkeley: Peachpit Press.

Miller, P. 1997. *Inside 3D Studio MAX.* Indianapolis: New Riders Publishers.

Omura, G., and B. R. Callori. 1993. *AutoCAD Release 12 for Windows—Instant Reference.* Alameda, CA: SYBEX Inc.

Payne, D. R. 1994. *Computer Scenographics.* Carbondale, IL: Southern Illinois University Press.

Pinnell, W. H. 1996. *Perspective Rendering for the Theatre.* Carbondale, IL: Southern Illinois University Press.

Potts, F., and D. H. Freidel Jr. 1996. *3D Studio MAX Design Guide.* Scottsdale, AZ: Coriolis Group.

Raker, D. 1976. *Inside AutoCAD: A Teaching Guide to the AutoCAD Microcomputer Design and Drafting Program.* Thousand Oaks, CA: New Riders Publishers.

Rose, R. 1990. *AutoCAD Onstage: A Computer-Aided Design Handbook for Theater, Film and Television.* White Hall, VA: Betterway Publications.

Sanchez, L. 1994. *Fallingwater in 3D Studio: A Case Study and Tutorial.* Sante Fe, NM: On Word Press.

Schaefer, A. T. 1988. *The AutoCAD Productivity Book: Tapping the Hidden Power of AutoCAD.* Chapel Hill, NC: Ventana Press.

Sperling, K. 1997. *Fractal Design: Painter 5 Complete.* Indianapolis: IDG Books Worldwide.

Sutton, J. 1996. *Fractal Design: Painter Creative Techniques.* Indianapolis: Hayden.

———. 1996. *Tutorials, 3D Studio MAX.* Kinetix, AutoDesk.

Vera, E., and L. Kirsher. 1998. *Poser 3: The Remarkable Figure Design and Animation Tool: Users Guide.* MetaCreations Corp.

INDEX

About the CD-ROM

CD Contents

- Sample files are included on this CD, to use for following exercises outlined in the book. Files are included for AutoCAD, 3D Studio MAX, Painter, and Poser.
- Note: The CD-ROM contains only samples files, NOT the applications used to create them.

System Requirements

Windows:
- Windows 95 or higher
- 200 mHZ Pentium II Processor (or higher)
- Minimum 32 MB of application RAM (more recommended)
- Color Display (24-bit recommended)
- CD-ROM Drive

Macintosh:
- System 7.5 (or higher)
- 200 mHZ Power PC Processor (or higher)
- Minimum 32 MB of application RAM (more recommended)
- Color Display (24-bit recommended)
- CD-ROM Drive
- Poser 3 requires System 8.0

These system requirements need to be met in order to run the applications associated with the sample files included on this disc.

Have a question about any of our electronic products? Call or e-mail our tech support hotline at (800) 793-2154 or techsupport@heinemann.com

AUTOCAD R12 AND READ ONLY FILES

If you are working in AutoCAD R12 you may experience some problems opening a file from the CD-ROM. This is because R12 must have a different file location for temporary files. Any file that has a "Read Only" property such as any file on a CD-ROM would cause this difficulty in R12. If you find that you cannot open a file in R12 you will have to reconfigure the program to send temporary files to a new location. The procedure is as follows:

When you attempt to open the file from the CD-ROM you will receive the following error message: To access files in a read-only directory you must configure a temporary file location other than "DRAWING". Click on OK. This returns you to the Open Drawing Box. Click on Cancel. Now you must reconfigure for a new temporary file location.

Click on File/Configure to begin reconfiguration. Hit Enter (Return) twice to get to the Configuration Menu list. Once you are in the Configuration Menu list type in the number for Configure Operating Parameters and hit Enter. You should now be in the Configure Operating Parameters list. Type in the number for Placement of Temporary Files and hit Enter.

The prompt on the screen will read: Enter directory name for temporary files, or DRAWING to place them in the same directory as the drawing being edited <DRAWING>. Now you will have to give AutoCAD a folder (directory) on your hard drive in which it can place these temporary files. Type in the letter that identifies your hard drive followed by :\ (colon backslash) and the name of the folder (directory). It does not matter what folder on your hard drive you select. For example, say that all of your AutoCAD files are in a folder named ACAD and the letter that designates your hard drive is C. Then at this prompt you could type in C:\ACAD. Hit Enter and you will be returned to the Configure Operating Parameters list. If this is not a valid folder on your hard drive AutoCAD will tell you so and you will have to try again. When you are returned to the Configure Operating Parameters list hit Enter again to select <0> Exit to configuration menu. You will be returned to the Configure Menu List. Hit Enter again to select <0> Exit to drawing editor. You will be prompted for whether you want to keep the configuration changes. Hit Enter again to select <Y> Keep configuration changes. You will be returned to the drawing editor.

Now you can open the file on the CD-ROM or any other Read Only file. When you attempt to do so you will see a message on the screen that reads: Unable to write to that directory. Do you want to continue? Click on Yes and the file will open.